HUGO GROTIUS
MARE LIBERUM
1609-2009

HUGO GROTIUS
MARE LIBERUM
1609-2009

Original Latin Text
(facsimile of the first edition, 1609)
and Modern English Translation

Edited and Annotated by
Robert Feenstra
Emeritus Professor of Roman Law at Leiden University

with a General Introduction by
Jeroen Vervliet
Director of the Peace Palace Library

BRILL

LEIDEN · BOSTON
2009

Colophon

Published in cooperation with the Peace Palace Library, The Hague

ISBN 978 90 04 17701 7
Copyright 2009 by Koninklijke Brill NV, Leiden, The Netherlands.
Koninklijke Brill NV incorporates the imprints Brill, Hotei Publishing,
IDC Publishers, Martinus Nijhoff Publishers and VSP.
All rights reserved. No part of this publication may be reproduced, translated, stored in
a retrieval system, or transmitted in any form or by any means, electronic, mechanical,
photocopying, recording or otherwise, without prior written permission from the publisher.
Authorization to photocopy items for internal or personal use is granted by Koninklijke Brill NV
provided that the appropriate fees are paid directly to The Copyright Clearance Center,
222 Rosewood Drive, Suite 910, Danvers, MA 01923, USA. Fees are subject to change.

Design
André van de Waal and Remco Mulckhuyse, Coördesign, Leiden

Photography
Joost Kolkman, Leiden
Koninklijke Bibliotheek, Den Haag, p. 3 - 160
Bert Mellink, D-Vorm, Leidschendam, p. XII

Paper
Arctic Volume White 130gr/m² with a FSC-certificate. The wood used in
its production originates from plantations and other controlled sources.

Printed by
Thieme GrafiMedia Groep

Bound by
Jansen Binders, Leiden

Contents

VII   PREFACE

IX   GENERAL INTRODUCTION by Jeroen Vervliet

XXXI   1 The Political Setting and Origins of *Mare liberum*
        1.1 *Mare liberum*, published anonymously at the time of the conclusion of the truce in 1609
        1.2 The assignment to Hugo Grotius by the Zeeland Chamber of the Dutch East India Company in 1608
        1.3 The seizure of a Portuguese carrack in the Straits of Singapore in 1603
        1.4 The sequel amongst the directors of the Dutch East India Company
        1.5 A policy brief by Hugo Grotius, 1604-1606

XIV   2 Legal Argument in *Mare liberum*

XIX   3 Aftermath. Bilateral Negotiations and a Battle of Books around *Mare liberum*
        3.1 Introduction
        3.2 Colonial conferences in London and The Hague (1613-1615)
        3.3 William Welwood's *An Abridgement of All Sea-Lawes* (1615)
        3.4 Hugo Grotius' *Defensio capitis quinti maris liberi* (1615)
        3.5 *De justo imperio Lusitanorum Asiatico* (1625) by Seraphin de Freitas
        3.6 Hugo Grotius' *De jure belli ac pacis* (1625)
        3.7 John Selden's *Mare clausum* (1635)
        3.8 Epilogue

XXXI   EDITOR'S INTRODUCTION by Robert Feenstra
        1 Existing Editions of *Mare liberum*
        2 *Mare liberum* and *De jure praedae*
        3 Translations of *Mare liberum*
        4 The Recently Edited Old English Translation by Richard Hakluyt
        5 Recent Research on Manuscript Leiden BPL 917
        6 The Objectives of the Present Edition
        7 The Verification of the References in the Margin and the Problem of Linking Them to the Text
        8 The List of Sources
        9 The Choice of the Editions Mentioned in the List
        10 Some Final Remarks on the Authors Cited

1   EDITION OF THE LATIN TEXT AND ENGLISH TRANSLATION

161   Abbreviations Used for References in the Editor's Introduction, in his Notes and his List of Sources

165   List of Sources

171   Index of Sources Not Mentioned in the List
        1 Roman and Canon Law Sources
        2 Ancient Non-Legal Sources

175   General Index

PREFACE

The quadricentenary of Hugo Grotius' *Mare liberum* has offered us the opportunity to realize a number of long-cherished ambitions. First of all the Director of the Peace Palace Library was able to show once again the value of the assets of his library in the field of the history of international law, in particular its world-famous Hugo Grotius collection, in which an 'editio princeps' of *Mare liberum* (1609) features prominently. Furthermore a specialist of Grotius' legal works, who had insisted long ago on the need of a reliable critical edition of *Mare liberum*, combined with a revised English translation, was given the opportunity to provide such an edition thanks to the support of the Peace Palace Library and a well-known Leiden publisher.

The General Introduction on the historical context of *Mare liberum* starts in 1609, simply, in order to underline the 400th birthday of the book. By choosing that approach the narrative sequence might be perceived as somewhat artificial since the story first meanders back in time through the years preceding the 1609 publication and then goes forward to its aftermath, offering examples from international practice as well as from the battle of books rising around *Mare liberum*.

The Editor's Introduction highlights the exceptional situation that an edition of a work of this kind could be realized by using the autographic manuscript of its author. This was of great help to a verification of the text and its numerous marginal references, resulting in corrections and new annotations. The English text was mainly derived from the English translation of a much larger work by Grotius, *De jure praedae commentarius* (of which the twelfth chapter was the basis for *Mare liberum*). This translation (by Gwladys L. Williams) was published in 1950 by the Carnegie Endowment for International Peace, which had already published an edition together with a translation of *Mare liberum* by Ralph Van Deman Magoffin in 1916. His translation was also used in the present edition, but only for Grotius' preface and chapter XIII, which were not translated by Williams. We would like to express our gratitude to the Carnegie Endowment for the fruitful use we could make of both publications.

This project was supported by many people but we will mention here only three names. Dr. Henk Nellen, the well-known biographer of Grotius, helped us in all possible ways in drafting our introductions. Kirsten Sierag was of incommensurable value for the final composition of the *Mare liberum* text and the annotations as well as in all other editorial activities. Onno Kosters carefully advised on the English versions of both introductions. We thank all three for their invaluable help. Nevertheless the responsibility for this 1609-2009 *Mare liberum* memorial volume resides entirely with the authors.

Jeroen Vervliet *Robert Feenstra*

Hvgonis Groti
MARE LIBERVM
SIVE
De iure quod Batavis competit ad Indicana commercia
DISSERTATIO.

Vltima Editio.

LVGDVNI BATAVORVM,
Ex Officinâ ELZEVIRIANA.
ANNO cIɔ. Iɔ. c. XVIII.

GENERAL INTRODUCTION
by Jeroen Vervliet

1 The Political Setting and Origins of *Mare liberum*

1.1 *Mare liberum*, published anonymously at the time of the conclusion of the truce in 1609

Mare liberum, 'The Free Sea', was published in April 1609. The book was written by Hugo Grotius, at the time 'Advocaat-Fiscaal' (public prosecutor) in the 'Hof van Holland en Zeeland' (Court of Appeal) in The Hague.

Interestingly, *Mare liberum* was published anonymously; soon, however, it became widely known that Hugo Grotius in fact authored this politically controversial booklet. The first edition of *Mare liberum* revealing the author's name was the Dutch translation issued in 1614[1]; the first Latin edition to show Hugo Grotius as the author was published in 1618. In the last years, *Mare liberum* has increasingly been perceived as a piece of propaganda justifying colonialism, colonial trade, and colonial domination[2].

The Latin text of the original edition of *Mare liberum*, or in full 'Mare liberum sive de iure quod Batavis competit ad Indicana commercia dissertatio' (The Free Sea or a Dissertation on the Right which the Dutch Have to Carry on Indian Trade), comprises only 66 pages, excluding the dedication and appendix, and consists of 13 chapters. Two chapters are comparatively quite long. Chapter V, 'That the sea leading to the Indians or the right of navigation thereon does not belong exclusively to the Portuguese by title of possession', covers 23 pages and would eventually receive an additional *Defensio* by Hugo Grotius in reaction to William Welwood's contesting critique in '*An Abridgement of All Sea-Lawes*' in 1613 (prophesying that the sea could indeed be the subject of ownership by a single sovereign). Chapter VII, 'That the sea or the right of navigation thereon does not belong to the Portuguese by title of prescription or custom' comprises 14 pages.

Publication of *Mare liberum* was deferred until the end of April 1609 in order to avoid jeopardising the ongoing negotiations on an armistice in the Dutch Revolt. This independence struggle and civil war against the Spanish monarchy went on since 1568. The Twelve Years' Truce was concluded on April 9, 1609.

< The first Latin edition to show Hugo Grotius as the author of *Mare liberum* was published in 1618 by Elzevier in Leiden. The first edition was published anonymously in 1609.

---

[1] More precisely the so-called 'third issue' of the 1614 Dutch edition.
[2] '*Mare Liberum* is essentially a propagandistic treatise and argues for Holland's merchants to freely access emporia in Asia by unimpeded navigation across the high seas. The freedom of navigation forms a subset to the overarching arguments on the freedom of access and trade'. Peter Borschberg, *Hugo Grotius' Theory of Trans-Oceanic Trade Regulation, Revisiting Mare Liberum (1609)*, International Law and Justice Working Papers, (Rev. Aug. 2006), p. 3. (Cited as 'Borschberg, *Hugo Grotius' Theory*'). Eric Wilson calls *Mare liberum* a propaganda instrument, investing the Dutch East India Company (VOC) with international legal personality and justifying private warfare; 'Simply put, the Text 'translates' the operational requirements of the World Economy into the terms of Naturalist jurisprudence'. See Eric Wilson, *Erasing the Corporate Sovereign, Inter-Textuality and an Alternative Explanation for the Publication of Hugo Grotius' Mare Liberum (1609)*, Itinerario, vol. 30/2 (2006), p. 78-103, at p. 78, p. 81, p. 83. Martine Julia van Ittersum, *Hugo Grotius in Context: Van Heemskerck's Capture of the Santa Catarina and its Justification in De Jure Praedae (1604-1606)*, Asian Journal of Social Science, vol. 31/3 (2003), p. 511-548, at p. 512: '… the natural law and natural rights theories that Grotius formulated in *De Jure Praedae* cannot be divorced from Dutch imperialism and colonialism in the early modern period'. (Cited as 'Van Ittersum, *Hugo Grotius in Context*').

Mare liberum advances and envisages an equal right of the Dutch to navigation and trade in the East Indies, still perceived by the Portuguese and hence by the Spaniards – the two countries were united in a personal union under the Spanish Crown – as an unconditional exclusive prerogative and acknowledged monopoly. The legally argued claim by Hugo Grotius in *Mare liberum* to unlimited seafaring and commerce – for a right of occupation of the sea cannot be settled by any single country – could have resulted in the suspension and cancellation of the truce talks, since the Spaniards were desperately adamant on the confirmation of the continuation of this exclusive right. The appearance of the controversial booklet had accordingly been postponed on the deliberate request of Johan van Oldenbarnevelt, the Advocate of Holland ('secretary' of the States of Holland, the highest civil authority), the most distinguished statesman in the truce negotiations. More in particular, the truce was threatened by the fact that Hugo Grotius' authorship of a political pamphlet on top of his role as a key person in the judiciary responsible for the defence of the interests of the States of Holland and Zeeland in criminal and fiscal cases could easily cause complexities, such as an undesirable interpretation of the official point of view. Clearly, omitting Grotius' name from the title page of *Mare liberum* was very much a precautionary measure.

1.2 The assignment to Hugo Grotius by the Zeeland Chamber of the Dutch East India Company in 1608

The Dutch East India Company (VOC), the Zeeland Chamber in particular, shooting for influence on the truce talks in 1608 (and 1609), assigned Hugo Grotius in November 1608 to publish on the right of the Dutch to freely navigate and conduct trade on the seas to the East Indies.

The intermediary intervention of Johan Boreel, a friend of Grotius', who declared that a valuable piece had already been written on this topic, made the publication of *Mare liberum* imminent. The twelfth chapter of an earlier scholarly work by Hugo Grotius, (later known as) *De jure praedae*, 'On the Law of Prize and Booty' (originally written between 1604 and 1606 but having remained unpublished) could simply and adequately serve the aforementioned goals. Only various modifications had to be implemented and a provocative introduction, viz. 'To the Rulers and To the Free Nations of the Christian World', had to be added[3]. Nevertheless – as said before – the forthcoming polemical paper came late and did not play any persuasive role as premeditated by the VOC.

In short, *Mare liberum* was probably published to invalidate the Spanish claims, which included the withdrawal by the Dutch from all commercial activities in Asia in exchange for a truce. By contrast, the *Mare liberum* pamphlet substantiated that no nation had exclusive rights to navigation and trade (through discovery, occupation,

---

[3] W. J. M. van Eysinga, *Huigh de Groot, een schets*, Haarlem 1945, p. 44-45. (Cited as 'Van Eysinga, *Huigh de Groot*').

1 The Political Setting and Origins of *Mare liberum*

prescription or donation by the Pope)[4].

Martine Julia van Ittersum, in *Profit and Principle: Hugo Grotius, Natural Rights Theories and the Rise of Dutch Power in the East Indies (1595-1615)*, argues that 'Dutch [...] expansion overseas in the early modern period is literally inconceivable without Grotius' natural law and natural rights theories'[5], i.e., that unimpaired 'freedom of trade and navigation was a natural right, innate to all peoples, including Dutch merchants and their indigenous trading partners', that the natural law principle 'pacta sunt servanda' (treaties must be honoured) forges 'the contractual obligations and their enforcement between the VOC and the Asian rulers', and that 'right to self-defense' entitles 'each private person' to resume 'his sovereign powers' and execute 'judgment in his own cause'[6].

1.3 The seizure of a Portuguese carrack in the Straits of Singapore in 1603

On February 25th, 1603, the Dutch Admiral Jacob van Heemskerck attacked and captured the Portuguese carrack Santa Catarina in the Straits of Singapore[7]. The Santa Catarina, a richly laden merchant-ship transporting a cargo from China and Japan to Malaysia, was assaulted in privateering and freebooting skirmishes. Seizing occurred frequently but the case of the Santa Catarina developed into a special occasion.

Asia had become the Portuguese colonial domain and the Dutch had only recently arrived. Natural law precepts such as freedom of trade and navigation were exercised by the Dutch, as was the right to self-defence and in particular the right to exact damages for injuries. The latter were used by Admiral Van Heemskerck as a justification for his own seizure of the Santa Catarina, because it was an individual's revengeful punishment in the absence of an independent judge in retaliation for mistreatment of Dutch merchants in Portuguese Asia[8]. The Amsterdam Admiralty Court endorsed Van Heemskerck's justification. The prize was sold in Amsterdam. The gain doubled the Dutch East India Company's financial means.

---

[4] Hedley Bull, *The Importance of Hugo Grotius in the Study of International Relations*, in: Hugo Grotius and International Relations, ed. by Hedley Bull, Benedict Kingsbury, Adam Roberts, Oxford 1990, p. 65-94, at p. 71.

[5] Martine Julia van Ittersum, *Profit and Principle: Hugo Grotius, Natural Rights Theories and the Rise of Dutch Power in the East Indies (1595-1615)*, Leiden-Boston 2006, p. xxxvii. (Cited as 'Van Ittersum, *Profit and Principle*').

[6] Van Ittersum, *Profit and Principle*, p. xxii-xxiii, see above, note 5.

[7] Peter Borschberg has identified the correct geographical location as the Singapore Straits, whereas in the past various places have been mentioned, of which the Straits of Malacca have been the most frequently cited. See Peter Borschberg, *Grotius, Maritime Intra-Asian Trade and the Portuguese Estado da India: Problems, Perspectives and Insights from De iure praedae*, in: Grotiana 26-28 (2005-2007), p. 31-60, at p. 35.

[8] Van Ittersum, *Profit and Principle*, p. liv-lv, see above, note 5. Martine Julia van Ittersum has produced evidence that 'Grotius' conceptualisation of natural rights and natural law in *De jure praedae* is based to a large extent on Van Heemskerck's own justification of privateering. A key notion of Grotius' rights theories – the individual's right to punish transgressors of the natural law in the absence of an independent and effective judge – follows logically from Van Heemskerck's reasoned decision to assault the *Santa Catarina* in revenge for Portuguese mistreatment of Dutch merchants in the East Indies'. See Van Ittersum, *Hugo Grotius in Context*, p. 511, see above, note 2.

1 The Political Setting and Origins of *Mare liberum*

The next chapter in the history of legitimation was Hugo Grotius' policy document *De jure praedae*, 'On the Law of Prize and Booty'.

1.4 The sequel amongst the directors of the Dutch East India Company

The Dutch East India Company ('Vereenighde Oostindische Companie' or 'VOC') was an enterprise chartered by the States General and being granted 'delegated, sovereign rights to maintain troops and garrisons, fit out warships, impose governors upon Asian populations, and conduct diplomacy with eastern potentates, as well as sign treaties and make alliances'[9] in order to fulfil its overseas commercial objectives in Asia.

In 1604, the Amsterdam Chamber of the VOC sent out a request to Hugo Grotius to write a justification for the taking of the Santa Catarina. The reason for this was that some VOC Directors required an assertion of the lawfulness of the capture and an alleviation of their moral scruples about the revenues that could be considered as plunder of an aggressive competing merchant.

In many shareholders' eyes costly and aggressive warfare by the VOC was not the way to attain their fortunes. Some amongst them even considered pulling out of the Dutch VOC and establishing a similar Asian trading company in France, because France – not at war with Spain and Portugal – could easily compete with the VOC and consequently beat the Dutch since the French were not burdened by the sinews of war. However, Grotius emphasized the importance of the buccaneering operations of the VOC as an instrument of warfare against the Spanish and Portuguese[10]. In the end, after an upheaval in the Dutch-French political relations the French King Henry IV dropped the French East India Company idea and redirected his interest to the West Indies[11].

The lawfulness of the seizure and booty acquisition was corroborated in 1606 through the policy document *De jure praedae*, 'On the Law of Prize and Booty'. Hugo Grotius explained that the VOC had become involved in a just war against the Portuguese. Exclusion of the Dutch from trade by the Portuguese was illegal, and, consequently, prize taking was legitimate. He produced evidence ('le triomphe du raisonnement juridique')[12] that resistance against the Portuguese and the seizure of the Santa Catarina was fully legitimate according to the laws of war as a rebuttal to violent attacks, as a means to preserve one's property, in order to restore one's rights or guarantee the return of goods, and as a punishment of committed crimes[13].

< Poster by J.B. Heukelom "Mare liberum" (1915) showing 'Hugo Grotius' on the stern and containing some verses inspired by Joost van den Vondel.

---

[9] Jonathan I. Israel, *The Dutch Republic, Its Rise, Greatness, and Fall 1477-1806*, Oxford 1995, p. 322.
[10] Henk Nellen, *Hugo de Groot, Een leven in strijd om de vrede, 1583-1645*, Amsterdam 2007, p. 83-84. (Cited as 'Nellen').
[11] Van Ittersum, *Profit and Principle*, p. 151-166, see above, note 5.
[12] Jules Basdevant, *Hugo Grotius*, in: Les Fondateurs du droit international, avec une introduction de A. Pillet, Paris 1904, p. 125-267, at p. 224.
[13] Van Eysinga, *Hiugh de Groot*, p. 23-24, see above, note 3. 'Authorities generally assign to wars three justifiable causes, defence, recovery of property, and punishment', see *Hugo Grotius, De Jure Belli ac Pacis*

1.5 A policy brief by Hugo Grotius, 1604-1606

The argument in *De jure praedae*, 'On the Law of Prize and Booty', intended and rendered by Hugo Grotius, leads convincingly to the view of 'Grotius as a VOC lobbyist and ideologue, eager to shape the foreign policy of the Dutch Republic in the 1600s and 1610s'[14].

Moral discontent about privateering certainly played a role at the outset of *De jure praedae*, but the argument that pacifist Mennonist VOC shareholders disagreed with capturing enemy cargo ships has been convincingly rejected by Martine Julia van Ittersum[15]. Personal reasons and political events for which *De jure praedae* remained unpublished were at stake as well, since the VOC might also have felt more at liberty in its privateering and freebooting as long as nothing was ever published formally on their behalf as official policy, and, finally, since its publication might threaten the pending truce[16].

De jure praedae remained in manuscript until it was discovered by accident as late as 1864 during the preparation of an auction of the Hugo Grotius legacy, in particular of the possessions of the Cornets de Groot family, descendants of Grotius. Simon Vissering, professor of law, and the historian Robert Fruin identified the value of the manuscript and its relation with *Mare liberum*. After Leiden University purchased the manuscript it was published by H.G. Hamaker, a classical scholar, in 1868[17].

2 Legal Argument in *Mare liberum*

Hugo Grotius, as if in an advocate's address to the court[18], treats the legality of warfare in general and of privateering and freebooting in particular throughout *Mare liberum*. Chapter 1 is on the Dutch right to navigate and trade in the Portuguese East Asian domains and the impossibility to exclude the Dutch because of natural law imperatives. In chapters 2-4 Grotius attacks the Portuguese claim to dominion in the East, chapters 5-7 are dedicated to free navigation and chapters 8-13 are on free trade.

Four reasons why war or buccaneering might be just in the case of the Luso-Dutch rivalry received greatest attention at the outset of *Mare liberum*: 1] the East Indies are accessible to all nations, 2] religion is not a ground for denying rights on property,

---

Libri Tres, Volume Two, the Translation, by Francis W. Kelsey, with the collaboration of Arthur E. R. Boak, Henry A. Sanders, Jesse S. Reeves and Herbert F. Wright, and an introduction by James Brown Scott, Oxford 1925, Book II (Chapter I, Paragraph II), p. 171. (Cited as 'Kelsey, *Hugo Grotius*').

[14] Van Ittersum, *Profit and Principle*, p. xi, see above, note 5.
[15] Van Ittersum, *Profit and Principle*, p. 118-122, see above, note 5.
[16] Van Ittersum, *Profit and Principle*, p. lvi-lvii, p. 187-188, see above, note 5.
[17] *Hugonis Grotii De jure praedae commentarius*, ex auctoris codice descripsit et vulgavit H. G. Hamaker, The Hague 1868.
[18] W. J. M. van Eysinga, *Quelques observations au sujet du Mare Liberum et du De Iure Praedae de Grotius*, in: Grotiana, vol. 9 (1941-1942), p. 61-75, at p. 63 (reprinted in: Sparsa Collecta, een aantal der verspreide geschriften van Jonkheer Mr. W.J.M. van Eysinga, ed. by F. M. van Asbeck e.a., Leiden 1958), [325-326].

2 Legal Argument in *Mare liberum*

sovereignty, and freedom of trade, 3] the sea and navigation over the sea cannot become a certain country's exclusive right since discovery, a donation by the Pope, prescription or plain war are unjustified ways to acquire property, and 4] trading cannot be exclusively possessed as a monopolistic right by any nation.

Subsequently, in *Mare liberum* Hugo Grotius disavows the Portuguese any 'ius dominii' (right of ownership) over East Indian territories, making use of natural law reasoning and Roman Law. Grotius examines the legality of 'inventio' (discovery)[19], Papal donation[20] and just war[21] ('bellum iustum') as ways for the Portuguese to acquire 'dominium' (ownership), or more distinctly formulated: to be allowed 'occupatio' (occupation). However, after having rejected the justified methods for receiving occupation rights as put forward by the Portuguese – because someone can only obtain territorial 'res nullius' (nobody's lands) through proper discovery and occupation – Grotius constitutes that the Indian population cannot be withheld any ownership rights because no just cause whatsoever entitles the Portuguese to demand another's property[22].

Through 'occupatio' someone may acquire 'proprium' (property). 'Inventio' (discovery) is criticized in *Mare liberum* as an unjust title for a legitimate establishment of a 'dominium' (ownership) because prior to any Portuguese occupation whatsoever another power was supposed to be the owner of the Asian lands. These lands had their own kings, government, laws and legal systems and the citizens had trade activities with the Portuguese, as with any other party. Accordingly, the Portuguese had no title to sovereignty[23].

The sea is not open to 'occupatio', because the sea is a 'res communis' (a common good). All things that by nature are for common use like air, sea and shore cannot be occupied, and the sea is for common use and cannot become anyone's property because it is limitless. Moreover, navigation and fisheries require such a common use[24]. The sea is 'res extra commercium'[25] (not an object of trade transactions, nor is the sea subject to a servitude for it is open by its nature to all persons). Common things ('res communes') have existed since the idyllic epoch of natural law[26], although over the course of time

Naval battle at Gibraltar on 25 April 1607. A Dutch fleet, under the command of Jacob van Heemskerck, surprised and engaged a Spanish fleet anchored at the Bay of Gibraltar. During the four hours of action, the entire Spanish fleet was destroyed.
ATLAS VAN STOLK, ROTTERDAM >

....

[19] Hugo Grotius, *Mare Liberum*, Caput II: The Portuguese do not effectively possess any part of the East Indies because the peoples have their own princes, kings, government and law systems; the Portuguese do not have any title to sovereignty because only discovery of a 'res nullius' yields rights.
[20] Hugo Grotius, *Mare Liberum*, Caput III: The Pope does not have any right of a secular leader entitling him to donate, still more convincingly the Pope cannot donate lands of a third person.
[21] Hugo Grotius, *Mare Liberum*, Caput IV: No just cause existed for the Portuguese to start a war and therefore no just title for possession was acquired.
[22] R. Feenstra, *Hugo de Groot's eerste beschouwingen over dominium en over de oorsprong van de private eigendom: Mare liberum en zijn bronnen*, Acta Juridica, vol. 25 (1976), p. 269-282, at p. 270-271.
[23] Hugo Grotius, *Mare Liberum*, Caput II, p. 6. Cf. Frans De Pauw, *Grotius and the Law of the Sea*, Brussels 1965, p. 33-34. (Cited as 'De Pauw').
[24] Hugo Grotius, *Mare Liberum*, Caput V.
[25] Hugo Grotius, *Mare Liberum*, Caput VI.
[26] Hugo Grotius, *Mare Liberum*, 'Dedicatio', 'Ad principes populosque liberos orbis Christiani' (To the Rulers and to the Free Nations of the Christian World); here the following general natural law concepts are mentioned: 'res communes', common goods for the use of mankind, and free navigation and free trade.

XV

many were acquired as personal property, with the exception of the sea.

Natural law stipulates free access to the world seas and oceans ('ius navigandi') and prescribes that the sea cannot be appropriated. Besides the pre-eminence of the freedom of navigation a similar natural law characteristic - trading without impediments ('libertas commerciorum') - forms the gist of *Mare liberum*[27]. *Mare liberum* treats the Dutch-Portuguese war in its entirety as a private one ('bellum privatum'), in which the Dutch East India Company had captured the Santa Catarina because of the infraction on the freedom of trade as a natural right and the illegality of the Portuguese trade monopoly[28]. After all, when in the absence of the sway of a State natural law rules are hampered, a private war is justified[29].

Denying in general the natural rights mentioned above would normally imply a justification for war. The Dutch have a right to navigate and trade freely, and if the Portuguese exclude the Dutch from seafaring and commerce in the East Indies they act unlawfully, as stated in Chapter I of *Mare liberum*[30].

Prescription and custom are no legal means either for the Portuguese to acquire monopolistic sea route rights etc., because prescription belonged to civil law domain only and was not applicable in legal disputes between kings or free people, especially when the law of nature commanded differently, and there could be no customary law contrary to the law of nature[31]. Even so, a Papal donation does not support the Portuguese claim to the sea and to exclusive navigation rights because the Pope is not entitled to act against natural law, that is to say, assign ownership of the sea as if it were private property, and he does not have any role within the commercial world[32].

In the field of natural law the 'recta ratio' or 'ratio summa' (the highest reason) shapes consensus and therefore law, the so-called 'ius naturae secundarium' (secondary natural law); it is herein that the Dutch assault on the Portuguese finds its justification. The primary law of nations is fully composed of basic natural law concepts. The 'ius gentium secundarium' (secondary law of nations) is a positivist dimension of the law of nations[33].

....

[27] W. E. Butler, *Grotius and the Law of the Sea*, in: Hugo Grotius and International Relations, ed. by Hedley Bull, Benedict Kingsbury, Adam Roberts, Oxford 1990, p. 209-220, at p. 211, p. 213. (Cited as 'Butler'). Borschberg, *Hugo Grotius' Theory*, p. 15, see above, note 2: 'The Dutch humanist understood unimpeded and peaceful maritime navigation as an extension of the *ius communicandi* and *ius commerciandi*, two natural rights that he adopts from the Spanish theologian Vitoria'.
[28] Hugo Grotius, *Mare Liberum*, Caput VIII.
[29] Benjamin Straumann, *Hugo Grotius und die Antike, Römisches Recht und römische Ethik im frühneuzeitlichen Naturrecht*, Studien zur Geschichte des Völkerrechts 14, Baden-Baden 2007, p. 127-157, at p. 19. (Cited as 'Straumann').
[30] Hugo Grotius, *Mare Liberum*, Caput I.
[31] Hugo Grotius, *Mare Liberum*, Caput VII. Cf. Wilhelm G. Grewe, translated and revised by Michael Byers, *The Epochs of International Law*, Berlin-New York 2000, p. 267. (Cited as 'Grewe'). And Martine Julia van Ittersum, *Mare Liberum versus the Propriety of the Seas? The Debate between Hugo Grotius (1583-1645) and William Welwood (1552-1624) and its Impact on Anglo-Scotto-Dutch Fishery Disputes in the Second Decade of the Seventeenth Century*, Edinburgh Law Review, vol. 10 (2006), p. 239-276, at p. 255. (Cited as 'Van Ittersum, *Mare Liberum*').
[32] Hugo Grotius, *Mare Liberum*, Caput VI. See also Grewe, p. 267, see above, note 31.
[33] Straumann, p. 24, p. 26-28, see above, note 29.

W. J. M. van Eysinga concludes that if Hugo Grotius had not written anything else but *Mare liberum*, his place in the development of the law of nations would already have been fully established. But he accomplished a lot more[34].

3 Aftermath. Bilateral Negotiations and a Battle of Books around *Mare liberum*

3.1 Introduction

In an 1891 issue of the 'Juridical Review'[35], Ernest Nys published 'Une bataille de livres, an Episode in the Literary History of International Law'. Indeed, many political debates on the seventeenth-century landscape of international relations, foreign policy, and colonialism were published in legal pamphlets and books. Hugo Grotius' *Mare liberum* yielded an avalanche of reactions and replies; within the frame of this introduction we restrict the Battle of Books to Welwood, Freitas and Selden, because they illustrate best what the discussion was about[36].

In the eighteenth century Cornelis Bynkershoek's view on the freedom of the sea, in which he elaborates on Hugo Grotius' ideas, is dominant. 'All prominent writers of the eighteenth century take up again the case of the freedom of the Open Sea, making a distinction between the maritime belt which is to be considered under sway of the littoral States, and on the other hand the High Seas, which are under no State's sovereignty'[37]. In 'De dominio maris' (1702) Bynkershoek explains 'the territorial sovereignty by restricting it to the range of a cannon-shot'[38].

---

[34] W. J. M. van Eysinga, *Grotius (1625-1925)*, Revue de droit international et de législation comparée, vol. 6 - Troisième série (1925), p. 271 (reprinted in: Sparsa Collecta, een aantal der verspreide geschriften van Jonkheer Mr. W.J.M. van Eysinga, ed. by F. M. van Asbeck e.a., Leiden 1958, p. 124). ('Si Grotius n'avait fait autre chose qu'écrire le Mare Liberum, sa place dans l'évolution du droit des gens serait déjà tout à fait indiquée. Mais il a fait beaucoup plus.') (Cited as 'Van Eysinga, *Grotius (1625-1925)*').

[35] Juridical Review (1891, vol. 3), Part I, p. 1-11, Part II, p. 131-137.

[36] Other authors: Walter Raleigh, *Observations Touching Trade and Commerce* (1610), A. Gentilis, *Hispanicae Advocationis libri duo* (1613), Julius Pacius, *De dominio Maris Hadriatici disceptatio pro Venetis* (1619), J. I. Pontanus, *Discussionum Historicarum libri duo* (1637), Jac. Gothofredus, *De imperio maris deque jure naufragii colligendi ὑπομνημα* (1637), Petrus Baptista Burgus, *De dominio Serenissimae Genuensis Reipublicae in Mari Ligustico libri II* (1641), C.-B. Morisot, *Orbis maritimi historia* (1643), J. Loccenius, *De jure maritimo et navali libri tres* (1650), Dirk Graswinkel, *Maris liberi vindiciae adversus Petrum Baptistam Burgum, Ligustici maritimi dominii assertorem* (1652), Dirk Graswinkel, *Maris liberi vindiciae adversus Gulielmum Welwodum Britannici maritimi dominii assertorem* (1653), John Burroughs, *The Sovereignty of the British Seas Proved by Records, History, and the Municipal Laws of this Kingdom* (1653), M. Schoock, *Imperium maritimum, ita explicatum, ut non solum ejus ostendatur praerogativae, verum etiam cuique genti, maxime Belgis foederatis, suus vindicatur honos* (1654), Paolo Sarpi, *Del dominio mare Adriatico* (1676), etc.

[37] L. Oppenheim, *International Law, a Treatise, Vol. I: Peace*, London 1912 (2nd ed.), p. 320 (*Part II, the Objects of the Law of Nations, Chapter II, the Open Sea, I, the Rise of the Freedom of the Open Sea, § 251*).

[38] Jeroen Vervliet, *The Peace Palace Library Centennial, the Collection as a Mirror of the Historical Development of International Law, 1904-2004*, The Hague 2004, p. 41.

3.2 Colonial conferences in London and The Hague (1613-1615)

The most essential problem to be solved in the 'Colonial Conferences' of 1613 and 1615 (and 1619) was the disputed right of English spice traders in the Indies. From the English point of view the Dutch unlawfully refused the English merchants the fulfilment of their desire to freely navigate and trade in the Indies. Reading more closely, we see that the Dutch deprived the English of a right they had so carefully safeguarded at the time of the 1608-1609 armistice talks with the Spanish. In the end, the Dutch sent an embassy to London to reach a settlement with the English, and Hugo Grotius became the most influential Dutch delegate and spokesman.

Grotius' line of reasoning[39] aimed at a concession to the English of the right to navigate and trade, limited, however, by existing contractual obligations and treaties between the Dutch and the Asian kings, princes and rulers. These mutual duties effectively meant a monopolistic situation in which the Dutch, in exchange of military protection, received an exclusive right to the spice harvest. At the same time, the English were though welcome to purchase these goods from the Dutch against reasonable prices[40]. This was Hugo Grotius' 'Pacta sunt servanda'-doctrine at its best; 'Freedom of trade and navigation was not indefinite, but circumscribed by contracts'[41].

'What really infuriated the English negotiators was Grotius' refusal to acknowledge that he had contradicted his own plea for freedom and navigation. They had quoted *Mare Liberum* […]'[42], because 'the authorship of *Mare Liberum* was already a public secret in England'[43]. The English considered all this as unjust and contrary to the law of nature, for Grotius' work implied limiting the universal freedom of commerce, confining the national sovereignty, extinguishing the liberty of the law of nations by contract, and curtailing inland monarchs bound by their own consent. In effect, Grotius advocated that both parties were bound to the contracts that they legitimately drafted[44].

The London negotiations did not turn out to be successful and the talks were continued in The Hague in 1615. The freedom of navigation and trade in the East Indies was still important. King James I had a keen interest in a well-forged agreement between the Dutch and English East India Companies[45]. On the agenda was an eventually fruitless item on closer cooperation between, or even a merger of the English and Dutch East India companies. For this, an unconditional, greater English contribution to the Asian

---

[39] Peter Borschberg in *Hugo Grotius' Theory of Trans-Oceanic Trade Regulation, Revisiting Mare Liberum (1609)*, IILJ Working Paper, 2005/14, p. 2, calls Grotius 'surprisingly consistent in his thinking on the wider issues of maritime trade and navigation, including the two colonial conferences of 1613 and 1615 and even beyond'.
[40] Van Eysinga, *Huigh de Groot*, p. 47-50, see above, note 3.
[41] Van Ittersum, *Profit and Principle*, p. 379, see above, note 5. Henk Nellen argues that as early as 1606 Hugo Grotius (in *De jure praedae*) aimed to counteract the English in this way. See Nellen, p. 84, see above, note 10.
[42] Van Ittersum, *Profit and Principle*, p. 430, see above, note 5.
[43] Van Ittersum, *Profit and Principle*, p. 375, see above, note 5.
[44] Van Ittersum, *Profit and Principle*, p. 490, see above, note 5. J. K. Oudendijk, *Status and Extent of Adjacent Waters, A Historical Orientation*, Leiden 1970, p. 38-39. (Cited as 'Oudendijk').
[45] Van Ittersum, *Profit and Principle*, p. 366, see above, note 5.

3 Aftermath. Bilateral Negotiations and a Battle of Books around *Mare liberum*

war effort (enabling the trade gains) was required[46]. In effect, however, the main themes of the diplomatic dialogue had shifted merely to herring fishery in the North Sea and whaling in the Spitzbergen area. We may therefore conclude this paragraph by quoting the Hugo Grotius scholar W. J. M. van Eysinga: 'On peut donc dire que la brochure de Grotius a été écrite contre le Portugal, qu'elle a été publiée contre l'Espagne, et qu'elle a conquis le monde contre la Grande-Bretagne'[47].

3.3 William Welwood's *An Abridgement of All Sea-Lawes* (1615)

William Welwood, Professor of Law in the University of St. Andrews from 1590-1611, published *An Abridgement of All Sea-Lawes* in reaction to Hugo Grotius' *Mare liberum* in 1613. William Welwood's 27th Chapter was a specific attack on Hugo Grotius' 5th Chapter. The 27th Chapter was translated into Latin and published as *De Dominio Maris* in 1615. It was particularly Grotius' notion of freedom of fishing that provoked Welwood's treatise[48]. W. G. Grewe even considers the proclamation by James I of a new maritime law policy, the Fishery Edict of 1609, as much an impulse behind the publication of *Mare liberum* as the impending Hispano-Dutch armistice[49].

The sea, in Welwood's opinion, can very well be divided by boundaries. It can even be acquired, it can equally be occupied and owned, and, finally, the sea is liable for the establishment of jurisdictional authority. That is to say, Welwood believes that the sea can be owned – although it changes continually – and similarly to how somebody might travel over land in possession of another, a person is able to navigate over a sea to which he has no title. Welwood draws a dividing line between a State's *dominium* or territory (including territorial seas) and the common sea and sets a limit at a hundred miles from the coast. And although factual occupation is not essential, coastal waters need to have the same owner as the adjacent lands. Therefore Welwood believes that ownership and jurisdiction and protection go hand in hand[50].

Welwood sees the seas as universes open for international commerce[51], but the freedom of the use of the sea is limited for the sake of fisheries because 'no foreign fishermen were permitted to fish […] unless they obtained licences […] in London and Edinburgh, all for a price […]'[52]. At the same time, although 'the law of nations (jus gentium) stipulated that the liberty of fishing was, yes, "common to all nations", [it] stipulated that they should do so "on their [own] seas and their [own] shores"'[53]. Nevertheless the Dutch

---

[46] Van Ittersum, *Profit and Principle*, p. 390-394, see above, note 5.
[47] Van Eysinga, *Grotius (1625-1925)*, p. 124, see above, note 34.
[48] Van Ittersum, *Mare Liberum*, p. 242, see above, note 31.
[49] Grewe, p. 265, see above, note 31.
[50] Oudendijk, p. 68-69, see above, note 44.
[51] Borschberg, *Hugo Grotius' Theory*, p. 39, see above, note 2.
[52] Van Ittersum, *Mare Liberum*, p. 257, see above, note 31.
[53] Van Ittersum, *Mare Liberum*, p. 247, see above, note 31.

envoys insisted on freedom of fishing. Welwood however blames Grotius for upholding an erroneous assumption of the abundance of fish[54]. According to Welwood, oceans, on the other hand, are known for their unlimited liberty, and are therefore the most free seas[55].

Hugo Grotius takes a contrary position: nobody is capable of appropriating the sea; there are no demarcation lines in the seas (the floodmark divides the State's *dominium* and the free sea); the sea is a common good for navigation and fisheries; no servitude in the public sense can be vested in the sea[56]. *Imperium* (sovereignty, consisting of jurisdiction in particular and protection in general) and *dominium* (ownership) are not necessarily entirely interconnected; the sea as a common good excludes ownership and occupation rights, and therefore at sea all States share jurisdiction competencies to defend free fishing and navigation and each individual State exercises jurisdiction over its own subjects[57].

Grotius 'castigated Welwood for his refusal to recognise that the sea, unlike the land, was incapable of occupation and possession'[58]. He denied Welwood legal knowledge (namely Roman law), and called him incapable of distinguishing properly between the law of nations and the civil law of one or more peoples[59].

3.4 Hugo Grotius' *Defensio capitis quinti maris liberi* (1615)

William Welwood's *An Abridgement of All Sea-Lawes* chiefly opposed Chapter V of *Mare liberum*, 'Mare ad Indos aut ius eo navigandi non esse proprium Lusitanorum titulo occupationis' ('That the sea leading to the Indians or the right of navigation thereon does not belong exclusively to the Portuguese by title of possession'). Hugo Grotius considered it most appropriate to contradict Welwood. The *Defensio* (compiled in 1615) or *Defensio capitis quinti maris liberi*[60] remained unfinished and was not published until 1872[61].

> PhD thesis by S. Muller Fzn. (Amsterdam 1872), in which he (as an appendix to his book) published, for the first time, the 1615 Latin manuscript by Hugo Grotius, *Defensio capitis quinti maris liberi oppugnati a Guilielmo Welwodo*, discovered at the 1864 auction of Hugo Grotius' papers.

---

54 Van Ittersum, *Mare Liberum*, p. 248, see above, note 31.
55 'mare vastum liberrimum' or 'that part of the main sea or great ocean which is far removed from the just and due bounds [...] pertaining to the nearest lands of every nation'. See *The Free Sea, Hugo Grotius, Translated by Richard Hakluyt, with William Welwod's Critique and Grotius's Reply*, edited and with an introduction by David Armitage, Indianapolis 2004, p. 74. (Cited as 'Armitage'). The translation of Hugo Grotius, Defense of Chapter V of the Mare Liberum, in 'Armitage', p. 77-130, is based on: Herbert F. Wright, *Some Less Known Works of Hugo Grotius*, in: Bibliotheca Visseriana, vol. 7 (1928), p. 133-238, at p. 154-205.
56 Armitage, p. 31-32, see above, note 55.
57 Oudendijk, p. 19, 20, 28, 30, 68, 69, see above, note 44.
58 Van Ittersum, *Mare Liberum*, p. 251, see above, note 31.
59 Van Ittersum, *Mare Liberum*, p. 253-254, see above, note 31.
60 Or in full, *Defensio capitis quinti maris liberi oppugnati a Guilielmo Welwodo juris civilis professore capite XXVII ejus libri scripti Anglia sermone cui titulum fecit Compendium legum maritimarum* (Defence of the Fifth Chapter of Mare Liberum opposed by William Welwood, Professor of Civil Law, in chapter 27 of his book, written in English, for which he made as a book title An Abridgement of All Sea-Lawes).
61 Oudendijk, p. 16, see above, note 44. *Defensio* remained a manuscript (as *De jure praedae*) until it was discovered at the 1864 auction of the Hugo Grotius legacy. S. Muller Fzn. published the Latin manuscript of the *Defensio* in *Mare Clausum. Bijdrage tot de geschiedenis der rivaliteit van Engeland en Nederland in de zeventiende eeuw* (Amsterdam 1872).

MARE CLAUSUM.

BIJDRAGE TOT DE GESCHIEDENIS DER RIVALITEIT VAN ENGELAND EN NEDERLAND IN DE ZEVENTIENDE EEUW.

ACADEMISCH PROEFSCHRIFT

TER VERKRIJGING VAN DEN GRAAD

VAN

Doctor in het Romeinsch en Hedendaagsch Recht,

AAN DE HOOGESCHOOL TE LEIDEN,

OP GEZAG VAN DEN RECTOR MAGNIFICUS

Dr. D. BIERENS DE HAAN,

HOOGLEERAAR IN DE FACULTEIT DER WIS- EN NATUURKUNDE,

IN HET OPENBAAR TE VERDEDIGEN

op Dinsdag, den 16 April 1872, te 3 uur,

DOOR

SAMUEL MULLER Fz.

GEBOREN TE AMSTERDAM.

AMSTERDAM,
FREDERIK MULLER.
1872.

The *Defensio* is not only a recapitulation and reiteration of the reasoning of *Mare liberum*, but 'must be considered as an important supplement to his earlier publication. In the first place the liberty of fishing with which *Mare liberum* hadn't to deal directly was now brought into full light and cleared up. So, if we want to learn what Grotius in this period thought about the status of the sea, we have to make use of the two works together'[62].

In the past a licence to partake in fishery had always been mandatory in Scotland and ever since Scotland and England were established as a union under James VI/I, the geography demanding this official permission had vastly expanded. This impediment had caused a severe blow to Dutch herring fishing.

Hugo Grotius sought support for the fishing theme in Roman law sources (Justinian's Digest and Institutes): 'May anyone be prohibited from fishing or navigating on the sea?'; 'Because the use of the sea is public under the law of nations, therefore *everyone* is free to let down his nets from the sea'; 'If anyone is prohibited from fishing or navigating on the sea, use is to be made of action for damages', etc[63].

Following the reasoning of the law of nature and nations Grotius still vindicated the idea that the sea can neither be divided nor owned; no *dominium* can be established over the sea. However, Grotius identifies a duty for the sovereign of a (maritime) State to exercise rights of protection and jurisdiction; thus he inclusively recognizes *imperium*[64].

3.5 *De justo imperio Lusitanorum Asiatico* (1625) by Seraphin de Freitas

The treatise *De justo imperio Lusitanorum Asiatico* (1625), written at request of the Spanish King Philip III by the Portuguese friar Seraphin de Freitas lecturing at the University of Valladolid in Spain, was a scholarly response to Hugo Grotius' *Mare liberum*. The late date of its publication was brought about by the ambition of the Spanish King to establish a well-balanced diplomatic relationship with the Dutch United Provinces[65], although the Truce was broken since 1621 and the war between the Spanish Crown and the rebellious Dutch had recommenced.

Several authors have presented evidence that Hugo Grotius was aware of the *De justo imperio Lusitanorum Asiatico*, but he never formally reacted, although he referred to Seraphin de Freitas as an honourable man having written a diligent essay[66].

Seraphin de Freitas argues that natural law may entitle any sovereign to refuse foreigners

---

[62] Oudendijk, p. 16, see above, note 44.
[63] Armitage, p. 80, p. 94, p. 95 (and p. 94-99, p. 114-115), see above, note 55.
[64] Butler, p. 214, see above, note 27.
[65] Monica Brito Vieira, *Mare Liberum vs. Mare Clausum: Grotius, Freitas and Selden's Debate on Dominion over the Seas*, Journal of the History of Ideas (2003), p. 361-377, at p. 362. (Cited as 'Vieira').
[66] C.H. Alexandrowicz, *Freitas versus Grotius*, British Yearbook of International Law, vol. 35 (1959), p. 162-182, at p. 162. (Cited as 'Alexandrowicz').

3 Aftermath. Bilateral Negotiations and a Battle of Books around *Mare liberum*

to travel and trade in his country[67], that the Portuguese hold exclusive sailing rights, and that the Portuguese territorial occupation through discovery (i.e. mainly in the wake of the direct sea route) was legally binding[68]. Furthermore, De Freitas argues that the sea – although a 'res communis', a common good – may be acquired, liable as it is to vesting property rights and quasi-occupation – thus subject to limitations because the high sea cannot remain in a state of lawlessness – whence exclusive navigational and jurisdictional zones originate[69].

Therefore Freitas suggests that no part of the world should be placed beyond the authority of a sovereign, and should therefore remain outside any legal jurisdiction[70]. The king of Spain, who knew no superior ('superiorem non recognoscens'), could exercise full sovereign rights over the sea, extend his jurisdiction, supervision and protection over all seas, notwithstanding the underlying financial burden. However, the vastness of the world seas complicates the effectivity of any occupation, but partial occupation is equally recognized. Letters of safe conduct (cartazes) were used to streamline claims to sovereignty of coastal States, and all other States that underwent a limitation and reduction in power since the Portuguese founded their colonial empire and built a 'mare clausum'[71].

3.6 Hugo Grotius' *De jure belli ac pacis* (1625)

B. M. Telders, in "Het leerstuk van de territoriale zee" (The Origin of the Theorem of the Territorial Sea)[72], concludes that Hugo Grotius made a 'volte face' in his opinion on the issue of appropriating the sea by occupation. J. K. Oudendijk, in 'Status and Extent of Adjacent Waters. A Historical Orientation,' shows starting points similar to *Mare liberum* and identifies minimal, gradual adjustments[73]. But to what extent did Hugo Grotius between 1609 and 1625 change his approaches as laid down in *Mare liberum* in comparison to *De jure belli ac pacis*?

In *De jure belli ac pacis*, Book II, Chapter III, Paragraphs VII, VIII and X, Hugo Grotius declares rivers, bays and straits as liable to ownership according to natural law and the law of nations: 'By occupation rivers can be acquired […]. It is sufficient that the greater part, that is that the sides, shall be enclosed by banks, and that the river by itself shall be small in extent in comparison with the land'; '[…] the sea also can be acquired by him who holds the lands on both sides, even though it may extend above a bay, or above and below as a strait, provided that the part of the sea in question is not so large

---

[67] Vieira, p. 364, see above, note 65.
[68] Alexandrowicz, p. 168-169, see above, note 66.
[69] Alexandrowicz, p. 172-178, see above, note 66.
[70] Borschberg, *Hugo Grotius' Theory*, p. 39, see above, note 2.
[71] Grewe, p. 259-260, see above, note 31.
[72] In: *Verzamelde geschriften, Vol. II*, Den Haag 1948, p. 109 et seq. See Oudendijk, p. 26, p. 40, see above, note 44.
[73] Oudendijk, p. 41-44, see above, note 44.

that, when compared with the lands on both sides, it does not seem a part of them.'; '[...] if a part of the sea can be added to estates of individuals, provided, of course, that it is enclosed and is so small that it can be considered a portion of an estate, and if the law of nature presents no obstacle to such procedure, why, also, may not a part of the sea enclosed by shores belong to that people, or to those peoples, to which the shores belong, provided that part of the sea, when compared in extent with the land of the country, is not larger than an enclosed inlet of the sea compared with the size of the private estate?'[74]. The words small, insignificant, not so great, etc., are indicative of the changes in point of view with respect to property ownership of the sea, 'dominium maris', in *De jure belli ac pacis* since *Mare liberum*.

The exclusive sovereign power of the coastal State, 'imperium', has therefore been modified substantially (since it ended at the flood line in *Mare liberum* and in the *Defensio*)[75]. 'We may assume that [Hugo Grotius] connected it with cannonshot [...]'[76] but imposing taxes for protection at sea and for maritime safety and thus improving the navigational and fishery use of coastal waters, although theoretically contrary to natural law and the law of nations, entered equally into the adjacent State's competence[77].

3.7 John Selden's *Mare clausum* (1635)

Although John Selden fully confirmed the unlawfulness of the Portuguese assertion of the exclusive authority over the sea, he did disagree with Hugo Grotius with respect to the littoral sea. Selden seeks to provide justification for the point of view that the sea is not common to all under all circumstances[78].

Traditionally the English had always claimed the control over the sea bordering their land[79]. Therefore Selden rebutted *Mare liberum,* jestingly naming his publication *Mare clausum*, the 'Closed Sea'. Selden's autobiographical notes ('*Vindiciae*') date his actual writing of *Mare clausum* to 1618, although it is clearly proven by now that 1619 is the proper year of composition, because it coincides with the presence of an official delegation of the Dutch States-General in London. King James I had requested the publication of Selden's work upon this occasion in order to be suitably armed for a settlement of the dispute (which was chiefly on herring fishing). Controversies during the revision of the manuscript, which arose, for instance, because James I hoped to avoid

---

[74] Kelsey, *Hugo Grotius*, p. 208-209, p. 211, see above, note 13; Van Ittersum, *Profit and Principle*, p. 418-419, see above, note 5. Oudendijk, p. 41-44, see above, note 44.
[75] Oudendijk, p. 50, see above, note 44.
[76] Oudendijk, p. 47, see above, note 44.
[77] Oudendijk, p. 48, see above, note 44.
[78] Selden explains that originally the sea – as did everything – belonged to all, but by law and custom it later became the property of princes and of individuals. See De Pauw, p. 13, see above, note 23.
[79] Cf. Alberico Gentili in *Hispanicae advocationis libri duo* (1613), in which it is defined that England not only has 'imperium' and 'dominium' over the sea but 'jurisdictio' as well; hence England's jurisdiction extends indefinitively. See De Pauw, p. 12, see above, note 23.

3 Aftermath. Bilateral Negotiations and a Battle of Books around *Mare liberum*

the annoyance of his brother-in-law the King of Denmark, Christian IV, led to Selden's decision to forbear publishing *Mare clausum*[80].

The formal publication by royal command of a revised edition of *Mare clausum* in 1635 intended to support the 'naval and commercial policy of Charles' (who had succeeded James I in 1625), 'the revival of Stuart claims to control the adjacent sea, the strengthening of the fleet, and the imposition of the new tax of "ship money"'[81].

Selden deals at length with the topics of natural law and the law of nations, and also touches upon the law of the sea, referring even more so than Hugo Grotius to classical authorship, but using contemporary sources as well. Selden recognizes occupation rights and private ownership of the sea and dominion over the sea and over parts of the sea, namely inland seas.

Consequently, Selden's reasoning makes possible imperial exercising of power over the sea, e.g., jurisdiction, granting fishing rights, exacting tolls, guaranteeing free passage. The world seas are divided amongst the various nations, concluded formally in covenants, as a result of which nations acquire property rights over seas. These claims to control are vindicated by Selden through a panoramic presentation of British history, legal history, and maritime law history. In this way Selden hopes to show that occupation of the sea, especially the seas by which Great Britain is surrounded, is possible and legitimate[82], and that the sea, as much subject to acquisition as the land, can be owned as a dominion and therefore the king of England is lord over the seas around the Great Britain[83]. Quintessential for vesting a dominion is the capacity of the navy to effectively rule the seas, a property Selden withholds from the Iberians[84].

In terms of pure legal argumentation Selden embarks upon a definition of dominion and the laws of God, natural law, laws of nations and Roman law and corroborates the new approaches of law of particular societies, that were integrated in and superseded the former kinds of law. Roman law became theory whereas municipal law history and English common law 'provided the basis for a refutation of the principle of communal ownership of the sea and for the ensuing historical demonstration of the exercise of dominion over the adjoining seas by the rulers of Britain from the time of the Romans to the seventeenth century'[85].

As the most famous response to *Mare liberum*, Selden's *Mare clausum* was never replied to by Grotius, because by then he had accepted responsibilities as an Ambassador and Counsellor to the Swedish Crown, and Sweden considered the Baltic Sea as its

---

[80] G. J. Toomer, *John Selden: A Life in Scholarship, Vol. I*, Oxford 2009, p. 388-389. (Cited as 'Toomer, *John Selden*').
[81] Toomer, *John Selden*, p. 391, see above, note 80.
[82] Toomer, *John Selden*, p. 395-437, see above, note 80.
[83] Butler, p. 211, see above, note 27. De Pauw, p. 9-13, see above, note 23.
[84] Grewe, p. 267, see above, note 31. R. P. Anand, *Origin and Development of the Law of the Sea, History of International Law Revisited*, The Hague, Boston, London 1983, p. 106.
[85] Paul Christianson, *Discourse on History, Law and Governance in the Public Career of John Selden, 1610-1635*, Toronto 1996, p. 9, p. 250, p. 279.

exclusive zone for navigation and trade. Moreover, Grotius preferred to refrain from any help offered to his former home country that had so mercilessly ignored him. Even Dirck Graswinckel, Hugo Grotius' friend in the days of the actual composition of *De jure belli ac pacis*, who officially responded on behalf of the Dutch through the pamphlet *Maris liberi vindiciae adversus virum clarissimum Johannem Seldenum* (1637), did not receive any support from Hugo Grotius in his endeavour[86].

3.8 Epilogue

Since Hugo Grotius' *Mare liberum* the leading idea has been that the open sea is free by nature, that it cannot be taken in possession through occupation and that it can never be under the sovereignty of any State[87].

Nevertheless, during the twentieth century, in particular after the Second World War, rights over the continental shelves exacted by coastal states and the establishment of economic zones up to 200 miles wide have set in motion a continuous limitation process of the freedom of the seas. However, a great number of maritime freedoms are enumerated in treaties, especially in the 1982 United Nations Convention on the Law of the Sea, and an even greater number of regulations have necessarily been issued worldwide, e.g. on exploitation of the sea (oil, minerals, natural resources and industrial deep seabed mining) and on biodiversity, fishery, conservation of nature, and the polar regions. Still, the freedom of the sea is always the leading idea[88].

The sea as a common good, as an element of the world's common heritage, and as a common natural preservation concern, is currently the best flag for the classification of Hugo Grotius' *Mare liberum*.

Allegory by Jacques de Gheyn on the blessings of peace, with a short poem by Hugo Grotius (1613). RIJKSMUSEUM, AMSTERDAM

---

[86] Nellen, p. 402-405, see above, note 10.
[87] L. Oppenheim, *International Law, a Treatise, Vol. I: Peace,* London 1912 (2nd ed.), p. 318 (*Part II, the Objects of the Law of Nations, Chapter II, the Open Sea, I, the Rise of the Freedom of the Open Sea*, § 250, § 254, § 259).
[88] Butler, p. 216-219, see above, note 27.

Pace viget Fortuna fauens, terrâq; mariq;
Jam blandiuntur omnia;   Hug. Grotius. Ætat. XIII

EDITOR'S INTRODUCTION
by Robert Feenstra

1 Existing Editions of *Mare liberum*

It is more than thirty years ago that I started reading the original text of *Mare liberum* critically. The first results were published in 1978 in two articles that are not easily accessible, since one is in Dutch[1], and the other in Spanish[2]. In both I insisted on the need for a critical edition. In 1996 I returned to the theme of the former of the two studies: the origins of *dominium* according to Grotius; this new publication (in French) was reprinted in 2005 and might be more easily accessible[3]. Meanwhile, a critical edition of *Mare liberum* has still not appeared and this gap has become even more conspicuous since the publication of such an edition of *De jure belli ac pacis* in 1993[4].

Let us consider the situation with respect to easily available editions of *Mare liberum*. Along with some of the 17th and 18th century editions[5] only one 'modern' edition can be mentioned: it dates from 1916 and was published by the Carnegie Endowment for International Peace, Division of International Law[6]. According to the title page, it is 'edited with an introductory note by James Brown Scott, Director [of the Division]', but his only contribution is the 'Introductory Note'[7]. The responsibility for the Latin text lies with the translator, Ralph Van Deman Magoffin[8]; also according to the title page,

< Portrait of Hugo Grotius, painter unknown.

HAAGS HISTORISCH MUSEUM, THE HAGUE

---

[1] R. Feenstra, *Hugo de Groot's eerste beschouwingen over dominium en over de oorsprong van de private eigendom: Mare liberum en zijn bronnen*, Acta Juridica 1976 [published in 1978 = Essays in honour of Ben Beinart, I], p. 269-282. (Cited as 'Feenstra 1978').

[2] R. Feenstra, *Grocio, Vitoria y el 'dominium' en el nuevo mundo*, Anuario Jurídico [Mexico], 3-4 (1976-1977) [published in 1978 or early 1979], p. 57-67 (many printing errors, no proofs seen).

[3] R. Feenstra, *Les origines du 'dominium' d'après Grotius et notamment dans son 'Mare liberum'*, in: Homenaje al profesor Alfonso García Gallo, I, Madrid 1996, p. 179-190; reprinted in R. Feenstra, *Histoire du droit savant (13e-18e siècle), Doctrines et vulgarisation par incunables*, [Variorum Collected Studies Series, CS 842], Aldershot 2005, as no. III. (Cited as 'Feenstra 1996-2005').

[4] Hugo Grotius, *De iure belli ac pacis libri tres*, curavit B. J. A. de Kanter - van Hettinga Tromp, *Editionis anni 1939 ... exemplar photomechanice iteratum, Annotationes novas addiderunt* R. Feenstra et C. Persenaire adiuvante E. Arps - de Wilde, Aalen 1993 (now available at Kloof Booksellers & Scientia Verlag, Amsterdam, www.kloof.nl). (Cited as 'Djbap 1993' or 'Feenstra, Djbap').

[5] Available as reprints or on microfiche, see below at notes 31 ff.

[6] *The Freedom of the Seas or the Right Which Belongs to the Dutch to Take Part in the East Indian Trade, a Dissertation by Hugo Grotius*, translated with a revision of the Latin text of 1633 by Ralph Van Deman Magoffin, edited with an introductory note by James Brown Scott, [Carnegie Endowment for International Peace, Division of International Law], New York [etc.] 1916. (Cited as 'Magoffin'). Two issues exist, see below, notes 84 and 85; I use the second issue.

[7] The formula on the title page is somewhat ambiguous and has indeed been misinterpreted by some later authors on *Mare liberum*, who consider Brown Scott as responsible for the statements in the notes added to the text and the translation; see e.g. Peter Borschberg, *Hugo Grotius' Theory of Trans-Oceanic Trade Regulation, Revisiting Mare Liberum (1609)*, Itinerario, vol. 29 (2005), number 3, p. 31-53 (cited as 'Borschberg (2005)'), at p. 51 (note 39 to p. 37). On Scott's 'Introductory Note' and Magoffin's 'Translator's Preface' cf. below, note 62. For the two different issues of Magoffin's edition and translation see below, notes 84 and 85; the second example given in note 85 shows that Borschberg, in the note cited above, refers to the first – deficient – issue of Magoffin's work.

[8] On the title page he is mentioned as Ph.D., Associate Professor of Greek and Roman History, The Johns Hopkins University. In 1923 he published an English translation of Cornelis van Bijnkershoek, *De dominio maris dissertatio* (Classics of International Law, vol. 11); at the time he was Head of the Department of Classics, New York University.

he 'translated with a revision of the Latin text of 1633'. In his 'Translator's Preface'[9] he specifies: 'The Latin Text is based upon the Elzevier edition of 1633, the modifications being only such as to bring the Latin into conformity with the present day Teubner and Oxford texts'.

In fact, two 1633 Elzevier editions exist, both printed in Leiden[10]. I have not been able to check which of the two was used by Magoffin. The choice of a 1633 and not an earlier edition[11] is important because the 1633 editions[12] are the first in which the marginal references are linked to the text by a letter or a number. We will see that this linking, copied in almost all later editions, is not always correct[13]. Magoffin made no effort to improve this. A much more important objection against his way of presenting the references, however, is that he does not render them literally but tacitly changes them into a modern form (or even tacitly adds some references), making any verification impossible. Sometimes he misunderstands them, which in some cases leads him to a completely false interpretation in the notes to the translation[14]. In other cases he simply omits a reference[15]. In short, the edition is completely unreliable[16].

Of course, a considerable part of the deficiencies of the Magoffin edition has to be ascribed to the fact that it was published on short notice during the First World War; it was to serve in a discussion on the freedom of the seas between the European belligerents and the United States as a neutral[17]. Between August 1914 and April 1917 James Brown Scott was a Special Advisor to the Secretary of State. It was in this context that he recommended a speedy publication of an edition of *Mare liberum*; this is the origin of the Magoffin edition, which appeared in the general series[18] of publication of the Division of International Law of the Carnegie Endowment for International Peace. Brown Scott must have been aware of some of the imperfections. In his annual report

Frontispiece of one of the two Leiden 1633 editions of *Mare liberum* published by Elzevier (also containing Paullus Merula's *de Maribus*.)

[9] On p. xi.
[10] See below, at notes 46 ff.
[11] This choice is not explained. Perhaps it was simply the oldest edition available to Magoffin, but he may also have been inspired by the fact that one of the two Leiden 1633 editions was used by the author of the translation into French, Alfred Guichon de Grandpont, published in 1845 (see below note 74), a translation which Magoffin claims to have consulted (Translator's Preface, p. xi). In any case, neither Magoffin nor Guichon uses the argument that these editions were revised by Grotius himself, an argument put forward in the Italian edition/translation of 2007 (see below, note 27) but without any evidence (see below, note 29).
[12] For a third 1633 edition, published by Blaeuw in Amsterdam, see below, at note 43.
[13] See below, at note 135.
[14] For examples, see edition, p. 3 note g, p. 9 note 2, p. 20 note c, p. 28 note 1, p. 35 note a and p. 58 notes a and b.
[15] For examples, see edition, p. 36 note d, p. 58 notes d and f, p. 64 note b, and p. 66 note c. There are, however, also cases where he adds useful references, see, e.g., p. 62 note 1 and p. 63 note 2.
[16] After having written this judgment my attention was drawn to a review of the Magoffin edition published in The English Historical Review, vol. 33, no. 229 (January 1918), p. 115-118, by Edward Bensly (cf. below, note 92). The long list of critical remarks (for his conclusions, see below, note 22) does not only concern the marginal references and the Latin text but also the translation into English. In my notes to the text and in my revisions of the translation I could still fully take into account Bensly's critics. (Cited as 'Bensly').
[17] See for this and the following details George A. Finch in his Preface to the 1950 edition of the English translation of *De jure praedae* (for the full title, see below, note 63), p. x-xi.
[18] Not in the series 'Classics of International Law', see below.

as Director of the Division, dated 5 April 1932, he stated that the 1916 edition could be improved by revision and then appear in the series 'Classics of International Law' as a companion volume to *De jure praedae*[19]. This plan did not succeed due to lack of funds[20]. In 1949 Scott's successor as Director of the Division, George A. Finch, wrote: 'It is now felt that the edition of Mare liberum published by the Endowment in 1916 answers the purpose of scholarship in this field at the present time'[21]. Although this opinion may not have been shared by many European scholars[22], the result was that the Magoffin edition tacitly became more or less the standard edition from 1950 onwards. It was reprinted in 1972[23] and 2001[24]. Two online versions are available; one has only the English translation[25], the other has the Latin text as well[26]. In 2007, a newly printed edition of the Latin text of *Mare liberum* (followed by an Italian translation) was published in Naples[27]. In a 'nota alla traduzione'[28] it is suggested that this Latin text was the one of 'l'edizione elzeviriana del 1633', recommended because it was 'riveduto da Grozio'[29]; in fact it was simply copied from the Magoffin edition along with all the errors in the text and the references[30].

---

[19] Finch, Preface, p. xi. On p. x Finch says that this has been part of Scott's original proposal of 1906 for the 'Classics' series. However, in the full text of this proposal, which was edited as Appendix C to the same 1950 edition (p. 388-393), Scott only speaks of 'a new and authoritative edition [of *De jure praedae*] ... which should contain the brief on the law of prize, with footnotes calling attention to the few and unimportant modifications of chapter 12 when published separately as the 'Mare Liberum' ...' It is clear that Finch gives a wrong interpretation of the words 'when published separately as the 'Mare Liberum''; no doubt they refer to the 1609 edition, not to a new edition in the 'Classics' series.

[20] Finch, Preface, p. xi-xii. For a small remainder of this plan see below, at notes 37 and 65.

[21] Finch, Preface, p. xii.

[22] In any case, not by those who might have read the review by Edward Bensly, cited above, note 16 (apparently this review was not present in the files of the Division of International Law of the Carnegie Endowment); cf. Bensly, p. 115 ('it cannot be regarded in any way as a definitive edition') and p. 118 ('it must be acknowledged that, before there is a second edition, translation and notes alike ought to be submitted to a searching revision').

[23] Arno Press, New York 1972.

[24] Union, N. J. Lawbook Exchange 2001.

[25] http://socserv.mcmaster.ca/econ/ugcm/3ll3/grotius/Seas.pdf. It was published by Batoche Books Limited, Kitchener (Ontario) 2000. The text of the translation is reproduced with a new pagination and a new numbering of the notes (continuous for the whole work); the text of the notes is put at the end of the translation. The revised issue of the 1916 edition has been used, cf. below, at note 85.

[26] http://oll.libertyfund.org/Texts/Grotius0110/FreedomOfSeas/0049_Bk.pdf. It was published by Liberty Fund, Inc., Indianapolis (no date), and available in different formats; one of these is 'a facsimile or image-based PDF made from scans of the original book'. The first (not revised) issue of the 1916 edition has been used, cf. below, at note 85.

[27] *Ugo Grozio, Mare liberum*, a cura di Francesca Izzo, [Quaderni del Dipartimento di Filosofia e Politica, Università di Napoli "L'Orientale"], [Napoli 2007].

[28] To be found on p. 32-34. The name of the translator is not mentioned there, nor on the title page; it only appears on the verso of the latter: Fabio Longobardi.

[29] See p. 32; in footnote 2 this is argued with the following words: 'l'opera di Grozio è inserita in una raccolta, da lui stesso curata come si evince dall' indice che riporta la firma di *Hugo* ...'. Indeed at the bottom of the page listing the contents of the 'raccolta' (see below, at notes 45 ff.) one finds 'Hugo'; that is, however, not a 'signature' but simply the indication by the printer that the next page begins with 'Hugo'!

[30] See below, at n. 97.

1 Existing Editions of *Mare liberum*

The alternative to using the unreliable Magoffin edition or one of its derivatives meant – until today – a recourse to one of the 17th or 18th century editions[31] (in an original copy, a reprint or on microfiche). A detailed description of them can be found in J. ter Meulen and P. J. J. Diermanse, *Bibliographie des écrits imprimés de Hugo Grotius*[32] (to be cited as TMD). Three categories are to be distinguished: 1) Separate editions[33]; 2) Editions in which *Mare liberum* is published together with treatises of other authors on related subjects[34]; 3) Editions in which it figures as an appendix to Grotius' *De jure belli ac pacis*[35].

To the first category belongs, of course, the *editio princeps*, published anonymously by Ludovicus Elzevirius in Leiden in the year 1609 (probably in April)[36]. Copies are rather rare; an early collotype reproduction of it exists, dating from 1951 and made available by the Carnegie Endowment to a limited number of libraries[37].

A counterfeit, bearing on the title page 'Impressa primum Lugduni Batavorum. In officina Ludovici Elzevirij. Anno M.DI.IX [1609]'[38], was probably printed in Antwerp shortly after the first edition[39].

A second edition, 'Ex officina Elzeviriana', appeared in Leiden 1618 with Grotius' name on the title page[40]; it was reprinted – along with John Selden's *Mare clausum*, London 1635 – by Biblio Verlag in Osnabrück 1978. The text corresponds, in principle, to the original 1609 edition; most of the errata have been corrected[41]. There is, however, no evidence that Grotius himself looked at it.

The text of the second edition was published anew by Iohannes Ianssonius in Amsterdam in 1632; just as the 1618 edition it was presented as the 'Ultima editio'[42].

....

[31] In the 19th century and in the beginning of the 20th (i.e., before Magoffin) no edition of *Mare liberum* was published.

[32] La Haye 1950, (reprint Zutphen 1995), p. 210-216, nos. 541-550. In 'remarque 12' under no. 541 (on p. 212-213) the authors refer to 27 editions of *De jure belli ac pacis* which add as an appendix an edition of *Mare liberum* (specified by giving the TMD numbers, cf. below, note 35). This has been overlooked in the Italian edition of 2007 (see above, note 27) where, on p. 32 n. 1, only those publishing the text separately or combined with works from other authors on related subjects are summed up as editions mentioned by TMD; as to the editions which do appear in the Italian translator's footnote, for 'Francoforte, 1683' read 'Francoforte, 1663'.

[33] TMD 541-544 and 547; for no. 544 it is not certain that it was a separate edition, see below, note 42.

[34] TMD 545, 546, 548-550

[35] TMD 544, 579-586, 588, 592-594, 596, 597, 599-603, 605-611 (cf. above, note 32).

[36] TMD 541. For further details see the 'remarques' (nos. 1-12) of Ter Meulen and Diermanse. The TMD information can be completed by consulting the on-line Short-title Catalogue, Netherlands (STCN), where, inter alia, typographical details and a list of copies available in the Netherlands can be found. The facsimile in the present volume is from the copy in the Royal Library in The Hague (KB).

[37] See below, note 65.

[38] TMD 542; cf. STCN. According to TMD the Errata of the *editio princeps* have been corrected. I have seen a copy in the Peace Palace Library (VP).

[39] Information kindly provided by Mr. Erik Geleyns (Royal Library, The Hague, STCN).

[40] TMD 543; cf. STCN. Copies inter alia at the Peace Palace Library (VP) and Leiden University Library (UBL).

[41] A few new printer's errors, however, were made; some of them have never been corrected in later editions, see edition, p. 28 note 1 and p. 39 note e; cf. also p. 28 note 2.

[42] TMD 544; cf. STCN. The only copies known to TMD and STCN (inter alia at the Peace Palace Library) are

Title page of the edition of Grotius' *De jure praedae commentarius* by the classicist H. G. Hamaker, The Hague 1868. The manuscript was discovered at the 1864 auction of Hugo Grotius' papers.

In 1633 another Amsterdam publisher, Gulielmus Blaeuw, reacted with an 'Editio nova, prioribus longe emendatior'[43]. One of the new elements was that the references in the margin were linked to the text by letters[44].

Meanwhile an edition of the second category had appeared for the first time: in 1633 *Mare liberum* was combined with other treatises under the title *Hugo Grotius de Mari libero et P. Merula de maribus*[45] in an edition published in Leiden by the 'officina Elzeviriana'[46], counting 308 pages[47]. In the same year the same publisher published a second version of the same treatises, with an identical title page, set in different type, and counting XV and 267 pages[48]. As noted above, both editions have in common that for the first time the marginal references are linked to the text, but in the one with 308 pages the links are by letters, in the one with 267 pages by numbers. The first system of linking has become the norm. It was already followed by the 1633 Amsterdam edition, mentioned earlier[49]. There is no evidence that Grotius himself was involved in any of the three 1633 editions; in all probability the linking system is therefore not authentic.

Returning to the list of editions found in the *Bibliographie* of Ter Meulen and Diermanse, we should note that after 1633 – apart from two German editions (of 1663 and 1669) in which *Mare liberum* is combined with different other treatises[50] – the text was only available as an appendix[51] to editions of *De jure belli ac pacis*. This combination, first found in the 1632 Amsterdam edition, by Ianssonius, became the convention since the 1667 Amsterdam edition by Blaeu[52]. About 18 editions followed in the next hundred years (see TMD); the series was closed by an edition published in Utrecht 1773,

....

bound together with an edition of *De jure belli ac pacis*, published also by Ianssonius, Amsterdam 1632 (TMD 570), which has on its title page 'Tractatu de Mari libero adaucta'. Ter Meulen and Diermanse do not exclude, however, that Ianssonius also issued separate copies.

[43] TMD 547; cf. STCN. Copies inter alia in Peace Palace Library (VP) and Leiden University Library (UBL).

[44] This was not the case in the editions I mentioned above; for the problems of linking, see below, at note 135. The Blaeuw edition probably followed the example of the two editions under the title *Grotius de Mari libero et P. Merula de maribus* (see below, notes 46-48).

[45] Two other treatises which follow after the one by Merula are not mentioned on the title page; for details, see TMD 545.

[46] TMD 545; cf. STCN. This edition was probably used for the French translation of 1845 (see below, note 74), by Magoffin (above, note 10 ff.) and for the Italian edition and translation (above, notes 27 ff.). Copy inter alia in the Peace Palace Library (VP).

[47] In order to distinguish it from the next edition it is easiest to add the number of pages. *Mare liberum* can be found on p. 1-106 (p. 101 incorrectly numbered as 201); on p. 65 'cap. III' is a printer's error for 'cap. VII'.

[48] TMD 546; cf. STCN. For the differences between TMD 546 and 545 – apart from what is mentioned below – see the 'remarques' under TMD 546. *Mare liberum* can be found on p. 1-83; on p. 46 'cap. III' is a printer's error for 'cap. VII'(just as in TMD 545). In the part not concerning *Mare liberum* a number of errors occur in the pagination. According to A. Willems (*Les Elsevier*, Bruxelles 1880, no. 385), TMD 546 is of a later date than TMD 545. Copies available inter alia at Peace Palace Library (VP) and Leiden University Library (UBL).

[49] See above, note 44.

[50] Both published at Frankfurt/Main in 1663 and 1669 respectively; see for details TMD 548 and 549.

[51] Without a separate title page; this is different from the Amsterdam 1632 edition (TMD 544), mentioned above at note 42.

[52] TMD 579; copy inter alia at the Peace Palace Library (VP).

HUGONIS GROTII

DE

JURE PRAEDAE

COMMENTARIUS.

Ex Auctoris Codice descripsit et vulgavit

H. G. HAMAKER, LITT. DR.

HAGAE COMITUM
APUD MARTINUM NIJHOFF.
CIƆIƆCCCLXVIII.

DE IURE PRAEDAE COMMENTARIUS

COMMENTARY ON THE
LAW OF PRIZE AND BOOTY

BY

HUGO GROTIUS

VOLUME I

A Translation of the Original Manuscript of 1604
by
GWLADYS L. WILLIAMS
with the collaboration of
WALTER H. ZEYDEL

OXFORD: AT THE CLARENDON PRESS
LONDON: GEOFFREY CUMBERLEGE
1950

1   Existing Editions of *Mare liberum*

for which the Utrecht professor of law Meinard Tydeman was responsible[53]. This last edition before Magoffin's is still available in many libraries and can be considered as the most reliable so far[54].

2   *Mare liberum* and *De jure praedae*

The lack of any edition of *Mare liberum* between 1773 and 1916 might seem surprising. Of course it could be argued that during this period no new edition of *De jure belli ac pacis* appeared either[55]. The position of the two works, however, was not the same since the discovery of the – autographic – manuscript of an unpublished work of Grotius in 1864. From that manuscript it became clear that the text of *Mare liberum* was based for the greater part on chapter XII of this hitherto unpublished work. An edition followed in 1868 under the title *Hugonis Grotii de jure praedae commentarius, ex Auctoris Codice descripsit et vulgavit H.G. Hamaker, Litt. Dr.*[56]. Naturally, in his preface Hamaker mentions *Mare liberum* and even publishes a passage from another hitherto unknown work of Grotius[57] in which *Mare liberum* is qualified as a part of his *commentarius* dealing – inter alia – with *universa belli praedaeque jura*[58]. In the text of his edition, however, Hamaker does not make any comparison to the printed text of *Mare liberum*[59]. In 1906 James Brown Scott, in his proposal to include works of Grotius in a series of 'Classics on International Law', suggested that an edition of *De jure praedae* should be prepared 'with footnotes calling attention to the few and unimportant modifications of chapter 12, when published separately as the 'Mare liberum''[60]. This was, however, not realized in the 'Classics' edition of *De jure praedae* which finally appeared in 1950[61]. On the other hand nobody seems to have thought to use Hamaker's text (or

< Title page of the English translation (Vol. I) of Hugo Grotius' *De jure praedae commentarius* by Gwladys L. Williams and William H. Zeydel published in 1950 in the 'Classics of International Law' series. It was the basis for the translation of *Mare liberum* hereafter.

---

[53]   TMD 611; microfiches available from Inter Documentation Company (IDC) in Leiden (Grotius Collection International Law, GRI-12/1).
[54]   It contains a number of improvements of the text and the marginal references, which already occur in earlier editions, in particular in those of 1689 (TMD 585-586), of 1712 (TMD 596-597), of 1720 (TMD 601-603) and of 1735 (TMD 605-606). I have cited some of these editions in my notes to the text; the 1712 edition seems to have supplied most improvements.
[55]   The first 'modern' edition of *Djbap* appeared only in 1919, cf. my additional notes in *Djbap* 1993, p. 926 ff.
[56]   Hagae Comitum 1868 (cited as 'Hamaker'). Since 2009 the text is also available at http://easy.dans.knaw.nl/dms or http://textlaboratorium.com/document/DeIurePraedae
[57]   Published in 1872 as *Defensio capitis quinti Maris liber* by S. Muller in his *Mare clausum, Bijdrage tot de geschiedenis der rivaliteit van Engeland en Nederland in de zeventiende eeuw*, Amsterdam 1872, p. 331-361 (cited as 'Defensio').
[58]   Hamaker, p. ix.
[59]   He does not exactly indicate in the Latin text of *De jure praedae*, cap. XII, p. 204-267, the beginning and the end of the section of this text which corresponds to that of *Mare liberum*: these can be found on p. 205 and 249 respectively (for cap. I-XII of *Mare liberum*; elements of cap. XIII on p. 249-252). For a special case see edition, p. 18 note 1.
[60]   See above, note 19.
[61]   See below, at notes 63 ff. In the meantime a translation of *De jure praedae* into Dutch – without the marginal references – had appeared: *Huigh de Groot, Verhandeling over het recht op buit*, vertaald door Dr. Onno Damsté, [Vereeniging voor de uitgave van Grotius], Leiden 1934. Oddly enough, nowhere in this edition is

XXXIX

Page of the collotype reproduction of the manuscript of De jure praedae, published in 1950 in the 'Classics of International Law' series as volume II of De jure praedae commentarius. The manuscript shows how Grotius started to reshape Chapter XII of De jure praedae into Mare liberum.

the manuscript) for publishing a new critical edition of *Mare liberum*. Even Brown Scott, in his 'Introductory Note' to the Magoffin edition of 1916 – though mentioning the Hamaker edition twice[62] – does not hint at this possibility.

Comparisons between *Mare liberum* and *De jure praedae* became much easier when, in 1950, a collotype reproduction of the manuscript was published in the series 'Classics of International Law' as volume II of *De jure praedae commentarius by Hugo Grotius*[63]. For scholars reading Latin, but unfamiliar with Grotius' handwriting, it is a great help that volume I of the edition contains an English translation of this text by Gwladys L. Williams (indicating in the margin the pages of the manuscript in bold type), including a translation and an identification of the marginal references[64]. Shortly after this the Carnegie Endowment made available the volume with a collotype reproduction of *Mare liberum*, already mentioned above[65], which was acquired by a limited number of libraries only. Because the Leiden University Library is one of these happy few, I was able to write my critical articles on some important passages of *Mare liberum*, but many others may not be in the privileged position of having at hand the three volumes dating from 1950-1951. When in 2007 I was asked to give a suggestion for a special publication commemorating the fourth centenary of *Mare liberum*, I proposed an

....

Mare liberum mentioned, of which three Dutch translations had been published in the 17th century, see below, at notes 66 ff.

[62] Introductory Note, p. v n. 2 and p. vii-viii n. 1 (where, for an analysis of *De jure praedae*, he refers to a well-known study on Grotius by Jules Basdevant). Magoffin himself, in his Translator's Preface, does not mention the existence of *De jure praedae* at all.

[63] *The Collotype Reproduction of the Original Manuscript in the Handwriting of Grotius* [*belonging to the State University of Leyden*], Oxford-London 1950. Reprints appeared in New York 1964 and 1995. The text of the ms. is now also available at the sites mentioned above, note 56; a new edition is planned, see J. Waszink, *Using the Work, Remarks on the Text of De iure praedae*, in: Grotiana, 26-28 (2005-2007), p. 215-245.

[64] *De iure praedae commentarius, Commentary on the Law of Prize and Booty by Hugo Grotius, a Translation of the Original Manuscript of 1604*, by Gwladys L. Williams with the collaboration of Walter H. Zeydel, Oxford-London 1950. Reprints appeared in New York 1964 and 1995. A new edition was published under the somewhat cryptic title *Commentary on the Law of Prize and Booty, Hugo Grotius, Edited and with an Introduction by Martine Julia van Ittersum*, [Natural law and Enlightment Classics – Major Legal and Political Works of Hugo Grotius], Liberty Fund, Indianapolis [2006]; only on the verso of the title page, in the middle of many other technical details, does it say: 'The text of this edition is a reprint of the translation of De jure praedae by Gwladys L. Williams published in 1950 [etc.]'. In a 'Note on the text' (on p. xxiii-xxvii) one can find which 'technical' changes and corrections were – tacitly – made in the original text and in the Index of authors cited by Walter H. Zeydel (for an example of an erroneous correction see below, note 173). All in all, the volume is more than a simple 'reprint'; the numbering of the pages is completely different. I have not referred to it in my notes on *Mare liberum*; there, citing 'Williams' means the original edition (or the 1964 and 1995 reprints); when a reference is cited, this implies the research of Walter H. Zeydel (on Zeydel, cf. below, note 151).

In translating the manuscript Williams has, in principle, not taken into account what Brown Scott called 'the few and unimportant modifications of Chapter 12, when published as the Mare liberum'. However, in the preface by George A. Finch, at p. xxiv, mention is made of Williams' efforts 'to decipher ... deleted material', i.e. 'deleted by Grotius himself in his revision [of chapter XII] for a separate publication'. Some remarks on this aspect appear in Williams' footnotes on p. 216, 244 and 261-262.

[65] At note 37; cf. the preface by George A. Finch to the 1950 translation, p. xi. In the Leiden copy of this volume an original letter from the Carnegie Endowment to the librarian, dated September 11, 1951, is found; the text was delivered in approximately one hundred unbound collotype sheets. Apparently, the collotype reproduction was made from a copy of the edition in the British Museum.

I. Ad Gentes omnes omnibus patet aditus iuris Gentium non permittente sed imperante.
II. Infideles ob hoc ipsum quod Infideles sunt, dominio publico, privato-ve capi non possunt, nec titulo inventionis, nec Pontificiæ donationis, nec belli.
III. Mare aut ius navigandi in eo proprium non fit occupatione, aut donatione Pontificia, aut præscriptione sive consuetudine.
IV. Ius mercandi cum gente altera proprium fieri non potest occupatione, aut donatione Pontificia, aut præscriptione sive consuetudine.

SEQVITVR EXAMEN.

CAPVT XII.

*In quo ostenditur etiamsi bellum privatum quispiam,
iustum fore, iustéque partam prædam Indicæ
Hollandorum societati.
In quo obiter certa inseruntur Problemata.*

SI ENIM factum istud ad doctrinam de belli ac prædæ iustitia supra traditam sedulo exigamus, omnino inveniri nihil poterit, quod non exactissime respondeat. Vt igitur omnia complectamur quæ ibi tradita sunt, primum ita agamus, quasi actio ista non publici, uti est revera, sed privati sit belli. Quod autem dico tale est. Separa a causa societatis Indicæ causam publicam Batavorum, et fac eam ipsam societatem non ex Batavis constare, qui bellum in Lusitanos iamdudum gerunt, sed alia aliqua puta Gallis, Germanis, Anglis, Venetis: Et diligenter vide, num quomnis, si se res ita haberet, prædam istam puram censeres, inspice quod societati Indicæ tum fecit subditus locus licuerit: deinde ad minimos societatis te convertere ac in singulis omnia causarum genera omnesque definitiones expende. Ac primum ad personas quod attinet, cum privati belli potestatem natura eius iuris domina atque imperatrix nemini mortalium neget, societatem Indicam excludi nemo dixerit: quod enim singulis seorsim, idem coniunctim pluribus iuris est. Causam ergo unde bellum oriatur, (hoc enim proxime consequitur) investigemus: Et quia monuimus, supra quæ causæ si iustæ essent bellum postea petitoris iustum facerent, easdem si id ius non recte præ se ferunt iustam ad defensorem transferre, quæramus ab ipsis Lusitanis, quid sit quod illi de societate Indica postulent. Non dubie respondebunt, hoc unum se postulare, ne quis præter se ad Indos mercandi causa accedat: quod etiamsi recte dicerent, non tamen continuo insidiæ et perfidia quarum quæ modo narravimus excusarentur.

MARE LIBERVM
SIVE
DE IVRE QVOD BATAVIS
COMPETIT AD INDICANA
COMMERCIA DISSERTATIO

VRYE ZEEVAERT
ofte
BEWYS
Van 't recht dat den Hollan=
ders toecompt over de
Indische coophandel.

Overghestelt uyt het Latynsche in onse
Neder-Duytsche sprake

tot vorderinghe des Vaderlants.

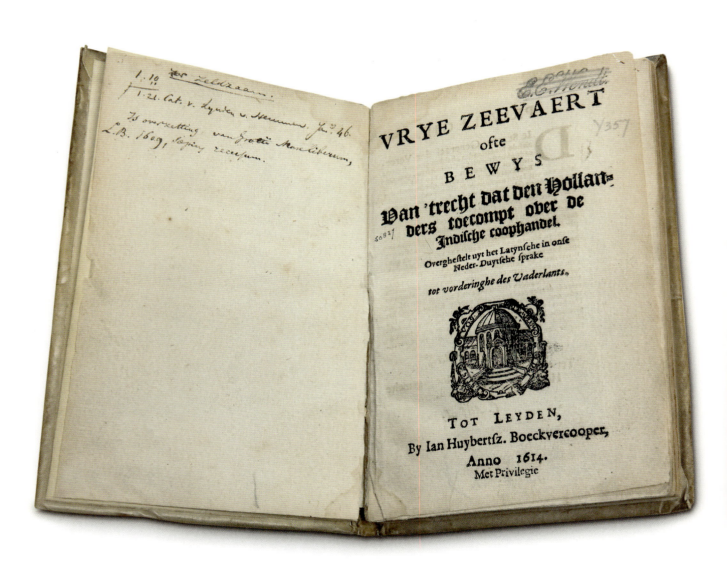

TOT LEYDEN,
By Ian Huybertsz. Boeckvercooper,
Anno 1614.
Met Privilegie

2 *Mare liberum* and *De jure praedae*

easily accessible reprint of the 1609 edition accompanied by a slightly revised text of the Williams translation as the main ingredients for a reliable new edition.

3 Translations of *Mare liberum*

Before going into detail on what is needed further for such an enterprise I have to complete my survey of the *status quaestionis* of editions by calling attention to available translations of *Mare liberum*. Just as for editions of the Latin text, the Ter Meulen and Diermanse bibliography should be the starting point.

There are three translations into Dutch, the first of which, dating from 1614, is of course the most interesting. The main title is *Vrije Zeevaert* but the subtitle and other details on the title page vary in the three different issues of this first edition, all published in the same year (1614) by Jan Huybertsz. in Leiden[66]. The most essential variations on the title page are that in the second issue (TMD 553) it is specified that the text was 'skimmed over and corrected for the second time by the author himself'[67] and that only the third issue (TMD 554) mentions Grotius' name (for the first time: the 1609 editions of the Latin text had not mentioned it). Unfortunately it is difficult to establish what will have been Grotius' corrections; only one seems evident to me[68]. Another variation is that only the third issue gives an indication of the name of the translator by mentioning the initials: 'P.B.'. Ter Meulen and Diermanse suggest – and in my opinion they may be right – that it was Petrus Bertius (1565-1629), at that time trustee of the 'Statencollege' at the University of Leiden and later professor of Ethics at that University[69]. The text of the translation gives the impression that the translator did his work seriously; although not taking over all the marginal references from the Latin text, he made a good selection of them and even added one[70].

The 1614 translation was reprinted in Haarlem in 1636 as part of a volume containing also two other works of Grotius in Dutch[71].

Later, two new translations followed: one appeared in Haarlem in 1639 and 1641 (bearing the name A. Iekerman as translator), and the other in Amsterdam in 1681 (translator Joan Goris)[72]. I did not check these editions.

< Title page of *Vrije Zeevaert*, the first Dutch translation of *Mare liberum*, published by Huybertsz. in Leiden. Three editions (issues) of this translation were published in 1614. This is the first issue. The second issue has a slightly different subtitle. The third issue mentioned Hugo Grotius for the first time as the author.

---

[66] TMD 552, 553 and 554; cf. STCN.
[67] 'Ten tweede mael oversien ende verbetert door den Auteur selffs. tot vorderinghe des Vaderlants'.
[68] The title of the first issue (TMD 552) has 'Vrye zeevaert ofte Bewys Van 't recht dat *den Hollanders* toecompt over de Indische coophandel'; in the second and third issues 'Hollanders' has been changed into 'de Ingesetenen deser geunieerde Landen'. The Latin title has 'Batavi' and at the beginning of the text the explanation is 'Batavis, hoc est Ordinum Federatorum Belgicogermaniae subditis': cf. my note 1 to p. 1 of the edition.
[69] On the role of Bertius see H. Nellen, *Hugo de Groot, Een strijd om de vrede, 1583-1645*, Amsterdam 2007, p. 167 and note 101 on p. 649. On the close relations between Grotius and Bertius in general see L. J. M. Bosch, *Petrus Bertius 1565-1629*, PhD. thesis Nijmegen 1979, p. 117-127 (and passim, see Index).
[70] See my note 1 on p. 61 of the edition.
[71] TMD 555; cf. STCN. The marginal references are incorporated in the text; some have been omitted.
[72] TMD 556 and 557 (1639 and 1641); TMD 558 (1681).

In Ter Meulen and Diermanse's list two translations into French are described: one by Antoine de Courtin, written before 1685 but published only in 1703 (in The Hague)[73], the other by Alfred Guichon de Grandpont which appeared in 1845 as a contribution to the journal *Annales maritimes et coloniales*[74]. Only the second translation is still of interest for the interpretation of *Mare liberum*. It has become easily accessible by a reprint from 1990[75], which unfortunately has a faulty title page, mentioning that it is the 'Traduction d'Antoine de Courtin (1703)'[76]. In his preface the translator – Guichon de Grandpont – severely criticizes precisely the Courtin translation. Guichon was a lawyer ('avocat') and, in my opinion, has rendered Grotius' text very well (he used one of the two Leiden editions from 1633[77]). As far as I can see, he has taken over all the marginal references, partly inserting them in the main text, partly presenting them as footnotes.

The TMD list of translations continues with the mention of the translation into English by Magoffin[78] as part of his edition of the Latin text discussed above. It will be clear that the translation of an edition with many deficiencies can only be of limited use[79]. Nevertheless it has some merits and I finally decided to incorporate two parts of it in my present new edition, i.e. the translation of Grotius' preface '*Ad principes populosque liberos orbis Christiani*' and of the last part of the treatise itself, chapter XIII. Both are missing in the Williams translation of *De jure praedae* because they do not belong to this work. For the preface[80] there were not many problems in using Magoffin's translation, because the Latin text is edited reasonably well and has no marginal references; I had to make only a limited number of changes to the translation. For chapter XIII the situation is somewhat more difficult[81], mainly because of the absence or incompleteness of some marginal references[82]. As to the rest of the Magoffin translation,

---

[73] TMD 559 and 559 A.

[74] TMD 560; *Dissertation de Grotius sur la liberté des mers, traduite du latin, avec une préface et des notes*, par A. Guichon de Grandpont, avocat, in Annales maritimes et coloniales, 30e Année, 3e Série, tome I, 1e section, Sciences et arts, tome 90 de la Collection, Paris 1845, p. 653-717.

[75] *Hugo Grotius, Mare liberum, La liberté des mers, 1609, Traduction d'Antoine de Courtin*, [Bibliothèque de philosophie politique et juridique, Textes et documents], Caen 1990.

[76] In the preface by Simone Goyard-Fabre the error on the title page is confirmed: 'La traduction que nous rééditons ici est celle donnée par Antoine de Courtin en 1703'.

[77] His choice can be explained by the presence of other treatises on the seas in the 1633 editions: he was writing for 'Annales maritimes' and mentions also the treatise by Merula *De maribus* (he apologizes for not dealing with it because it has passages in Hebrew, see p. 660).

[78] Mentioned shortly as TMD 561, with a reference to the full description of the Magoffin edition in TMD 551. As a 'remarque' under TMD 561 the authors refer to an English translation of chapter V of *Mare liberum* by Herbert F. Wright in his study *Some Less Known Works of Hugo Grotius*, [first part: 'The works of Hugo Grotius on fisheries in his controversy with William Welwood', no. 1: 'Chapter V of the Mare liberum'], in: Bibliotheca Visseriana Dissertationum ius internationale illustrantium, tom. VII (Lugduni Batavorum 1928), p. 131-238, at p. 137-153. Wright does not refer to the Magoffin edition and translation; although his translation is different he seems to have used Magoffin's – unreliable – version of the Latin text.

[79] See above, at notes 14 and 15: the changes in the Latin version of the references has led him, in some cases, to a completely false interpretation in the notes to the translation. Cf. also Bensly's review (above, note 16).

[80] For which we only have the Latin version as it appears in the edition, no manuscript version.

[81] Although for this chapter a manuscript version is available.

[82] See edition, p. 62 note a, p. 64 note b and p. 66 note d.

3 Translations of *Mare liberum*

I have sometimes used it for amending some passages of the Williams translation which I did not find satisfactory[83].

One aspect of Magoffin's work remains to be mentioned here, because I found no printed allusions to it elsewhere[84]: the existence of a second issue, in which a number of changes have been made. In part these are corrections, in part additions; the latter are even to be found in the Translator's Preface. The title page has been printed anew, with slight typographical differences. The easiest way to distinguish is to look at p. 64 of the translation, where the last sentence is changed into its opposite meaning[85]. The 1972 and 2001 reprints are of the second – and of course best – issue. Of the two online versions one[86] also has the second issue, the other[87], however, the first.

There is one German translation available: it was made by Richard Boschan and published in 1919 in Leipzig as part of a series 'Philosophische Bibliothek'[88]. The translator does not specify which edition of the Latin text he used and I have not been able to discover it. Identification is particularly difficult because Boschan does not give a literal translation of the marginal references to the sources. He does not neglect them but states in his preface that he will only take them into account as far as they 'specifically enlighten Grotius' working-method'[89]. Nevertheless, in the preface he includes a list of names and authors cited and in the text of his translation there are a number of footnotes which show that he has checked the references seriously. He sometimes rightly criticizes them, and sometimes unjustly. In a few cases he gives solutions for insufficiencies, which I have not found elsewhere. I have mentioned some of these criticisms and solutions in the notes[90].

---

[83] For this purpose, I have also compared the old translation by Hakluyt (see below, section 4) as well as, in a few cases, the Wright translation (cf. above, note 78).

[84] There is, however, a handwritten notice about it in the author's copy of TMD (at no. 551) in the Peace Palace Library. My attention was drawn to this notice by C. G. Roelofsen at the occasion of the publication of the *Grotius Reader*, ed. by L. E. van Holk and C. G. Roelofsen, The Hague 1983, where a reprint of the Magoffin translation of chapters I, II, V and VIII of *Mare liberum* can be found on p. 59-93. This reprint proved to have been made from another copy than the one in my possession. In the Peace Palace Library (VP) a copy of the first issue has the shelf mark S 95 d 6, a copy of the second issue has 196 A 7.

[85] The first issue reads: 'So far is that from being the case, that any one nation may justly oppose in any way, any other two nations that desire to enter into a mutual and exclusive contractual relation'; the second issue has: 'For surely no one nation may justly oppose in any way two nations that desire to enter into a contract with each other'. Another example can be found on p. 44 note 3, where the first issue identifies Rodericus Zuarius with 'Philippus Zuerius (? – 1606) of Antwerp' and the second issue simply refers to 'Rodericus Zuarius, Consilia published in 1621'. Apart from that, in both issues the reference is completely mutilated, cf. my edition, p. 36 notes 2, c and d. For Zuarius cf. below, at note 174.

[86] The version mentioned above, note 25 (Batoche).

[87] The version mentioned above, note 26 (Liberty Fund).

[88] *Hugo Grotius, Von der Freiheit des Meeres*, übersetzt und mit einer Einleitung, erklärenden Anmerkungen und Register versehen von Richard Boschan, [Der Philosophischen Bibliothek Band 97], Leipzig 1919; see TMD 562. According to K.-H. Ziegler, *Völkerrechtliche Aspekte der Eroberung Lateinamerikas*, Zeitschrift für neuere Rechtsgeschichte, 23 (2001), p. 1-29, at p. 19 n. 141, is this 'seinerzeit verdienstvolle Übersetzung ... in manchen Teilen nicht juristisch präzise genug'. His translation is not mentioned by Williams but it does figure in Armitage's edition of Hakluyt's translation (see below, note 98), p. xxi n. 2.

[89] 'nur insoweit, als durch sie seine Arbeitsweise in ein bezeichnendes Licht gerückt wird' (p. 10).

[90] See edition, fol. 5 r note 2, p. 3 note i, p. 4 note b, p. 9 note 2 and note a, p. 20 note f and p. 42 note d.

Overview of the various translations of *Mare liberum*: English (the longstanding edition by Magoffin, second issue), Korean, Spanish, Italian, French, Polish, German.

The last of the translations mentioned by Ter Meulen and Diermanse (in 1950) is one into Italian by F. Carfì, published in Florence in 1931-1933 as a contribution to the journal *L'Alfieri*, and also separately as a book in 1933[91].

After the 1950 TMD bibliography several new translations have appeared: in 1955 into Polish, in 1956 into Spanish (reprinted in 1979), in 1984 into Korean and in 2007 for a second time into Italian[92]. I will only give some comments on the Spanish and the second Italian translation[93].

The first edition of the Spanish translation, by V. Blanco García and L. García Arias, was published in 1956; a reprint followed in 1979[94]. The translation is said to be based on the Latin text of the Amsterdam Blaeuw edition of 1633 (TMD 547) but to follow the Magoffin edition of 1916 for the citations by Grotius[95]. We have already seen what that means. Of Magoffin's most serious errors in interpreting the references they have copied the great majority; in only two cases have they added critical observations[96].

The new Italian translation is combined with the edition of the Latin text of 2007, already mentioned and criticized in section 1 (above at notes 27 ff.). The translation copies all the shortcomings of the Magoffin edition, neglecting even some critical comments from the Spanish translators[97].

---

[91] For further details see TMD 563 and 564; the full title of the edition as a book is given in the list of Abbreviations (below, p. 163). The translator in the 2007 edition (see below, note 164) says not to have been able to find a copy of the 1933 book (but heavily criticizes the text as it appeared in *L'Alfieri*); I have seen, however, a copy in the Peace Palace Library (VP) and made some use of it. The translation seems to be partly based on the Magoffin edition, which, however, is not mentioned; only in L'Alfieri II-3 (1931), p. 17, Carfì calls his translation 'dall'edizione elzevíriana dell'anno 1663 [sic]'. (1633 is meant).

[92] A translation into Norwegian, accompanied by an edited version of the text from 1609, has been published in November 2009: *Mare liberum: Det frie hav, En avhandling om retten Nederlenderne har til å drive handel i Ostindia*, redigert og oversatt av Andreas Harald Aure, Oslo 2009. I am much indebted to Mr. Aure, who put a question to me which led to an improvement of my edition and who drew my attention to the review of the Magoffin edition by Edward Bensly (see above, note 16).

[93] As to the Polish and the Korean translations (both available at the Peace Palace Library) it may suffice to give the (short) titles: *Hugo Grotius, Wolność Mórz* ... [ed. by] Remigiusz Bierzanek, Warszava 1955; *Hugonis Grotii Mare liberum* ... translated by Seok Hyun Kim, Seoul 1984. Both translations seem to be based on the Magoffin edition, the Polish one looks more independent and avoiding some of Magoffin's errors but at one point the Korean translation takes over a useful comment of Magoffin not figuring elsewhere, see edition, p. 62 note 1.

[94] *Hugo Grocio, De la libertad de los mares*, Prólogo de Luis García Arias, Traducción de V. Blanco García y L. García Arias, Madrid 1979 (the 1956 edition has – after the main title – only 'Estudio preliminar por Luis García Arias').

[95] See p. 48 n. 66, where the editors wrongly qualify the Amsterdam Blaeuw edition as the 'edición elzeviriana', published by Magoffin.

[96] See p. 99 n. 49 (Johannes Faber), and p. 115 n. 70 (Rodericus Zuarius); on the other hand they added details on Estius (see edition, p. 3 note g) and maintained (on p. 105) 'Alvarez' (cf. below, at note 198).

[97] See p. 136 n. 48 (Johannes Faber), and p. 145 n. 68 (Rodericus Zuarius).

4 The Recently Edited Old English Translation by Richard Hakluyt

Much more important than these modern translations is no doubt an old English translation by one of Grotius' contemporaries, Richard Hakluyt the younger (died November 1616), edited for the first time by David Armitage in 2004[98]. The manuscript of this translation – a fair copy in Hakluyt's own hand – was found in Inner Temple Library in London[99]. According to Armitage, the occasion for the translation and the reason it was not published (in Hakluyt's lifetime or shortly afterwards) can only be matter for speculation. He calls the translation quite literal in its adherence to Grotius' Latin syntax and adds that in his edition 'to clarify the meaning of the text, spelling and punctuation have been modernized throughout'. Because the manuscript does not include Grotius' marginal annotations, Armitage has supplied them from the 1609 text of *Mare liberum* and 'expanded, supplemented, and corrected [them] as necessary'[100].

It will be clear that not only Hakluyt's translation by itself but also Armitage's additions and annotations, referring to the 1609 edition (and other sources, like the manuscript of *De jure praedae* and Williams' translation of it with identification of the sources) proved to be of the utmost importance for my project of a new edition of *Mare liberum*. In a certain number of cases I made changes in Williams' translation when I preferred the more literal adherence to Grotius' text of Hakluyt. On the other hand, I found more examples of errors in Hakluyt's translation than those mentioned by Armitage[101]. As to the latter's additions of the sources and their identification I have some objections, but for the greater part they have their origin in the fact that he follows Williams too strictly, in particular in the incorrect way of linking the references to the text (originating from the 1633 and later editions). Only in some exceptional cases have

---

[98] *The Free Sea, Hugo Grotius, Translated by Richard Hakluyt with William Welwod's Critique and Grotius's Reply*, edited and with an introduction by David Armitage, [Natural law and Enlightenment Classics – Major Legal and Political Works of Hugo Grotius], Liberty Fund, Indianapolis [2004] (cited as 'Armitage').

[99] Armitage, p. xxi ff. (also for what follows in the next lines).

[100] Armitage, p. xxiii.

[101] For examples I refer to the following pages of the Hakluyt translation:

p. 8 l. 11-12 'notwithstanding necessity was driven from equal judges of extreme servitude' (criticized also by Armitage in his note 3 but amended by him in a wrong way: the text of 1609 has 'extrem*ae* servitutis', not 'extrem*a*'; cf. my translation on fol. 5 recto, inspired by the German translation);

p. 29 l. 11-12 'Paulus thought they were to be forbidden' (it should be: 'Paulus thought [the owner of the preserve] would have been entitled to avail himself of the interdict [Uti possidetis]', see the Williams translation (slightly improved by me) on p. 24 of the present edition).

p. 30 l. 16-17 'Johannes Faber, "When the sea shall depart ..."'(it should be: 'Johannes Faber ... when he asserted'); Hakluyt had not corrected the printer's error 'cesserit' (instead of 'asserit'), mentioned in the Errata of the 1609 edition, cf. p. 24 note 3 of the present edition. For similar cases where Hakluyt neglects the errata, see p. 11 note 1 and p. 27 note 1 of this edition.

p. 51 l. 1-4 (passage in which 'navium exercitio' is opposed to 'institorum usus'): Hakluyt has not understood the Roman Law terminology and the contradistinction between both; for a correct translation see p. 54 of the present edition.

p. 60 l. 16 'these multitudes' (it should be 'those to go unpunished'). Hakluyt has not corrected the printer's error 'multos' (instead of 'inultos'), mentioned in the Errata of the 1609 edition, cf. p. 66 note 2, of the present edition.

I made allusions to Armitage's 'apparatus' in my edition of the references[102].

One of Armitage's comments merits special attention: in a footnote to the translation of Hakluyt[103] he refers to an interesting passage in the manuscript of *De jure praedae* which is not found in the Latin text of the 1609 edition of *Mare liberum*[104]. Although he does not mention it explicitly, the reason for this discrepancy between manuscript and edition is undoubtedly the fact that in the ms. this passage is crossed out for a particular reason.

5 Recent Research on Manuscript Leiden BPL 917

This brings us to a last aspect of the 'status quaestionis' that should be considered before approaching a new edition of *Mare liberum*. One of Armitage's pupils, Martine Julia van Ittersum, has recently written a series of articles on the manuscript of *De jure praedae*, in particular on its use in preparing the edition of *Mare liberum*[105]. There are many examples of changes in the text like the ones just mentioned: not only of crossing out passages of the original text, but also of adding new passages to it and even of crossing out newly added passages. Van Ittersum has developed a special technique of dating these revisions on the basis of ink-colour[106]. I cannot go into details and have to refer the reader to her studies, not only for these revisions of the text[107] but also for the printing story of *Mare liberum*[108]. One aspect of this story, however, should be mentioned here for a better understanding of the present edition.

When the Zeeland VOC directors commissioned Grotius to publish *Mare liberum* by a letter of 4 November 1608, he asked his friend Daniel Heinsius to oversee the publication[109]. Grotius himself had of course to prepare the text for the printer. From a

---

[102] See the present edition, p. 6 note i, p. 39 note e, 42 note c and 50 note a.
[103] P. 14 n. 6 (in the text the reference mark should figure after 'so famous many ages since', not after 'Horace').
[104] See ms. fol. 98 r and edition p. 6, with my note 1.
[105] The most important article is M. J. van Ittersum, *Preparing Mare Liberum for the Press: Hugo Grotius' Rewriting of Chapter 12 of De Jure Praedae in November-December 1608*, in: Grotiana 26-28 (2005-2007) [published in one volume in 2008], p. 246-280 (cited as Van Ittersum, *Preparing Mare Liberum*). Before this article she had already mentioned a detail in her *Mare Liberum in the West Indies? Hugo Grotius and the case of the Swimming Lion, a Dutch Pirate in the Caribbean at the turn of the Seventeenth Century*, Itinerario, 31 (2007), no. 3, p. 59-94, at p. 79-80 (cited as 'Van Ittersum, *Mare Liberum in West Indies*'). Later followed her *Dating the Manuscript of De Jure Praedae (1604-1608): What Watermarks, Foliation and Quire Divisions Can Tell Us about Hugo Grotius' Development as a Natural Rights and Natural Law Theorist*, History of European Ideas, 35 (2009), p. 125-193 (cited as 'Van Ittersum, *Dating the Manuscript*'). Still forthcoming (?) is her *The Wise Man is Never Merely a Private Citizen: the Roman Stoa in Hugo Grotius' De Jure Praedae (1604-1608)* (contribution to a conference 'Cosmopolitan Politics: on the History of a Controversial Ideal' (Frankfurt am Main, December 2006); the author kindly provided me with a copy of her text, cited by me as 'Van Ittersum, *The Wise Man*').
[106] See particularly Van Ittersum, *Preparing Mare Liberum*, p. 261-265.
[107] Some of these revisions described by van Ittersum are mentioned in my notes to the edition, but not all.
[108] See Van Ittersum, *Preparing Mare Liberum*, p. 256-258.
[109] For details on the history of the publication see Nellen, *Hugo de Groot* (above, note 69), p. 94-97, mainly based on letters of Grotius to Heinsius, published in *Briefwisseling van Hugo Grotius*, ed. by P. C. Molhuysen

5 Recent Research on Manuscript Leiden BPL 917

line-count made in his own manuscript (now BPL 917 in Leiden)[110] it can be concluded that, in order to enable two compositors to work simultaneously – one setting the type for the first half of the text, the other doing the same for the second half – he had to deliver to the printer a copy in two halves. We do not know who made this scribal copy[111], but in comparing the printed text to the original manuscript we have to keep in mind that differences may be due not only to printer's errors in a strict sense, but also to the copying.

6 The Objectives of the Present Edition

In the preceding sections of this Introduction some occasional remarks have already been made on the origins and different aspects of my project for the present publication. Its objectives may be summarized as follows.

The first objective is to offer a reliable edition of the Latin text, based on a facsimile of the first edition, the only one which Grotius may have given some attention to himself. A number of corrections have to be made in this printed text. A first category is constituted by those mentioned in the List of Errata on fol. 6 v of the edition. A second consists of errata discovered by close reading and by collation with the manuscript Leiden BPL 917; although strictly speaking they might not be printer's errors (they might stem from the copyist[112]) I will refer to them as such.

As far as the main text is concerned these corrections are given in footnotes identified by Arabic numerals[113]; corrections in Grotius' references to his alleged sources in the marginalia are included in the lettered footnotes which first repeat in bold printing what is found in the margin of the facsimile edition and then add identification and further comment[114].

....

et al., vol. I, [Rijks Geschiedkundige Publicatiën, Grote Serie, vol. 64], 's Gravenhage 1928, Nos. 148, 149, 151-156, 159, 161, 164, 165 (the relevant texts of these letters have also been published by C. van Vollenhoven, in a study reprinted in his *Verspreide Geschriften*, I, Haarlem – 's Gravenhage 1934, p. 503-507.

Apart from the interesting allusions to the possibility of a French translation of *Mare liberum* (a plan that did not succeed; cf. *Briefwisseling*, I, nos. 148, 151, and 152) I would like to draw attention to some passages referring to the correction of the proofs. Apparently Heinsius himself was, at first, not in the picture for this task: Grotius makes suggestions that either Gerard Tuning or Dominicus Baudius (both Leiden professors) could be asked (*Briefwisseling*, I, nos. 153 and 154). It is not clear whether this had any result; maybe Heinsius did some of the work after all.

Finally, in a letter of 7 March 1609 (*Briefwisseling*, I, no. 161), Grotius says, after thanking Heinsius for all his help: 'Errata annotavi et gaudeo me tam paucis defunctum, ut nunc est Typographorum genus'. May we conclude that the small list on fol. 6 v of the edition was composed by Grotius himself?

[110] For details see Van Ittersum, *Preparing Mare Liberum*, p. 258; the suggestion about the line count was made to her by Dr. Nellen.
[111] One copyist or two? Van Ittersum speaks of one, Nellen thinks of two. I am inclined to follow Van Ittersum.
[112] Cf. above, at the end of section 5; for an example see p. 4 note b. Not all differences between the edition and the manuscript need to be printer's errors or copyist's errors: for a special problem see p. 18 note f.
[113] They are attached to the Latin text (in the margin) as well as to the English translation.
[114] They are only attached to the English translation; the link with the Latin text can easily be established

A special problem in giving the results of a comparison between the text of the edition and the manuscript Leiden BPL 917 is whether mention should be made – in a footnote – of cases in which a passage in the printed text figures in the manuscript only as an addition to the original text. My policy has been to do this only when the addition evidently had its origin in the adaptation of the text for the edition. In some cases I have made an exception when the addition – even if probably not being an adaptation for the edition – is an important element in understanding the rest of the text[115].

The second objective is to make available a usable English translation in the shape of a slightly revised text of the translation of chapters I to XII as part of the *De jure praedae* manuscript by Gwladys L. Williams[116], completed by an – equally revised – text of the translation of *Mare liberum* by Ralph van Deman Magoffin for Grotius' preface and for chapter XIII[117]. The revisions are of various kinds. Some are based on comparisons with other translations, mainly the old English translation by Hakluyt[118] but also some translations into other languages (the 1614 translation into Dutch, the 1845 one into French and the 1919 one into German). Other revisions are inspired by reading the sources mentioned by Grotius, in particular the juridical texts[119].

This brings me to the third objective of this edition: the verification of the references in the margin. This is a point I already became familiar with in my edition of *De jure belli ac pacis* published in 1993. The main problem there was to make choices: not all the sources could be verified in the time available for research. Mutatis mutandis the situation is the same for *Mare liberum* and I decided to apply the same restrictions as in the 'Additional Notes' of the 1993 edition of Grotius' main work[120]: to exclude authors of literary texts from classical antiquity, biblical texts and early Christian sources; to take the end of the 6th century as a rough dividing line and to verify from the period before only the legal texts, i.e. mainly those of Justinian's *Corpus iuris civilis*[121]; to verify

---

because of the repetition of the marginal references in bold type.

[115] See e.g. p. 26 note 2 and p. 42 note 1.

[116] See above, at note 64. I took over the indication, in the margin, of the pages of the manuscript.

[117] See above, at notes 80ff. The translations sometimes have a different approach of some technical details, e.g. in the case of passages in Greek. As a rule I let the differences exist; the only thing I unified (in the sense of Williams) is that when Grotius puts some words or passages in capitals (in the manuscript and in the printed text), I changed this everywhere into lower case italics.

Both translations have introduced paragraphs. These do not occur in the Latin text of the manuscript nor in the editions of the 17th and 18th centuries. Magoffin has introduced them also in the Latin text (this was followed in the Italian edition of 2007). The French translation of 1845 already has paragraphs; this is also the case for the German translation of 1919. In the translation of the present edition I have copied the paragraphs of Williams and Magoffin respectively.

[118] Sometimes I have also compared the English translation of chapter V by Herbert F. Wright, mentioned above, note 78.

[119] Williams was not very familiar with Roman law terminology, e.g. *accessio*, *iniuria* and *occupatio*.

[120] See *Djbap (1993)*, p. 933-934 (in my introduction to the 'Additional Notes').

[121] The ancient legal texts outside the *Corpus iuris civilis* mentioned in *Djbap (1993)*, p. 939, do not occur in *Mare liberum*. In the latter there is, however, one ancient legal text not mentioned in *Djbap*: constitutions of Theodoric, King of the Ostrogoths (died 526), transmitted by Cassiodorus (died c. 575) in his *Variae* (published in the 16th century); see the present edition, p. 66 note c. – The excluded texts can be found in the 'Index of Sources not Mentioned in the List' (below, p. 171-174)

6 The Objectives of the Present Edition

all the texts written after the end of the 6th century, which leads primarily to the fields of jurisprudence, moral theology and historiography. For the excluded texts I simply adopt the verifications given by Williams and Magoffin. Only in cases where Grotius omits a citation in the margin or where serious difficulties could arise to identify the source have I made a few exceptions[122].

A last and rather specific objective of the present edition is to provide the reader with the Latin text of some relevant passages which have been crossed out in the manuscript and are therefore mentioned neither in the edition of *Mare liberum* nor in the edition and the translation of *De jure praedae*[123].

7 The Verification of the References in the Margin and the Problem of Linking Them to the Text

In the verification of the references in the margin I have, in principle, followed the method used in the 'Additional Notes' in the 1993 edition of *De jure belli ac pacis*[124]. This method differs in some respects from what has been practiced by Williams[125] in her translation of *De jure praedae*.

The reference is mostly[126] identified by an indication of the page(s)[127] in the edition in which it was checked. These editions are given in a highly abbreviated form: only the name of the author and a short title reference (the title has been omitted when there can be no doubt which work is meant). These abbreviations are explained in the List of Sources (see below, p. 165-169).

When Grotius' reference (sometimes with a short addition by me) indicates the part of the work (book, chapter, section, number, etc.) sufficiently clearly, I have only indicated the page or pages that might be meant. If, however, Grotius' indication has been added to or changed in any way, I give it in full as it should be and only then add the page reference, beginning with the abbreviation 'ed.' (for edition). To draw the reader's attention to the changes I have made in the indication of the part of the text referred to, I have sometimes used bracketed exclamation marks.

In some instances the edition commits an error in the name of an author. In such cases I have placed the correct name in brackets after the erroneous name[128].

For some authors Grotius' indication of the divisions of the work is of such a character that a great many pages have to be leafed through before the intended passage is found. In those cases it has been my aim to give further specifications, introduced by the word

---

[122] Cf. inter alia, p. 63 note 3.
[123] Cf. above, note 64, at the end, and the text at notes 104 and 106.
[124] *Djbap (1993)*, p. 934 ff.
[125] Williams' method has, grosso modo, been followed by Armitage in his edition of Hakluyt's translation.
[126] Not in the case of texts of the *Corpus iuris civilis* and the *Corpus iuris canonici*.
[127] This is the most important difference compared to the method of Williams and Armitage.
[128] See e.g. edition, p. 28 note 1.

'at', sometimes followed by a number in the edition I used. Here I am forced, however, to admit that I did not have time to do this for all the sources I consulted[129].

In some cases I add to the identification of the reference a short commentary. This may consist of a proposed textual emendation in the reference[130] or a remark concerning other editions of the work cited in which printer's errors occur, etc.[131]. On occasion, however, I go a step further and express an opinion concerning the likely provenance of Grotius' reference[132]. Sometimes I have also noted examples that Grotius adopted a *Mare liberum* reference in *De jure belli ac pacis*[133]. In none of these cases – either in the case of textual emendations or printing errors, or in indications of provenance or repetitions – do I make any claims to being exhaustive. I wish to add that I did not refrain from sporadic references to detailed studies I have written on certain passages[134].

As to problems concerning the linking of Grotius' references to the text, there is a clear difference between *Mare liberum* and *De jure belli ac pacis*. In the latter work a number of these links – concerning additions made by Grotius in the 1642 and 1646 editions – are authentic since the author made them himself. In *Mare liberum* the links occur for the first time in the 1633 edition(s) and were probably established by some assistant of the publisher, without any consultation of the author. They were maintained – with a few exceptions – in all subsequent editions and translations[135]. In the 1609 and 1618 editions no links are found and they do not appear either in the manuscript of *De jure praedae*; it was only in the printed edition of the latter that Hamaker introduced them. Williams, in her annotated translation, took them over. In using this translation for my edition of *Mare liberum* I was faced with the problem[136] whether I should maintain these links or create my own. I decided to change the Hamaker-Williams links only where I thought it necessary for a correct interpretation of Grotius' text. In closely comparing the 1609 edition with the manuscript I found only a limited number of cases where a change was desirable. In some instances splitting a cluster of references seemed the best solution.

---

[129] See e.g. edition, p. 58 note e.
[130] See e.g. edition, p. 3 notes d, g and i, p. 4 note b, p. 6 note g, p. 9 notes a and d, p. 11 note a, and p. 20 note c.
[131] See e.g. edition, p. 9 note b.
[132] See below, at the end of section 9.
[133] See e.g. edition, p. 3 note i and p. 62 note a.
[134] See above, at the beginning of this Introduction; cf. e.g. p. 14 notes a, b and c, as well as p. 16 note b.
[135] An example of incorrect links can be found in the case of the references on p. 5 of the ed. 1609, mentioned in my notes a, b, c and d: in the ed. 1633, p. 22 and 23, these four references have been put together in two notes whereby my note c is split into two sections. In later editions (including Magoffin's) my note a has become the first note and notes b, c and d are put together as the second note. In fact, all four references should appear in separate notes with different links as they are presented by Hamaker on the basis of the ms.; this division and linking is also clearly meant in the 1609 edition.
For another example see edition, p. 36 note 3.
[136] Of course I had to make links in the English text because it was difficult to do so in the facsimile of the 1609 edition.

8 The List of Sources

Just as in *De jure belli ac pacis*[137], my List of Sources has a twofold function: it serves to give further specifications of the editions I use and refer to in my notes in an abbreviated form, and it serves as an Index of authors cited by indicating the pages in the edition of *Mare liberum* on which references to the relevant source occur. As to the latter purpose, I have also included passages in the text where a particular author but not a particular work is named.

I follow a special policy as regards references to standard texts concerning Roman and Canon law; that is, texts which occur in the editions of the *Corpus iuris civilis* and the *Corpus iuris canonici* as used in Grotius' day. There is no point in giving page references relating to these 16th and early 17th century editions. In most cases I did no more than check the relevant texts in 19th and 20th century standard editions, and change Grotius' references into modern ones (with numbers only)[138]. For the benefit of non-specialist readers I indicate these editions here (they do not belong to the List of Sources, which only contains editions that could have been used by Grotius; however, the list does include the standard abbreviations under which these sources are cited and a special index of the Roman and Canon law texts follows on p. 165-169).

For the *Corpus iuris civilis* I use the so-called *editio stereotypa*, which consists of three volumes. The most accessible of these is a 1954 Berlin reprint, which reproduces the 16th edition of vol. I, the 11th edition of vol. II and the 6th edition of vol. III. In the first volume one finds *Institutiones*, recognovit P. Krueger, and *Digesta*[139], recognovit Th. Mommsen, retractavit P. Krueger (first edition Berlin 1872, many later editions; cited by Grotius with the medieval abbreviation ff.). The second part contains the *Codex Iustinianus*, recognovit et retractavit P. Krueger (first edition Berlin 1877, many later editions). The third contains *Novellae*, recognovit R. Schoell, absolvit G. Kroll (first edition Berlin 1895, many later editions; it also contains an edition of the *Authenticum*, the only version in which the *Novellae* were known in the Middle Ages).

For the *Corpus iuris canonici* the edition used is that of E. Friedberg, Leipzig 1879-1881 (reprint Graz 1959). The first volume contains the *Decretum Gratiani*, the second the *Decretales*, both those of Gregory IX (*Liber Extra*) and the later collections such as (*Liber*) *Sextus, Clementinae, Extravagantes* (*communes* and *Joannis XXII*).

---

[137] In the following pages many passages are an adapted version of §§ 8 and 9 (p. 937-944) of my Introduction to the *Annotationes novae* in the 1993 edition of *De jure belli ac pacis*.

[138] In one case there is a special difficulty, caused by the fact that Grotius cites a text in two different ways: as '*l. ult.*' [*lex ultima*] and as '*l. Praescriptio*' [being the first word of the text]. See my comments p. 20 note d, p. 25 note a, p. 39 note d, p. 40 note b, p. 41 note b and p. 44 note c.

[139] In a number of cases Grotius, when he is citing texts of the Digest, adds the name of the Roman jurist who is mentioned as author of the work from which Justinian's compilers of the Digest took over the text. Again, for the benefit of non-specialist readers I included these names in my List of Sources with reference to the pages where Grotius mentions them (in the main text). For biographical details see W. Kunkel, *Herkunft und soziale Stellung der römischen Juristen* (2nd ed.), Graz-Wien-Köln 1967 (reprint Köln-Weimar-Wien 2001).

16th and 17th century editions of the *Corpus iuris civilis* also include a number of sources that are not to be found in the standard editions noted above, primarily[140] the *Libri feudorum* and the Gloss of *Accursius*. Those interested in these texts can consult a reprint of the last so-called Gothofredus edition with the Gloss, Lyon 1627: *Corpus iuris civilis Iustinianei, studio et opera Ioannis Fehi*, 6 vol., Osnabrück 1966[141].

9 The Choice of the Editions Mentioned in the List

As a rule, I have attempted to verify the sources that do not fall under the exceptions mentioned above in an edition that Grotius could have used.

Only in a few cases can we establish with any degree of certainty which edition Grotius actually used. One of these is that only one edition of a work cited appeared before the moment Grotius refers to it[142].

One might be tempted to assume that a particular edition was used if it was one that Grotius owned himself. But a certain amount of caution is called for here. This is not the place to dwell upon Grotius' library[143]; nevertheless, it is perhaps worth mentioning the following.

It is a well-known fact that an inventory of Grotius' library was compiled on 25 March 1620, showing the state of his collection at the moment of his incarceration in August 1618[144]. Much of this inventory is so sketchy, however, that where more than one edition existed it is not possible to ascertain the exact edition Grotius owned. Moreover, it is not certain that books cited in *Mare liberum* and occurring in the list were already in his possession when he wrote that part of ms. Leiden PBL 917.

What seems to be somewhat more important than the inventory are the books of Grotius' library which still exist, such as a number of those bought after his death by Queen Christina of Sweden. Some of the latter books are still in Swedish libraries[145],

---

[140] In addition, the *Novellae Leonis*, the novels of the Byzantine emperor Leo VI (886-912), can be mentioned; they have been added to most editions of the *Corpus iuris civilis* without the Gloss since 1571.

[141] Sometimes this edition can also be used to identify references to Doctores on the Civil law.

[142] This would, e.g., seem to be the case for Albericus Gentilis, De iure belli; see the List of Sources, below p. 165-169

[143] The most recent general study on this subject is E. Rabbie, *The History and Reconstruction of Hugo Grotius' Library, a Survey of the Results of Former Studies with an Indication of New Lines of Approach*, in: Bibliothecae selectae da Cusano a Leopardi, ed. E. Canone, Firenze 1993, p. 119-137. For the books cited in his juridical works see R. Feenstra, *Ius commune et droit comparé chez Grotius, Nouvelles remarques sur les sources citées dans ses ouvrages juridiques, à propos d'une réimpression du De iure belli ac pacis*, Rivista internazionale di diritto comune, 3 (1992), p. 7-36); reprinted in R. Feenstra, *Legal Scholarship and Doctrines of Private Law, 13th-18th centuries*, [Variorum Collected Studies Series, CS 556], Aldershot 1996, as no. VI (cited as Feenstra 1992-1996); cf. also P. Borschberg, *Hugo Grotius "Commentarius in Theses XI", an Early Treatise on Sovereignty, the Just War and the Legitimacy of the Dutch Revolt*, Berne etc. [1994], p. 47-101 ('Considerations relating to the principle sources utilized by Grotius for the '*Commentarius in Theses XI*').

[144] See P. C. Molhuysen, *De bibliotheek van Hugo de Groot in 1618*, Mededeelingen der Nederlandsche Akademie van Wetenschappen, Afd. Letterkunde, Nieuwe reeks, 6 (1943), p. 45-63 (in our List of Sources cited as 'Inv.').

[145] See F. Dovring, *Une partie de l'héritage littéraire de Grotius retrouvée en Suède*, Mededelingen der Koninklijke

9 The Choice of the Editions Mentioned in the List

others in Leiden University Library[146] and they include titles cited in *Mare liberum*[147]. Of these we can at least be certain about the editions he owned, but whether he actually used these editions when writing the *Mare liberum* part of the Leiden manuscript is not always clear.

As to books which Grotius apparently did not own but which he borrowed[148], mention should be made of the fact that in 1604 his friend Jan ten Grootenhuis sent him an edition of Victoria's *Relectiones theologicae* – one of the main sources of *De jure praedae* and *Mare liberum* – which can probably be identified as the *editio princeps*, published in Lyon 1557[149].

In spite of all these reservations with regard to Grotius' book collection, I do indicate in the List of Sources whether a particular work can be found in the inventory of 1620 (with the reference 'Cf. Inv.' followed by the number). As for the books from his library still extant I refer in the List of Sources to footnote 147 of the present introduction, where the relevant works are listed.

The List of Sources made for the additional notes in the 1993 edition of *De jure belli ac pacis* mentions for every source[150] whether it is referred to by Grotius in one of his other major legal works. The most important of these is of course *De jure praedae*, whose chapter XII was the basis for *Mare liberum*. It is obvious that an edition of this last work, in its turn, should mention every work referred to in *De jure belli ac pacis* and in the other chapters of *De jure praedae*. I have done this in adding the general references 'Cf. Djbap' and 'Cf. Djp o.p.' [= *De jure praedae*, other parts than the one used for *Mare liberum*], followed by the number of citations. For *Djbap*, it will be easy to find the passages via the 'List of Sources' of the 1993 edition. For *Djp*, the 'Index of authors cited'[151] in the English translation by Williams (1950) should be used; the Latin text of the reference can be found in the 'collotype reproduction' of the ms. Leiden BPL 917 (the folio numbers are mentioned in the margin of the translation)[152].

Nederlandsche Akademie van Wetenschappen, Afd. Letterkunde, Nieuwe reeks, 12 (1949), p. 237-250, and *Nouvelles recherches sur la bibliothèque de Grotius en Suède et en Italie*, ibidem 14 (1951), p. 331-340 (hereafter cited as 'Dovring I and II').

[146] See E. M. Meijers, *Boeken uit de bibliotheek van De Groot in de Universiteitsbibliotheek te Leiden*, Mededelingen der Nederlandsche Akademie van Wetenschappen, Afd. Letterkunde, Nieuwe reeks, 12 (1949), p. 251-279 (hereafter cited as 'Meijers'); cf. also F. F. Blok, *Contributions to the History of Isaac Vossius' Library* [= Verhandelingen der Koninklijke Nederlandse Akademie van Wetenschappen, Afd. Letterkunde, Nieuwe reeks, 83], Amsterdam-London 1974 (hereafter cited as 'Blok'), in particular p. 34-43 (The Grotiana in the 'Gerardus Johannes Vossius' auction catalogue; these books are not to be found in Leiden University Library).

[147] Among the authors mentioned in the List of Sources this is the case for *Ayala* (Blok, p. 40 no. 22), *Jason de Maino in Cod.* and *in Dig.* (Dovring II, no. 11) and *Thomas Aquinas, Summa* (Dovring I, no. 16).

[148] For some orientation, see my Introduction to the *Annotationes novae* in the 1993 edition of *De jure belli ac pacis*, p. 941 n. 86.

[149] See my 1993 Introduction, p. 940 n. 77.

[150] In Djbap there is one reference to chapter 5 of his *Mare liberum*, see p. 189 n. 1. and p. 958 in the 1993 edition.

[151] Made by Walter H. Zeydel, research assistant on the Classics of International Law, who has also located most of the passages cited; cf. Preface to the translation, p. xxv.

[152] It is more difficult to trace these passages in the edition of the Latin text by Hamaker, which has no index

I have conducted no systematic research of this kind as far as Grotius' other works are concerned, although some attention was, of course, given to the other legal works. The principal of these, as far as references to sources are concerned, is his *Florum sparsio ad jus Justinianeum*. Although planned at a much earlier date (Grotius announced it already in 1613), this work did not come out until 1642. I had to abandon a plan to include references to this work in my edition, even in the List of Sources[153]. The same applies to the additions Grotius made in his own copy of the *Inleidinge tot de Hollandsche Rechtsgeleerdheid*, now part of the collection of the University Library at Lund[154].

Among the minor legal works[155] there is one which, due to its date – 1607, i.e., practically contemporary with *Mare liberum* – deserves some attention: a memorandum in Latin made for the government of the United Provinces regarding possible negotiations on a peace treaty with Spain[156]. A number of authorities referred to there also occur in *Mare liberum*. In the List of Sources I will refer to it as 'Mem. 1607', followed by the page number in the 1955 edition by W. J. M. van Eysinga.

Finally, we must consider the possibility that Grotius simply copied references to a source from another source without verifying them himself. Sometimes Grotius expressly mentions it: this is particularly the case for the references given by Vasquius[157]. In many other cases it is evident that Grotius has copied references tacitly; when possible I have made an effort to mention this in my notes. The main authors from whom Grotius has taken over references without saying so are Albericus Gentilis[158], Franciscus de Victoria[159] and Rodericus Zuarius[160]. A most interesting case of a reference taken over from Vasquius (not in a quotation but in a paraphrase of his text) concerns Alphonsus de Castro, *De potestate legis poenalis*: Grotius even mentions the page number given by Vasquius, which is in itself a printer's error in Vasquius' text and therefore enables us to identify the edition of Vasquius' work used by Grotius, as well as the edition of Alphonsus de Castro's work used by Vasquius[161]. The mere fact, however, that Grotius copied certain references from one of his main sources should not release

---

and does not give the folio numbers in his text.

[153] For some details on *Florum sparsio*, see my 1993 Introduction, p. 943.

[154] For some details, see also my 1993 Introduction, p. 943.

[155] Cf. the list given in my 1993 Introduction, p. 942 n. 90.

[156] Text edited by W. J. M. van Eysinga, *Eene onuitgegeven nota van De Groot*, Mededelingen der Nederlandsche Akademie van Wetenschappen, Afd. Letterkunde, Nieuwe reeks, 18 (1955), p. 235-252, reprinted in his *Sparsa collecta*, Leiden 1958, p. 488-504.

[157] The references in the long quotations from Vasquius on p. 44-49 begin with 'all.' [= 'allegans']. Apart from Vasquius I found the following examples: p. 53 note h ('Castr. ex Cyno et aliis'), p. 58 note a ('Doctores in l. qui iure familiaritatis, ff. de acq. poss. et alleg. per Covar.'), and p. 65 note f ('Silv. in verbo restitutio … alleg. Gerar., Oldradum et Archid.').

[158] See p. 2 note d, p. 3 notes g and i, p. 4 note b and p. 43 note b.

[159] See p. 6 note g and p. 9 notes b (also an error is taken over), g, h and i.

[160] See p. 26 note e, p. 27 note a (also specification of a column), p. 28 note e, p. 35 note a and p. 36 notes c and d; cf. also p. 26 note 2.

[161] See p. 44 note 1; at the same time this case presents an example that the figuring of a book in the inventory of 1618 does not mean that he used it when writing Djp and Ml.

9 The Choice of the Editions Mentioned in the List

us from verifying these references[162]. I have, as far as possible, consistently checked them and discovered that Grotius sometimes copied mistakes and sometimes made mistakes while copying.

10 Some Final Remarks on Authors Cited

Most of the names of legal authors mentioned in the List of Sources may be known to readers who are more or less familiar with the history of legal science in the Middle Ages and Early Modern Times[163]. There are, however, some names (also of sources) which have caused difficulties to editors or translators of *Mare liberum* and for which it was not possible to add information in the notes – or the List of Sources – of the present edition. In this section an effort will be made to give some more details[164].

To begin with there are two 12th century Glossators whose names are only mentioned in the text of *Mare liberum* without a reference in the margin but who nevertheless merit some attention.

The first is Placentinus, an Italian jurist who taught in Bologna and Montpellier (where he probably died in the early 1180s, not in 1192 as is usually assumed[165]). At p. 26 an opinion of his is quoted indirectly: Grotius found it in a quotation by Zuarius from Johannes Faber (for both see below). The identification by Zeydel is unsatisfactory[166].

The second Glossator is Johannes Bassianus, also an Italian jurist, teacher of the famous Azo. At p. 40 he is cited as Iohannes for an interpretation of D. 44, 3, 7, transmitted by the Accursian Gloss; Grotius found it in a quotation by Cujacius[167]. He is not identified by Zeydel, who only suggests that perhaps Johannes Andreae could be meant[168].

Among the 14th and 15th century sources some difficulties have been caused by the *leges Hispanicae*, Johannes Faber, the two 'Angeli' (de Ubaldis and Aretinus) and Alvarotus.

---

[162] The mere mention of the name of an author is, in principle, not considered as a reference.
[163] For a first orientation, mainly as to dates, see W. H. Bryson, *Dictionary of Sigla and Abbreviations to and in Law Books before 1607*, Charlottesville 1975 (reprint Buffalo (N.Y.) 1996).
[164] I will – inter alia – deal with several names which have caused confusion in the notes of Magoffin. Some others have already been dealt with in my notes to the text, see p. 9 note 2 and p. 20 note c; cf. also his mentioning of the name Estius as a source in a passage which has only the word 'est', see p. 3 note 9. I may add that even for Antiquity Magoffin has succeeded to make a gaffe – still repeated in the Italian translation 2007 – by interpreting 'Gordiani epistola' on p. 5 (Magoffin, p. 11-12) as a letter of a Benedictine monk (468-533) instead of a letter (constitution) of the emperor Gordianus (238-244), mentioned in the inscription of C. 8, 40, 13 cited by Grotius; cf. already Bensly, p. 118.
[165] See A. Gouron, *La date de la mort de Placentin; une fausse certitude*, Tijdschrift voor Rechtsgeschiedenis, 61 (1993), p. 481-492.
[166] In his Index to *De jure praedae* (see above, note 64) he mentions him as 'Placentinus, Petrus (1135-1192)'; Magoffin does not give an identification. The quotation is indirect, see edition, p. 26 note 2. In the printed edition of 'Placentinus' *Summa Institutionum* (Mainz 1535) ad Inst. 2, 1, 5 (on p. 18) he expresses himself in different terms.
[167] Edition, p. 40 note 2.
[168] See his Index s.v. Andrea. Magoffin does not give an identification.

The *leges Hispanicae* are not only mentioned twice in the text of *Mare liberum*[169], but also once in the preface (without specification)[170]; a Castilian codification from the beginning of the 14th century, known as *Las Siete Partidas* is meant[171]. Grotius has, however, certainly not seen an edition of this text; he has taken over the references to it from a *consilium* of Rodericus Zuarius (Rodrigo Suárez), a famous Castilian jurist from the end of the 15th (and the beginning of the 16th?) century[172], who may have used a manuscript or an incunabulum-edition of the Siete Partidas. A collection of his *consilia* was first printed (together with another work) in Medina del Campo 1550 and 1555, then in Lyon 1559 and again in Spain in 1568, 1588 and 1599[173], but Grotius must have consulted a publication containing only two of them, as part of the well-known *Tractatus de mercatura* edited by Benvenuto Straccha[174]. This has not been remarked by Zeydel, who only refers to the 1614 edition of the collected works of Zuarius[175]. The latter's references to the *Siete Partidas* in most of these editions do not always seem to correspond with the numbering in the 1555 edition of that codification, which I used[176].

Johannes Faber is a well-known 14th century French jurist, in France mostly cited as Jean Faure[177]. Magoffin confounds him with a 16th century bishop of Vienna[178]. Of his commentary on the Institutes many editions were published in the 16th century but Grotius did not use any of these; he took over the reference from Zuarius[179].

Angelus de Ubaldis (brother of Baldus de Ubaldis) was a 14th century Italian jurist,

---

[169] Edition, p. 36 note 2 and note d and p. 41 note c.
[170] Edition, fol. 5 r note 1.
[171] See A. Wolf in *Handbuch der Quellen und Literatur der neueren europäischen Privatrechtsgeschichte* (ed. by H. Coing), I, München 1973, p. 672-673.
[172] See Nic. Antonio, *Bibliotheca Hispana nova*, II, Matriti 1788, p. 271-272.
[173] Born in Salamanca, he became professor in Valladolid, where, somewhat later, he was appointed as '*oidor*' (*auditor*) in the *Audiencia y Chancilleria*, a high royal court, see Antonio, *Bibliotheca*, p. 272, as well as A. Pérez Martin and J. M. Scholz, *Legislación y jurisprudencia en la España del Antiguo Régimen*, Valencia 1978, p. 334. I could use the edition *Allegationes et consilia quaedam*, Lugduni 1559, where I found the text meant by Grotius as Allegatio XVII. The collection was later also published in his *Opera omnia*, Francofurti 1594, Duaci 1614, Antverpiae 1618 and 1661. Magoffin, p. 44 n. 3, mentions an edition of 1621 (see above, note 85), which I could not find. Williams and Zeydel (Index) used the ed. Douai 1614; it is not clear why Van Ittersum in her edition of the Index (see above, note 64) changed the name 'Suárez' into 'Juárez'.
[174] Full title in the List of Sources at Zuarius. Consilium I gives the text that was published as 'Allegatio XVII' in the edition Lugduni 1559, mentioned above, note 173. Grotius refers to Consilium I, so he will not have used the 1559 edition or the 1594 edition of Suarez' *Opera omnia*. It is of course possible that he consulted another edition of Straccha's *Tractatus de mercatura*.
[175] Cf. above, note 173.
[176] The two references mentioned in *Mare liberum*, p. 36 note d, use a different numbering; the reference at p. 40 note c, however, has the same numbering.
[177] See K. Weidenfeld in *Dictionnaire historique des juristes français (XIIe-XIIIe siècles*, ed. by P. Arabeyre, J.-L. Halpérin and J. Krynen, Paris 2007, p. 321-322. He was born circa 1275 and died 1340; he is also cited as Johannes Fabri or Johannes de Runcinis (de Roussines).
[178] Magoffin, p. 34 n. 2: 'Johannes Faber (c. 1570- c. 1640) was Bishop of Vienna and Court preacher to Emperor Ferdinand. He was popularly known as 'Malleus Haereticorum'. The confusion between the French jurist and the German bishop, who wrote a *Malleus in haeresim Lutheranam* is also found elsewhere, but Magoffin makes it worse by adding wrong dates. It was already criticized by Bensly, p. 118.
[179] Edition, p. 36 note 2.

10 Some Final Remarks on Authors Cited

whom some editors and translators have confounded with Angelus (de Gambilionibus) Aretinus, a 15th century jurist (also Italian). Again, it was Magoffin who started the confusion by ascribing to Angelus Aretinus all references to 'Ang.' and all mentions of 'Angelus' in Grotius' text[180], whereas in the only marginal note where indeed Angelus Aretinus is meant he is simply cited as 'Aretinus'[181]. Williams did not follow Magoffin; she rightly attributes to Angelus de Ubaldis all references to 'Ang.' occurring in the manuscript which correspond to those in *Mare liberum*. She makes a mistake, however, in identifying a reference in the manuscript, fol. 113 r, not taken over in *Mare liberum* (p. 50): a commentary on the Institutes is ascribed to Angelus de Ubaldis[182]. The error was probably made by Zeydel, who in his Index mentions an edition Pavia 1489 of such a commentary whose existence is extremely doubtful. A second (double) error was made by Williams and Zeydel where they interpret the reference 'd[icto] loc[o] n. 38' (on the same fol. 113 r and taken over in *Mare liberum*, p. 50) as referring to another passage in the supposed commentary of Angelus de Ubaldis on the Institutes; this reference is to Vasquius[183].

Jacobus Alvarotus (or de Alvarotis) is an Italian jurist from the first half of the 15th century who is mainly known as the author of a commentary on the *Libri feudorum*, which was the result of a lecture at the University of Padua[184]. Grotius mentions him only in the text, together with the better-known and more than a century older Andreas de Isernia[185]. The combination of the two names may have been taken over from Zuarius; Grotius did probably not consult the two authors[186]. A printing error in the 1618 edition of *Mare liberum* – 'Alvotus' instead of 'Alvarotus' – repeated in all editions up to and including the 1773 one[187], led to a false identification by Magoffin. He supposes a misprint for 'Alvarus (Alvarez)', without any further specification[188]. Some later translators, who may have used the 1609 edition, rightly mention Alvarotus[189] but others follow

---

[180] See Magoffin, p. 35, 48, 49, 50, 52 and 55, corresponding to p. 27, 39, 40, 41, 44 and 47 of the 1609 edition of *Mare liberum*.

[181] Edition, p. 42 and note c: the mention of 'ff.' instead of 'Inst.' is an error taken over from Balbus. Magoffin, p. 51 (not mentioned in his Index), refers wrongly to 'rubr. Digest I, 8 (De divisione rerum)'. Williams, p. 248, corrects the error, but Armitage, p. 42 n. 17, puts again 'Angelus on Digest. I, 8' (in his bibliography he mentions only the commentary of Angelus de Ubaldis on the Digest and no work of Angelus Aretinus).

[182] Williams, p. 253; cf. edition, p. 50 note 1. Armitage, p. 47 n. 42, simply puts 'Angelus on Inst. 2, 1, 5' (a work which he does not mention in his bibliography, where Angelus Aretinus is missing; see above, note 181).

[183] See edition, p. 50 note a; this error was also adopted by Armitage. Both errors were already mentioned in Feenstra (1992-1996), p. 28 n. 119. A commentary of Angelus de Ubaldis on the Institutes was also invented in the English translation of *De jure belli ac pacis*; see Djbap 1993, p. 1030, and Feenstra (1992-1996), p. 15.

[184] On this lecture and an early German translation of its summaries see R. Feenstra, *Kaiserliche Lehnrechte, Die Libri Feudorum in deutscher Fassung nach Alvarotus und andere Inkunabeldrücke zum Lehnrecht*, Tijdschrift voor Rechtsgeschiedenis, 63 (1995), p. 337-354 at p. 340 ff.

[185] A Neapolitan jurist, who died c. 1316 (and not 1553 as Magoffin p. 36 n. *, says).

[186] Edition, p. 28 note e.

[187] Edition, p. 28 note 1.

[188] Magoffin, p. 36 note *.

[189] Boschan, p. 53, and the Polish translation (above, note 93), p. 48 n. 62.

Magoffin; the Italian translation even identifies Alvarez as Pelajo Alvarez[190], whereas the Spanish translation gives no specification at all.

There is one legal source from the end of the 15th century which should perhaps be briefly mentioned here, although it does not occur in Grotius' references in *Mare liberum*. In several passages he makes allusions to the so-called *Donatio Pontificis Alexandri* of 1493, which was used by the Portuguese as an argument for their pretensions. In 1941 a German author, E. Staedler, published an article[191] on the question which source Grotius might have used for his statements made on this *Donatio*. Staedler found it in the preface to a work of a Portuguese historian, cited by Grotius twice for other reasons: Hieronymus Osorius, *De rebus Emmanuelis Lusitaniae Regis virtute et auspicio gestis*[192]. This preface was written by the jurist Johannes Metellus[193]. Staedler calls attention to a passage where Metellus gives a summary of Pope Alexander's bull *Inter cetera* of 4 May 1493 (holding the so-called *Donatio*) and argues that Grotius must have used it, even if he does not mention it. Staedler only refers to the edition of *Mare liberum* and not to *De jure praedae*, where indeed Metellus is cited twice in another context[194]. What Staedler and others could not know, however, is that Metellus was cited a third and a fourth time in the margin of passages that were crossed out[195]. One of these concerns precisely the *Donatio Alexandri*[196].

As to the 16th century, there are three authors who merit some attention here[197].

Johannes Franciscus Balbus, who is cited at least seven times and who certainly has been consulted by Grotius himself[198], is very poorly identified by Magoffin as 'a priest and jurisconsult at Muentz-hof'[199]. Balbus was an Italian jurist, born in Avigliana before 1480; he studied in Turin, where he became a professor of civil law circa 1508 and published in 1511 his *Tractatus de praescriptionibus*, dedicated to duke Carlo II of Savoy, whose *consiliarius* he later became. The date of his death is unknown; he is not mentioned as being alive after 1518[200]. The *Tractatus de praescriptionibus* is his only major work, wholly in the Bartolist tradition. It had many separate editions in the 16th century and figured also in the collections of *Tractatus universi juris* of 1549 and 1584[201].

---

[190] Not in the text but only in the Index.
[191] E. Staedler, *Hugo Grotius über die "donatio Alexandri" von 1493 und der Metellus-Bericht*, Zeitschrift für Völkerrecht, 25 (1941), p. 257-274.
[192] See List of Sources.
[193] Staedler calls him a Spanish jurist, but on the title page he is mentioned as Sequanus, i.e. from the Franche Comté (Burgundy); cf. the Index of Zeydel, who calls him Jean Matal.
[194] Hamaker, p. 329 and 332; Williams, p. 353 and 356.
[195] Edition, p. 10 note 1 and p. 56 note 1.
[196] Edition, p. 56 note 1.
[197] As is explained in the edition, p. 4 note 3, Andreas Alciatus should not figure among the authors cited in *Mare liberum*; the List of Sources in Djbap 1993, p. 1029 (at 'Alciatus, Responsa') should be corrected: instead of 'Djp (2)' read 'Djp (1)'.
[198] He copies an error of Balbus on p. 42 (see note c).
[199] Magoffin, p. 47 n. 3, copied inter alia by the Italian translation 2007, but already criticized by Bensly, p. 118, who shows the origin of the erroneous statement.
[200] See P. Craveri, in *Dizionario biografico degli Italiani*, V (1963), p. 407-409.
[201] After the Turin edition 1511 I found reliable mentions of editions Trino 1523, Lyon 1532, 1542 and 1544,

10 Some Final Remarks on Authors Cited

Andreas Fachinaeus, whose *Controversiarum iuris libri decem* is cited twice and was probably consulted by Grotius himself[202], has also been a victim of Magoffin's incompetence in the field of legal sources. The abbreviation 'Fachin.' is tacitly solved as 'Fachinham', a name identified as 'Nicholas Fachinham (? – 1407), a Franciscan who taught theology at Oxford'[203]. Fachinaeus was an Italian jurist (Fachinei or Facchinei), born in Forlì in the middle of the 16th century; he studied in Padua, where he started teaching. In 1587 he was called to the University of Ingolstadt, where he taught ten years with much success and started writing the first book of his *Controversiae*. In 1597 he went to Pisa; he died shortly after 1607[204]. His work is partly in the Bartolist tradition but also shows humanist interests. From the Leiden manuscript it can be gathered that Grotius only got to know the *Controversiae* in a later stage of the composition of *De jure praedae*[205].

Albericus Gentilis (1552-1608) and his *De iure belli* call for a special mention here, not only because of its influence on Grotius on which many discussions have already been published[206] but also because recently a very substantial annotated translation into Italian of his book[207] has appeared which is of the utmost importance for the identification of sources also mentioned by Grotius in *Mare liberum* (and for a great part copied from Gentili).

It is not only proper names of individual authors that sometimes have caused difficulties, but also some denominations like 'Glosa' and 'Doctores'.

As to 'Glosa'[208], I have made a difference between the Civil law and the Canon law texts. For 'Gl.' or 'Glosa' in Civil law texts I have put '[Accursian] Gloss', for the Canon law texts I have not added the name of the author; in both cases the gloss is specified by its initial word(s)[209].

'Doctores', when used in Civil law context, mostly denotes authors from the period after the Accursian Glossa ordinaria, i.e., from about 1250 onwards. In a more general context it can denote not only jurists but also theologians, e.g. when Grotius mentions

---

Cologne 1565 and 1573, Venice 1582 and Cologne 1590 (which I used).

[202] Edition, p. 42 notes a and b.

[203] Magoffin, p. 50 n. 3, copied inter alia by the Polish, the Spanish and the 2007 Italian translation.

[204] See V. Ventura, in *Dizionario biografico degli Italiani*, XLIV (1994), p. 94-95.

[205] Edition, p. 42 note 1.

[206] See Feenstra (1992-1996), p. 20, for references,

[207] Alberico Gentili, *Il diritto di guerra* (*De iure belli, libri III, 1598*), Introduzione di Diego Quaglioni, Traduzione di Pietro Nencini, Apparato critico a cura di Guiliano Machetto e Christian Zendri, Milano 2008.

[208] Magoffin, Williams and Armitage translate Grotius' references to 'Gl[osa]' into 'Glossators' which seems very unfortunate.

[209] For the [Accursian] Gloss on the Corpus iuris civilis a reprint of the edition Lyon 1627 can be used, see above at note 141. For the Glossa ordinaria on the parts of the Corpus iuris canonici old editions are to be used; for the authors of the different parts and for further details see E. J. H. Schrage, *Utrumque Ius, Eine Einführung in das Studium der Quellen des mittelalterlichen gelehrten Rechts*, [Schriften zur Europäischen Rechts- und Verfassungsgeschichte, 8], Berlin 1992, p. 90 ff.

'Doctores Hispani'. Usually the great theologians of the Middle Ages are called 'Scholastici'[210], a term which, however, can sometimes also denote authors of the so-called Second Scholasticism (16th and early 17th century).

At the end of this Introduction I would like to express my gratitude to the people and institutions who have in various ways helped to accomplish this edition.

Besides the three persons mentioned at the end of the preface of this book I am indebted to various people who contributed to my research. I would particularly like to thank the following people (in alphabetical order): Professor E. C. Coppens (Nijmegen), Mrs. M. C. I. M. Duynstee (Leiden), Dr. D. Osler (Frankfurt am Main), Professors A. J. B. Sirks (Oxford) and L. C. Winkel (Rotterdam).

Among the libraries it goes almost without saying that I have always enjoyed tremendous support from the Peace Palace Library in The Hague, in particular from its Director, Mr. J. Vervliet, the initiator of the present edition. I am further indebted to the Library of the Max-Planck-Institut für europäische Rechtsgeschichte in Frankfurt am Main (in particular Mrs. U. Pohl), to the University Library of Leiden and the Royal Library at The Hague.

Autumn 2009 *R. Feenstra*

Addendum

On the very moment of sending this introduction to the press a new edition and translation (into Dutch) by A. Eyffinger was published: *Hugo de Groot, De vrije zee, een uiteenzetting over het recht van de Nederlanders om handel te drijven in Oost-Indië, door Arthur Eyffinger* [The Hague, 2009]. To take his publication into account in the present edition was, of course, impossible.

---

[210] Cf. Feenstra (1992-1996), p. 22 n. 78.

THE FREE SEA
OR A DISSERTATION ON
THE RIGHT WHICH THE DUTCH HAVE
TO CARRY ON INDIAN TRADE

LEIDEN

From the bookshop of Louis Elzevier

IN THE YEAR 1609

MARE LIBERVM
SIVE
DE IVRE QVOD BATAVIS
COMPETIT AD INDICA-
NA COMMERCIA
DISSERTATIO.

auctore Hugone Grotio.

LVGDVNI BATAVORVM,
Ex officinâ Ludovici Elzevirij.
ANNO CIƆ. IƆI. IX.

CAPITA DISSERTATIONIS.

Cap. I. *Iure gentium quibusvis ad quosvis liberam esse navigationem.*

Cap. II. *Lusitanos nullum habere ius dominij in eos Indos ad quos Batavi navigant titulo inventionis.*

Cap. III. *Lusitanos in Indos non habere ius dominij titulo donationis Pontificiæ.*

Cap. IV. *Lusitanos in Indos non habere ius dominij titulo belli.*

Cap. V. *Mare ad Indos, aut ius eo navigandi non esse proprium Lusitanorum titulo occupationis.*

Cap. VI. *Mare aut ius navigandi proprium non esse Lusitanorum titulo donationis Pontificiæ.*

Cap. VII. *Mare aut ius navigandi proprium non esse Lusitanorum titulo præscriptionis, aut consuetudinis.*

Cap. VIII. *Iure gentium inter quosvis liberam esse mercaturam.*

Cap. IX. *Mercaturam cum Indis propriam non esse Lusitanorum titulo occupationis.*

Cap. X. *Mercaturam cum Indis propriam non esse Lusitanorum titulo donationis Pontificiæ.*

Cap. XI. *Mercaturam cum Indis non esse Lusitanorū propriā iure præscriptionis, aut consuetudinis.*

Cap. XII. *Nulla æquitate niti Lusitanos in prohibendo commercio.*

Cap. XIII. *Batavis ius commercij Indicani, qua pace, qua induciis, qua bello retinendum.*

AD PRIN

THE CHAPTERS OF THE DISSERTATION

I	That by the law of nations navigation is free for everybody to whomsoever.	p. 1 - 4
II	That the Portuguese have no right of dominion, by title of discovery, over those Indians to whom the Dutch sail.	p. 4 - 7
III	That the Portuguese have no right of dominion over the Indians by title of Papal donation.	p. 7 - 9
IV	That the Portuguese have no right of dominion over the Indians by title of war.	p. 9 - 11
V	That the sea leading to the Indians or the right of navigation thereon does not belong to the Portuguese by title of possession.	p. 11 - 36
VI	That the sea or the right of navigation thereon does not belong to the Portuguese by title of Papal donation.	p. 36 - 38
VII	That the sea or the right of navigation thereon does not belong to the Portuguese by title of prescription or custom.	p. 38 - 51
VIII	That by the law of nations trade is free between whomsoever.	p. 52 - 54
IX	That trade with the Indians does not belong to the Portuguese by title of occupation.	p. 55
X	That trade with the Indians does not belong to the Portuguese by title of Papal donation.	p. 55 - 56
XI	That trade with the Indians does not belong to the Portuguese by right of prescription or custom.	p. 57 - 59
XII	That the Portuguese cannot appeal to any equity in their prohibition of trade.	p. 59 - 62
XIII	That the Dutch are to maintain the right to carry on Indian trade by peace, by truce, or by war.	p. 62 - 66
	[Two letters of the King of Spain]	p. [67 - 68]

AD PRINCIPES
POPVLOSQVE LIBEROS
ORBIS CHRISTIANI.

ERROR est non minus vetus quam pestilens, quo multi mortales, ij autem maxime qui plurimum vi atque opibus valent, persuadent sibi, aut, quod verius puto, persuadere conantur, iustum atque iniustum non suapte natura, sed hominum inani quadam opinione atque consuetudine distingui. Itaque illi & leges & æquitatis speciem in hoc inventa existimant, ut eorum qui in parendi conditione nati sunt dissensiones atque tumultus coerceantur: ipsis vero qui in summa fortuna sunt collocati, ius omne aiunt ex volūtate, voluntatem ex utilitate metiendam. Hanc autem sententiam absurdam plane atque naturæ contrariam auctoritatis sibi nonnihil conciliasse haud adeo mirum est, cum ad morbum

* 2   com-

TO THE RULERS AND TO THE FREE NATIONS OF THE CHRISTIAN WORLD.

The delusion is as old as it is pernicious with which many men, especially those who by their wealth and power exercise the greatest influence, persuade themselves, or as I rather believe, try to persuade themselves, that justice and injustice are distinguished the one from the other not by their own nature, but in some fashion merely by the opinion and the custom of mankind. Those men therefore think that both the laws and the semblance of equity were devised for the sole purpose of repressing the dissensions and rebellions of those persons born in a subordinate position, affirming meanwhile that for themselves, being placed in a high position, all right is to be measured by their will and this will by what is expedient to them. This opinion, absurd and unnatural as it clearly is, has gained some authority but this should by no means occasion surprise, inasmuch as there has to be taken into consideration not only the common disease

communem humani generis, quo sicut vitia ita vitiorum patrocinia sectamur, accesserint adulantium artes quibus omnis potestas obnoxia est. Sed contra extiterunt nullo non sæculo viri liberi, sapientes, religiosi, qui falsam hanc persuasionem animis simplicium evellerent, cæteros autem eius defensores impudentiæ convincerent. Deum quippe esse monstrabant conditorem rectoremque vniuersi, imprimis autem humanæ naturæ parentem, quam ideo, non uti cætera animantia, in species diuersas, variaque discrimina segregasset, sed unius esse generis, una etiam appellatione voluisset contineri, dedisset insuper originem eandem, similem membrorum compagem, vultus inter se obversos, sermonem quoque & alia communicandi instrumenta, ut intelligerent omnes naturalem inter se societatem esse atque cognationem. Huic autem a se fundatæ aut domui aut ciuitati summum illum principem patremque familias suas quasdam scripsisse leges, non in ære aut tabulis, sed

Preface

[Fol. 2 verso]

of the human race by which we pursue not only vices and their purveyors, but also the arts of flatterers, to whom power is always exposed.

But, on the other hand, there have stood forth in every age independent and wise and devout men able to root out this false doctrine from the minds of the simple, and to convict the others, who defend it, of shamelessness. For they showed that God was the founder and ruler of the universe, and especially that being the father of all mankind, he had not separated human beings, as he had the rest of living things, into different species and various divisions, but had willed them to be of one race and to be known by one name; that furthermore he had given them the same origin, the same structural organism, the ability to look each other in the face, language too, and other means of communication, in order that they all might recognize their natural social bond and kinship. They showed too that he is the supreme lord and father of this family; and that for the house or the state which he had thus founded, he had drawn up certain laws not graven on tablets

lis, sed in sensibus animisque singulorum, ubi
invitis etiā & aversantibus legendæ occur-
rent. his legibus summos pariter atque infi-
mos teneri. in has non plus regibus licere,
quā plebi aduersus decreta decurionum, de-
curionibus contra præsidium edicta, præsidi-
bus in regum ipsorum sanctiones. Quin illa
ipsa populorum atque urbium singularum iura ex illo fonte dimanare, inde sanctimo-
niam suam atque maiestatem accipere. Sicut
autem in ipso homine alia sunt quæ habet
cum omnibus communia, alia quibus ab alte-
ro quisque distinguitur, ita earum rerum
quas in usum hominis produxisset natura
alias eam manere communes, alias cuiusque
industria ac labore proprias fieri voluisse. de
utrisque autem datas leges, ut communibus
quidem sine detrimento omnium omnes
uterentur, de cæteris autem quod cuique
contigisset eo contentus abstineret alieno.
Hæc si homo nullus nescire potest nisi homo
esse desierit, hæc si gentes uiderunt quibus
ad ue-

Preface

[Fol. 3 recto]

of bronze or stone but written in the minds and on the hearts of every individual, where even the unwilling and the refractory must read them. That these laws were binding on great and small alike; that kings have no more power against them than have the common people against the decrees of the magistrates, than have the magistrates against the edicts of the governors, than have the governors against the ordinances of the kings themselves; nay more, that those very laws themselves of each and every nation and city flow from that divine source, and from that source receive their sanctity and their majesty.

Now, as there are some things which every man enjoys in common with all other men, and as there are other things which are distinctly his and belong to no one else, just so has nature willed that some of the things which she has created for the use of mankind remain common to all, and that others through the industry and labor of each man become his own. Laws moreover were given to cover both cases so that all men might use common property without prejudice to anyone else, and in respect to other things so that each man being content with what he himself owns might refrain from laying his hands on the property of others.

Now since no man can be ignorant of these facts unless he ceases to be a man, and since races

ad verum omne cæcutientibus sola naturæ fax illuxit, quid vos sentire ac facere æquum est, principes populique Christiani? Si quis durum putat ea a se exigi quæ tam sancti nominis professio requirit, cuius minimum est ab iniuriis abstinere, certe quid sui sit officij scire quisque potest ex eo quod alteri præcipit. Nemo est vestrum qui non palam edicat rei quemque suæ esse moderatorem & arbitrum: qui non fluminibus locisque publicis cives omnes uti ex æquo & promiscue iubeat, qui non commeandi commercandique libertatem omni ope defendat. Sine his si parva illa societas, quam rempublicam vocamus, constare non posse iudicatur (& certe constare non potest) quamobrem non eadem illa ad sustinendam totius humani generis societatem atque concordiam erunt necessaria? Si quis adversus hæc vim faciat, merito indignamini, exempla etiam pro flagitij magnitudine statuitis, non alia de cau-

Preface

[Fol. 3 verso]

blind to all truth except what they receive from the light of nature, have recognized their force, what, O Christian Kings and Nations, ought you to think, and what ought you to do?

If anyone thinks it hard that those things are demanded of him which the profession of so holy a name requires, the very least obligation of which is to refrain from injuries, certainly everyone can know what his own duty is from what he prescribes for others. There is not one of you who does not openly proclaim that every man is entitled to manage and dispose of his own property; there is not one of you who does not order that all citizens have equal and indiscriminate right to use rivers and public places; not one of you who does not defend with all his might the freedom of travel and of trade.

If it be thought that the small society which we call a state cannot exist without these principles (and certainly it cannot), why will not those same principles be necessary to uphold the social structure of the whole human race and to maintain the harmony thereof? If anyone rebels against these principles you are justly indignant, and you even decree punishments in proportion to the magnitude of the offense, for no other reason

de causa nisi quia ubi ista passim licent status imperii tranquillus esse non potest. Quod si rex in regem, populus in populum inique & violente agat, id nonne ad perturbandam magnæ illius civitatis quietem & ad summi custodis spectat iniuriam? Hoc interest, quod sicut magistratus min res de vulgo iudicant, vos de magistratibus, ita omnium aliorum delicta cognoscenda vobis & punienda mandavit rex universi, vestra excepit sibi. Is autem quanquam supremam animadversionem sibi reservat, tardam, occultam, inevitabilem, nihilominus duos a se iudices delegat qui rebus humanis intersint, quos nocentium feliciissimus non effugit, conscientiam cuique suam & famam sive existimationem alienam. Hæc tribunalia illis patent quibus alia præclusa sunt: ad hæc infirmi provocant: in his vincuntur qui vincunt viribus, qui

*4   licen-

Preface

[Fol. 4 recto]

than that a government cannot be tranquil where trespasses of that sort are allowed. If king acts unjustly and violently against king, and nation against nation, such action involves a disturbance of the peace of that universal state, and constitutes a trespass against the supreme ruler, does it not? There is however this difference: just as the lesser magistrates judge the common people, and as you judge the magistrates, so the king of the universe has laid upon you the command to take cognizance of the trespasses of all other men, and to punish them; but he has reserved for himself the punishment of your own trespasses. But although he reserves to himself the final punishment, slow and unseen but none the less inevitable, yet he delegates to intervene in human affairs two judges whom the luckiest of sinners does not escape, namely, every man's own conscience and his fame (or other men's estimation of them). These two tribunals are open to those who are debarred from all others; to these the powerless appeal; in them are defeated those who are wont to win by might, those who

licentiæ modum non statuunt, qui vili putant constare quod emitur humano sanguine, qui iniurias iniuriis defendunt, quorum manifesta facinora necesse est & consentiente bonorum iudicio damnari, & sui ipsorũ animi sententia non absolvi. Ad utrumq; hoc forum nos quoque novam causam afferimus: non hercule de stillicidijs aut tigno iniuncto, quales esse privatorũ solent, ac ne ex eo quidẽ genere quod frequens est inter populos, de agri iure in confinio hærẽtis, de amnis aut Insulæ possessione: sed de omni prope oceano, de iure navigandi, de libertate commerciorum. Inter nos & Hispanos hæc controuersa sunt: Sitne immensum & vastum mare regni unius nec maximi accessio: populone cuiquam jus sit volentes populos prohibere ne uendant, ne emant, ne permutent, ne denique commeent inter sese: potueritne quisquam quod suum nunquam fuit elargiri, aut inuenire quod iam erat alienum: an ius aliquod tribuat manifesta longi temporis

iniu-

Preface

[Fol. 4 verso]

are licentious out of measure, those who consider cheap anything bought at the price of human blood, those who defend injuries by injuries, men whose wickedness is so manifest that they must needs be condemned by the unanimous judgment of the good, and not be absolved by the sentence of their own souls.

To this double tribunal we also bring a new case. It is in very truth no petty case such as private citizens are wont to bring against their neighbors about dripping eaves or inserting a beam in a wall; nor is it a case such as nations frequently bring against one another about boundary lines or the possession of a river or an island. No! It is a case which concerns practically the entire expanse of the high seas, the right of navigation, the freedom of trade! Between us and the Spaniards the following points are in dispute: Can the vast, the boundless sea be the accessory of one kingdom alone, and that not the greatest? Can any one nation have the right to prevent other nations which so desire, from selling to one another, from bartering with one another, actually from communicating with one another? Can any nation give away what it never owned, or discover what already belonged to someone else? Does a manifest injury of long time create a specific right?

iniuria. In hac disceptatione ipsis qui inter Hispanos præcipui sunt divini atque humani iuris magistri calculum porrigimus, ipsius denique Hispaniæ proprias leges imploramus.[1] Id si nihil iuvat, & eos quos ratio certa cōvincit cupiditas vetat desistere, vestrā principes maiestatem, vestram fidem quotquot estis ubique gentes appellamus. Non perplexam, non intricatam movemus quæstionem. Non de ambiguis in religione capitibus, quæ plurimum habere videntur obscuritatis, quæ tantis tam diu animis decertata, apud sapientes hoc fere certum reliquerunt, nusquam minus inveniri veritatem quam ubi cogitur assensus. Non de statu nostræ reipublicæ, & libertate armis haud parta sed vindicata: de qua recte statuere ij demum possunt qui iura patria Belgarum, mores avitos, & institutum non in leges regnum, sed ex legibus principatum accurate cognouerint. in qua tamen quæstione æquis iudicibus extremæ servitutis depulsa necessitas,[2] subtilius

[1] 'ipsius denique Hispaniae proprias leges imploramus': see below p. 36 notes 2 and d as well as p. 41 note c. Cf. also Borschberg *Hugo Grotius' theory* (see above Introduction, note 7), p. 37 and note 40 on p. 51.

[2] 'in qua tamen quaestione aequis iudicibus extremae servitutis depulsa necessitas ... nihil dubitandum reliquit': this passage seems to have been wrongly interpreted by most translators (with the exception of Boschan, p. 21; the 1614 Dutch translation simply omits the whole passage); cf. also Introduction, note 101. Instead of Magoffin's text I have given here a translation of my own.

Preface

[Fol. 5 recto]

In this controversy we appeal to the principal authorities on divine and human law among the Spaniards; we actually invoke the very laws of Spain itself[1]. If that is of no avail, and greed forbids to desist those whom good reason convinces, we appeal, ye princes, to your majesty, and ye nations – how many and wherever you may be – to your faith.

It is not an involved, it is not an intricate question that we are raising. It is not a question of ambiguous points of theology which seem to be wrapped in the deepest obscurity, which have been debated already so long and with such heat, that wise men are almost convinced that truth is never so rarely found as when assent thereto is forced. It is not a question of the status of our commonwealth and of our liberty, not created but vindicated by taking arms. On this point only those can reach a right decision who have an accurate knowledge of the ancient laws of the people of the Low Countries, of their ancestral customs and of the fact that we have not founded a state in defiance of the laws but a government based upon the laws; in this matter, however, there has been left no room for doubt[2]: to equal judges not by the necessity (to which we were driven by extreme servitude);

lius inquirentibus decreti tot nationum publica auctoritas, infensis etiam & malevolis adversariorum confessio nihil dubitandum reliquit. Sed quod hic proponimus nihil cum istis commune habet. nullius indiget anxiæ disquisitionis. non ex divini codicis pendet explicatione, cuius multa multi non capiunt, non ex unius populi scitis quæ cæteri merito ignorant. Lex illa e cuius præscripto iudicandum est inventu est non difficilis, utpote eadem apud omnes: & facilis intellectu, utpote nata cum singulis, singulorum mentibus insita. Ius autem quod petimus tale est, quod nec rex subditis negare debeat, neque Christianus non Christianis. A natura enim oritur, quæ ex æquo omnium parens est, in omnes munifica, cuius imperium in eos extenditur qui gentibus imperant, & apud eos sanctissimum est qui in pietate plurimum profecerunt. Cognoscite hanc causam principes, cognoscite populi. si quid iniquum postulamus, scitis quæ vestra

Preface

[Fol. 5 verso]

to those making more subtile inquiry not by the public authority of a decree of so many nations; to the malicious and ill-willers not by the confession of our adversaries.

But what we here submit has nothing in common with these matters. It calls for no troublesome investigation. It does not depend upon an interpretation of Holy Writ in which many people find many things they cannot understand, nor upon the decrees of any one nation of which the rest of the world very properly knows nothing.

The law by which our case must be decided is not difficult to find, seeing that it is the same among all nations; and it is easy to understand, seeing that it is innate in every individual and implanted in his mind. Moreover the law to which we appeal is one such as no king ought to deny to his subjects, nor a Christian to non-Christians. For it is a law derived from nature, which is an equal parent to us all, whose bounty falls on all, and whose sway extends over those who rule nations, and which is held most sacred by those who are most advanced in piety.

Take cognizance of this cause, ye Princes, take cognizance of it, ye Nations! If we are making an unjust demand, you know

stra & è vobis eorum qui viciniores nobis estis apud nos semper fuerit auctoritas. monete parebimus. Quin si quid a nobis hac in re peccatū est, iram vestram, odium denique humani generis non deprecamur. Sin contra se res habet, quid vobis censendum, quid agendum sit, vestræ religioni & æquitati relinquimus. Olim inter populos humaniores summum nefas habebatur armis eos impetere qui res suas arbitris permitterent. contra qui tam æquam conditionē recusarent, ij nō ut unius sed ut omnium hostes ope communi cōprimebantur. itaque eam in rem videmus icta federa, iudices constitutos. Reges ipsi validæque gentes nihil æque gloriosum, ac magnificum deputabāt, quam aliorum coercere insolentiam, aliorum infirmitatem atque innocentiam sublevare. Qui si mos hodieque obtineret, ut humani nihil a se alienum homines arbitrarentur, profecto orbe non paulo pacatiore uteremur. refrigesceret enim multorum audacia, & qui iustitiam utilitatis causa

Preface

[Fol. 6 recto]

what your authority and the authority of those of you who are our nearer neighbors has always been with us. Caution us, we will obey. Verily, if we have done any wrong in this our cause, we will not deprecate your wrath, nor even the hatred of the human race. But if we are right, we leave to your sense of righteousness and of fairness what you ought to think about this matter and what course of action you ought to pursue.

In ancient times among the more civilized peoples it was held to be the greatest of all crimes to make war upon those who were willing to submit to arbitration the settlement of their difficulties. On the contrary, those who would decline so fair an offer, were repressed by common effort, not as enemies of any one nation, but as enemies of them all alike. So for this very object we see that treaties were made and judges appointed. Kings themselves and powerful nations used to think that nothing was so chivalrous or so noble as to coerce the insolent and to help the weak and innocent. If this custom were held also today, that men thought no human thing strange into them, we should surely live in a much more peaceable world. For the presumptuousness of many would abate, and those who now

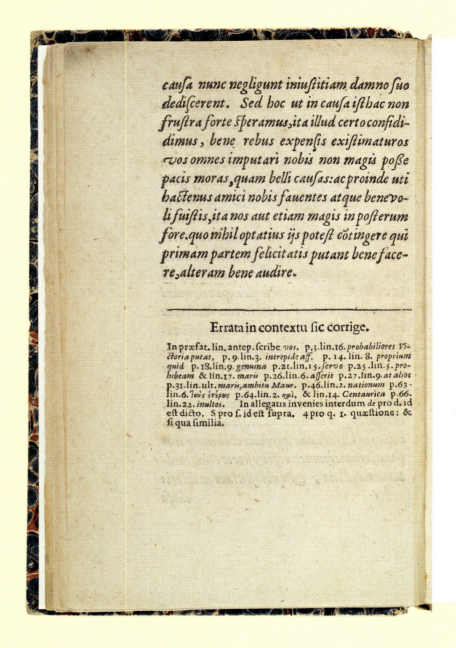

[1] On the origin of this list of 'errata' see Introduction, note 109 in fine. On 'errata' in general, see Introduction, section 6.

[2] In line 8 of the Latin text there is a printer's error: 'S pro s. id est supra' instead of '5 pro s. id est supra'. Examples of this 'erratum' can be found on p. 58 (note f) and p. 64 (note b). Of the two other non-specified 'errata' in the references ('in allegatis') examples can be found on p. 9 note d and 58 note d (examples of 'de pro d. id est dicto') and on p. 3 note g and 11 note a (examples of '4 pro q. i. [id est] quaestione').

Preface

[Fol. 6 verso]

neglect justice on the pretext of expediency would unlearn the lesson of injustice at their own expense.

But as in this cause perhaps we do not hope for that in vain, so at all events we are confident that you will all recognize after duly weighing the facts in the case that the delays to peace can no more be laid to our charge than can the causes of war; and as hitherto you have been indulgent friends, even favorably disposed to us, we feel sure that you will not only remain in this mind, but be even more friendly to us in the future. Nothing more to be desired than this can come to men who think that the first condition of happiness is good deeds; the second, good repute.

Errors of the press are to be corrected as follows

[There is no need to translate the list of printer's errors[1]. In the present edition the corrections of these errors are mentioned in the notes with the sign 'Err.' (to distinguish them from other corrections which are not in the list[2])]

MARE LIBERVM
SIVE
DE ·IVRE QVOD BATAVIS
COMPETIT AD INDICA-
NA COMMERCIA
DISSERTATIO.

CAPVT I.

Iure gentium quibusvis ad quosvis liberam esse navigationem.

[1] [2] [3] PROPOSITVM est nobis breviter ac dilucide demonstrare, jus esse Batavis, hoc est Ordinum Federatorum Belgicogermaniæ subditis, ad Indos, ita uti navigant navigare, cumque ipsis commercia colere. Fundamentum struemus hanc juris Gentium, quod primarium vocant, regulam certissimam, cujus perspicua atque immutabilis est ratio : licere cuivis genti quamvis alteram adire, cumque ea negotiari. Deus hoc ipse per naturam loquitur, cum ea cuncta quibus vita indiget, omnibus locis suppeditari a natura non vult : artibus etiam alijs alias gentes dat excellere. Quo ista? nisi quod voluit

---

[1] 'the Dutch': the Latin term *Batavi*, used by Grotius – not only here but also in the general title of Ml, in the heading of Chapter XIII and at various places in the text – should properly speaking be rendered literally as 'Batavians'. For obvious reasons I have refrained from using this term; it would have made the text less accessible. It should be noted, however, that in this opening sentence Grotius found it necessary to give a definition of the term (a definition which I have not found elsewhere).

[2] Instead of 'uti navigant navigare' the ms. reads 'uti faciunt navigare'.

[3] Instead of 'perspicua atque immutabilis' the ms. reads 'perpetua atque immutabilis'.

THE FREE SEA
OR A DISSERTATION ON
THE RIGHT WHICH THE DUTCH HAVE
TO CARRY ON INDIAN TRADE

Chapter I

*That by the law of nations navigation is free
for everybody to whomsoever.*

Our intention is to demonstrate briefly and clearly that the Dutch[1], that is to say, the subjects of the Estates [General] of the confederated Dutch Provinces, have the right to sail to the Indians as they are now doing[2] and to engage in trade with them. I shall base my argument on the following unimpeachable rule of [that part of] the law of nations [*jus gentium*] which they call primary [*jus gentium primarium*], the reason of which [rule] is self-evident[3] and immutable, to wit: Every nation is free to travel to every other nation and to trade with it.

God himself says this speaking through the voice of nature, as it is not his will that all the necessities of life shall be supplied to every region by nature; he grants pre-eminence in different arts to different nations. Why are these things so, if not because it was his will

[96']*

---

* The bracketed, bold-face numerals in the margin of the English text represent the corresponding page numbers in the manuscript of *De jure praedae*, cf. Introduction, note 116 (96' means folio 96 verso).

MARE

luit mutua egestate & copia humanas foveri amicitias, ne singuli se putantes sibi ipsis sufficere, hoc ipso redderentur insociabiles? Nunc factum est ut gens altera alterius suppleret inopiam, divinæ justitiæ instituto, ut eo modo (sicut Plinius dicit) quod genitum esset uspiam, apud omnes natum videretur. Poëtas itaque canentes audimus:

Panegyr.

Virgil.   *Nec vero terræ ferre omnes omnia possunt.*
Item:
   Excudent alij: & quæ sequuntur.
Hoc igitur qui tollunt, illam laudatissimam tollunt humani generis societatem, tollunt mutuas benefaciendi occasiones, naturam denique ipsam violant. Nam & ille quem Deus terris circumfudit Oceanus, undique & undique versus navigabilis, & ventorum stati aut extraordinarij status, non ab eadem semper, & a nulla non aliquando regione spirantes, nonne significant satis concessum a natura cunctis gentibus ad cunctas aditum? Hoc

5.4.Nat.qu. Seneca summum Naturæ beneficium putat, quod & vento gentes locis dissipatas miscuit, & sua omnia in regiones ita descripsit, ut necessarium mortalibus esset inter ipsos commercium. Hoc igitur jus ad cunctas gentes æqualiter pertinet: quod clarissimi jurisconsulti eo usque producunt, ut negent ullam

Inst. de rerum divis. §. 1. rempublicam aut Principẽ prohibere in universum

Chapter I

that human friendships should be fostered by mutual needs and resources, lest individuals, in deeming themselves self-sufficient, might thereby be rendered unsociable? In the existing state of affairs, it has come to pass, in accordance with the design of divine justice, that one nation supplies the needs of another, so that in this way (as Pliny[a] observes) whatever has been produced in any region is regarded as a product native to all regions. Thus we hear the poets sing,

> Nor yet can ev'ry soil bear ev'ry fruit;

and again,

> Others [the seething bronze] will mould [in lines
> More fair . . . .]

together with the remainder of the same passage[b].

Consequently, anyone who abolishes this system of exchange abolishes also the highly prized fellowship in which humanity is united. He destroys the opportunities for mutual benefactions. In short, he does violence to nature herself. Consider the ocean, with which God has encircled the different lands, and which is navigable from boundary to boundary; consider the breath of the winds in their regular courses and in their special deviations, blowing not always from one and the same region but from every region at one time or another: are these things not sufficient indications that nature has granted every nation access to every other nation? In Seneca's[c] opinion, the supreme blessing conferred by nature resides in these facts: that by means of the winds she brings together peoples who are scattered in different localities, and that she distributes the sum of her gifts throughout various regions in such a way as to make reciprocal commerce a necessity for the members of the human race.

Therefore, the right to engage in commerce pertains equally to all peoples; and jurisconsults of the greatest renown extend the application of this principle[d] to the point where they deny that any state or prince has the power to issue a general prohibition

---

[a] **Panegyr.**: Plinius, Panegyricus [XXIX, 7].
[b] **Virgil.**: Virgilius, Georgica [II, 109], and Aeneis [VI, 847 f.].
[c] 3. 4. Nat. qu.: Seneca, Naturales quaestiones, III, 4 [V, 18].
[d] **Inst. de rerum divis. §. 1.** [continuation on p. 3:] et L. nemo igitur ff eod. vide Gent. de iure belli lib. 1. c. 19 [/] vid. L. mercatores C. de comm.: Inst. 2, 1, 1, and D. 1, 8, 4; see Gentilis, De iure belli I, 19 [ed. p. 138-149]. See [also] C. 4, 63, 4 [§ 3] (in the ms. this last reference appears to be a later addition: it could have been taken over from Gentilis, p. 145).

LIBERVM. 3

versum posse, quo minus alij ad subditos suos accedant, & cum illis negotientur. Hinc jus descendit hospitale sanctissimum: hinc querelæ: ^a*&L. nemo igitur ff eod. vide Gent. de iure belli lib.1.c.19 vid. L.mercatores C. de Comm.*

Quod genus hoc hominum, quæve hunc tam barbara morem
Permittit patria? hospitio prohibemur arenæ. ^a*Virgil. X. Aen.*

Et alibi
littusque rogamus
Innocuum, & cunctis undamque auramque patentem. ^b*7. Aeneid.*

Et scimus bella quædam ex hac causa coepisse, ^c*Diod.11. Platar. Pericle.*
ut Megarensibus in Athenienses, Bononiensibus in Venetos: Castellanis etiam in Americanos has justas potuisse belli causas esse, & ^d*Sig. ult. de reb. Ital.*
cæteris probabiliores. Victoria putat, si peregrinari & degere apud illos prohiberentur, si ^e*Vict.de Indis parte 2,n.1.2. 3.4.5.6.7. Adde Covar. in c. peccatū. §.9.n.4. ibi: Quinta.*
arcerentur a participatione earum rerum quæ jure gentium aut moribus communia sunt, si denique ad commercia non admitterentur. ^f*Num. c. 20.*
Cui simile est quod in Mosis historia, & inde ^g*August.lib.4. qu 44. super. Num. Et est c. ult.23.4.2.*
apud Augustinum legimus, justa bella Israëlitas contra Amorræos gessisse, quia innoxius transitus denegabatur: qui IVRE HVMANÆ SOCIETATIS æquissimo patere debebat. Et hoc nomine Hercules Orchomeniorum, ^h*Sophocl. Trachin.*
Græci sub Agamemnone Mysorum Regi arma intulerunt: quasi libera essent naturaliter itinera ut Baldus dixit: accusanturque a Ger- ⁱ*3.Cons.293.*
manis

A 2

---

[1] 'probabiliores. Victoria putat': the full stop before Victoria is a printer's error, see Err.

^a **Virgil. 1. Aen.**: Virgilius, Aeneis, I [539 f.].
^b **7. Aeneid.**: Virgilius, Aeneis, VII [229 f.]. Cf. below, p. 20 note f.
^c **Diod. 11. Plutar. Pericle.**: Diodorus Siculus, XI [XII, 39]; Plutarchus, Pericles [XXIX, p. 168 B].
^d **Sig. ult. de reb. [read: re.] Ital.**: Carolus Sigonius in the last book of his *De regno Italiae* [*quinque reliqui libri*] (= lib. XX, ed. p. 194 and 196). The reference was taken over from Gentilis, De iure belli, I, 19, ed. p. 145; my identification is borrowed from Gentilis, De iure belli (Italian translation), p. 130, referring to an edition Venetiis 1591 of *De regno Italiae quinque reliqui libri*. Confusion has been caused by the fact that Sigonius' work was published in two parts: *Historiarum de regno Italiae libri quindecim* and *De regno Italiae quinque reliqui libri*. Interpreters who only used an edition of the first part [must] have looked in vain in chapter XV, see Boschan, p. 26 n. 7 (who explicitly says so) and Williams, p. 219 and 410 (who simply does not specify). Bensly, p. 117, has found the right passage in the second part.

^e **Vict. de Indis parte 2, n. 1. 2. 3. 4. 5. 6. 7. Adde Covar. in c. peccatū. §. 9. n. 4. ibi: Quinta.**: Victoria, De Indis, pars 2 [= 3], num. 1-7, ed. p. 257-261. Add Covarruvias in reg. Peccatum, p. 500 (cf. Djbap, p. 642).

^f **Num. c. 20**: Numeri XX [14-22].

^g **August. lib. 4. qu 44 super. Num. Et est c. ult. 23. 4. (read: q.; see Err.) 2.**: Augustinus, Quaestiones in Heptateuchum, IV, qu. 44, on Numeri, also to be found in Decretum Grat.,

forbidding others to enjoy access to or trade with the subjects of that state or prince. This doctrine is the source of the sacrosanct law of hospitality. It is the basis of the Trojan complaints:

> What kind of men are these? What land allows
> So barbarous a custom? We are barred
> From welcome to its shores . . . ^a

This other passage, too, is pertinent:

> A harmless landing-place we crave, and air
> And water, which are free to all. . . ^b

Moreover, we know that certain wars have been undertaken precisely on such grounds. This was true, for example, of the Megarean war against the Athenians^c, and of the Bolognese war against the Venetians^d. Similarly, Victoria^e holds¹ that, if the Spaniards should be prohibited by the American Indians from travelling or residing among the latter, or if they should be prevented from sharing in those things which are common property under the law of nations or by custom – if, in short, they should be debarred from the practice of commerce – these causes might serve them as just grounds for war against the Indians; and, indeed, as grounds more plausible than others [discussed by Victoria in an earlier section of the same work]. A like example is recorded in the story of Moses^f and in a passage from Augustine^g based upon that story. I allude to the fact that the Israelites waged war justly against the Amorites because the right of inoffensive transit through the Amorite territory was denied them, even though such transit ought to be freely permitted according to the absolutely just *law of human fellowship*. Hercules, too, made war upon the King of the Orchomenians^h, and the Greeks (under the leadership of Agamemnon) upon the King of the Mysians, on this same ground, namely, that highways are (so to speak) free and open by natural disposition, as Baldusⁱ has declared.

[97]

Causa 23, 2, 3 [cf. below, p. 61 note e). The reference was taken over from Gentilis, De iure belli, I, 19 [ed. p. 138]. Gentilis has 'et c. ult. 23. q. 2'; Grotius changed 'et' into 'Et est' ('also to be found in'). In two of the three 1633 editions (TMD 545 and 546) 'est' was changed into 'Est.' This has induced Magoffin (p. 9 n. 5) to interpret 'Est.' as referring to an author called 'Estius': 'Estius (?-1613) was a Dutch commentator of the Epistles of St. Paul and the works of St. Augustine'. This absurd interpretation was taken over by the editor of the Spanish translation (p. 66 n. 12), who added information on Estius (Willem van Est, 1542-1613, professor of theology at the University of Douai); the editor of the Italian translation 2007 followed his Spanish colleague (p. 111 n. 12).

h **Sophocl. Trachin.:** Sophocles, Trachineae [found in Apollodorus, Bibliotheca, II, 7, 7]. Cf. Bensly, p. 117

i **3. Cons. 293:** Baldus, Consilia, IV [!], cons. 293, ed. fol. 63 v. Copied from Gentilis, De iure belli, I, 19, [ed. p. 138], who has the same error ('3. Cons.' instead of '4. Cons.'). The erroneous reference was repeated in Djbap, p. 196 (see my note on p. 959). The editors of Gentilis, De iure belli (Italian translation), at page 124 n. 2, tried to emend G.'s reference to Baldus in another way, which would seem completely unsatisfactory; in any case their contention that the ed. 1598 would read '3. Cons. 203' (instead of '3 Cons. 293', as the ed. 1612 has) is not right, although the printing is somewhat defective. The correct identification (IV, 293) was already given by Boschan, p. 27 n. 8, and by myself in Djbap, p. 959. The error is found in all editions of Ml.

manis apud Tacitum Romani, quod colloquia congressusque gentium arcerent, fluminaque & terras & cœlum quodammodo ipsum clauderent. Nec ullus titulus Christianis quondam in Sarracenos magis placuit, quam quod per illos terræ Iudææ aditu arcerentur. Sequitur ex hac sententia Lusitanos, etiamsi domini essent earum regionum ad quas Batavi proficiscuntur, injuriam tamen facturos si aditum Batavis & mercatum præcluderent. Quanto igitur iniquius est volentes aliquos a volentium populorum commercio secludi, illorum opera quorum in potestate nec populi isti sunt, nec illud ipsum, qua iter est; quando latrones etiam & piratas non alio magis nomine detestamur, quam quod illi hominum inter se commeatus obsident atque infestant?

4. Histor.

Alut.;. cons. 130. Cov. cap. peccatum p.2.§.9. Bart. ad L. 1. C. de Pagan.

CAPVT II.

Lusitanos nullum habere ius dominii in eos Indos ad quos Batavi navigant titulo inventionis.

NON esse autem Lusitanos earum partium dominos ad quas Batavi accedunt, puta Iavæ, Taprobanæ[1], partis maximæ Moluccarum, certissimo argumnto colligimus, quia

---

[1] 'Taprobana' is traditionally translated as Ceylon, but Williams has proven that Grotius used it here for Sumatra (see Williams, p. 5 n. 1, p. 184 n. 1 and p. 221 n. 1; cf. however below, p. 33 n. 1).

Yet again, according to Tacitus[a], the Germans accused the Romans of preventing conferences and assemblages among the various tribes, and of blocking off lands, rivers, and, in a sense, the very skies. Nor did the Christians in earlier times find any more acceptable justification for their crusades against the Saracens than the charge that the latter were barring the Christians from access to the land of Palestine[b].

From the doctrine above set forth, it follows that the Portuguese, even if they were the owners of the regions sought by the Dutch, would nevertheless be inflicting an injury if they prevented the Dutch from entering those regions and engaging in commerce therein. How much more unjust, then, is the existing situation, in which persons desirous of commerce with peoples who share that desire, are cut off from the latter by the intervention of men who are not invested with power either over the said peoples or over the route to be followed! For there is no stronger reason underlying our abhorrence even of robbers and pirates than the fact that they besiege and render unsafe the thoroughfares of human intercourse.

Chapter II

That the Portuguese have no right of dominion, by title of discovery, over those Indians to whom the Dutch sail.

In any case, we hold that the Portuguese are not the owners of the regions visited by the Dutch (that is to say, Java, Sumatra[1], and most of the Moluccas), on the basis of the incontrovertible argument

---

[a] 4. Histor.: Tacitus, Historiae, IV [64].
[b] Alci. [read: Alex.] 7. cons. 130. Cov. cap. peccatum p. 2. §. 9. Bart. ad. L. 1. C. de Pagan.: Alexander Tartagnus, Consilia, VII, 130, ed. fol. 83r-84v; Covarruvias in reg. Peccatum, p. 506 (in § 10 instead of § 9). Bartolus on C. 1, 11, 1, ed. VII, fol. 25 r. – 'Alci.' instead of 'Alex.' is an error; the ms. has 'Alex.' This is probably not a printer's error in the strict sense, but a copyist's error (see Introduction, at note 111): Hamaker also misread the ms., followed by Williams. All editions of MI have copied this error. Among the translators only Boschan, p. 27 n. 9, seems to have noticed that the reference could not be right; he claims, however, only to have looked in vain in Alciatus' Pandectarum commentaria. Nobody mentions the simple fact that book VII of the Consilia of Alciatus has only 27 numbers. The reference to Alexander Tartagnus and Covarruvias, for that matter, was probably copied by Grotius from Gentilis, De iure belli, I, 19 [ed. p. 138], just as the references in notes d, g and i on p. 3.

LIBERVM.

quia dominus nemo est eius rei quam nec ipse unquam nec alter ipsius nomine possedit.[1] Habent insulæ istæ quas dicimus & semper habuerunt suos Reges, suam rempublicam, suas leges, sua jura: Lusitanis mercatus, ut aliis gentibus conceditur: itaque & tributa cum pendunt, & jus mercandi à Principibus exorant, dominos se non esse, sed ut externos advenire satis testantur: ne habitant quidem nisi precario. Et quanquam ad dominium titulus nõ sufficiat, quia & possessio requiritur, cum aliud sit rem habere, aliud jus ad rem consequendam, tamen ne titulum quidem dominij in eas partes Lusitanis ullum esse affirmo, quem non ipsis eripuerit Doctorum, & quidem Hispanorum sententia. Primum si dicent inventionis præmio eas terras sibi cessisse, nec jus, nec verum dicent. Invenire enim non illud est oculis vsurpare, sed apprehendere, vt Gordiani epistola ostenditur: unde Grammatici invenire & occupare pro verbis ponunt idem significantibus: & tota Latinitas quod adepti sumus, id demum invenisse nos dicit, cui oppositum est perdere. Quin & ipsa naturalis ratio, & legum diserta verba, & eruditiorum interpretatio manifeste ostendit ad titulum dominii parandum eam demum sufficere inventionem quæ cum possessione conjuncta est,

L. Si Barsatorem C. de fidejuss. Non Marc. c. 4. in verbo occupare. Vid. Conan. comm. Iuris Civil. li. 3 c. 3. in fine. Vide Donell. de Iure Civili li. 4. c. 10. Instit. de rerum divis. §. illud quæsitum est.

---

[1] 'possedit': in the ms. a short sentence follows which is crossed out: 'Non enim de Malacca, non de Goa loquimur, coloniis Lusitanorum' ('We do not speak of Malacca, nor of Goa, colonies of the Portuguese'). This crossing out could date from the time when the ms. was prepared for publication but it is not mentioned by Armitage nor by van Ittersum (cf. below, p. 6 note 1).

Chapter II

that no one is owner of a thing which has never been taken into his possession either by his own direct action or by another party acting in his name[1]. The islands in question now have, and always have had, their own rulers, governments, laws and rights. The Portuguese, like other peoples, are permitted to carry on trade there. Indeed, by paying the tributes levied and also by the very act of petitioning the rulers for the right of trade, the Portuguese themselves testify clearly enough to the fact that they are not the owners of those lands but foreign visitors. Their very residence in the islands is allowed as a favour. Moreover, aside from the fact that title does not suffice to constitute ownership, since possession is also a requisite (for possession of a thing is different from the right to seek possession thereof), I go so far as to assert that the Portuguese do not even have any title to ownership of the said regions which has not been taken from them by the pronouncements of – notably Spanish – Doctores.

In the first place, if the Portuguese maintain that those territories have passed into their hands as a reward for discovery, their contention will find support neither in law nor in fact.

For discovery consists, not in perceiving a thing with the eye, but in actual seizure, as is intimated by the Emperor Gordian in one of his letters[a]. Thus the philologists[b] treat the expressions 'to discover' (*invenire*) and 'to take possession of' (*occupare*) as synonymous terms; and, according to all Latin usage, we have 'discovered' only that which we have acquired (*adepti*), the opposite process being that of 'loss' (*perdere*)[c]. Furthermore, natural reason itself, the express statements of the law, and their interpretation by men of considerable learning[d], all clearly indicate that discovery suffices to create a title to ownership only when possession is an accompanying factor[e];

---

[a] **L. Si Barsatorem C. de fideiuss.**: C. 8, 40 (41), 13. As to Gordianus, mentioned in the text, see Introduction, note 164.

[b] **Non [read: Non.] Marc. c. 4 in verbo occupare**: Nonius Marcellus [De compendiosa doctrina], IV, on word *occupare*.

[c] **Vid. Conan. comm. Iuris Civil. li. 3 c. 3 in fine**: See Connanus, Commentaria iuris civilis, ed. I, fol. 160v-161r.

[d] **Vide Donell. de Iure Civili li. 4. c. 10**: See Donellus, Commentaria de iure civili, ed. I, p. 247-248.

[e] **Instit. de rerum divis. §. illud quaesitum est**: Inst. 2, 1, 13.

MARE

est, ubi scilicet res mobiles apprehenduntur, aut immobiles terminis atque custodia sepiuntur: quod in hac specie dici nullo modo potest. Nam praesidia illic Lusitani nulla habent. Quid quod ne reperisse quidem Indiam ullo modo dici possunt Lusitani, quae tot à saeculis fuerat celeberrima. Iam ab Horatij tempore: [1]

Impiger extremos currit mercator ad Indos
Per mare pauperiem fugiens.

Taprobanes pleraque quam exacte nobis Romani descripsere? Iam vero & caeteras insulas ante Lusitanos non finitimi tantum Persae & Arabes, sed Europaei etiam, praecipue Veneti noverant. Praeterea inventio nihil iuris tribuit, nisi in ea quae ante inventionem nullius fuerant. Atqui Indi cum ad eos Lusitani venerunt, etsi partim idololatrae, partim Mahumetani erant, gravibusque peccatis involuti, nihilominus publice atque privatim rerum possessionumque suarum dominium habuerunt, quod illis sine justa causa eripi nō potuit. Ita certissimis rationibus post alios auctores maximi nominis concludit Hispanus Victoria: *Non possunt*, inquit, *Christiani seculares aut Ecclesiastici potestate civili & principatu privare infideles, eo duntaxat titulo, quia infideles sunt, nisi ab eis alia iniuria profecta sit.* Fides enim, ut recte inquit Thomas, non tollit [2] [3] [4]

Marginalia: L.3.§. Neratius in fine.ff. de acq.possess. — Lib.1.epist.1. — Vide Plin. Nat.histor. lib.6.c.22. — L.3.ff. de acquir. rerum dom. — Covar. in c. peccatū. §.10. n.2.&4.&5. — De potest. civili parte 1. num 9. — 2.2.q.10.art.12.

---

[1] 'celeberrima': in the ms. a short sentence follows which is crossed out: 'Alia enim Indiae alia Americae ratio est' ('There is one reason for India, another for America'). This crossing out probably dates from the time when the ms. was prepared for publication, see Armitage, p. 14 n. 6, who, instead of 'Indiae' and 'Americae', wrongly reads 'India' and 'America'; cf. van Ittersum, Preparing Mare liberum, p. 260.

[2] 'Taprobanes': Williams has retained the Latin form here because there is a discrepancy between Grotius' use of the term (for Sumatra, see above, p. 4 note 1) and the proper interpretation of the same term in Classical Latin.

[3] After 'noverant' a passage was added and then crossed out in the top margin of the ms.: 'Et quamvis antea noti non fuissent Indi, tamen hac ratione, ut optime collegit Victoria, cum primum alteri alteros viderunt non magis Indos Hispani invenisse, quam Indi Hispanos dici poterunt'. This was probably crossed out at the time when another addition, touching more or less on the same point, was added in the bottom margin of the ms. (see below, p. 7 note 1). The first addition might have been inserted when, in a later passage (Ml p. 9), he referred to Victoria I, 31 (= II, 7), see below p. 7 note 1 and p. 9 notes j and k.

[4] 'Christiani': read 'Christian rulers, whether lay or clerical' (see note f).

Chapter II

that is to say, only in cases where movable articles are seized[a], or immovable property is marked off by boundaries and placed under guard. In the particular case under discussion, it is in nowise possible to maintain that this requisite has been met; for the Portuguese have no garrisons stationed in those East Indian lands.

Besides, what answer can be made to the objection that the Portuguese cannot in any sense at all be said to have found the East Indies, a region exceedingly well known for so many centuries past[1]? Even as early as the time of Horace [we find these lines[b]]

> The busy trader flees from poverty,
> Across the seas to India's farthest isle.

And what of the fact that the Romans[c] have described for us with the utmost exactitude many things of Taprobane[2]? The other islands, too, were already known not only to the neighbouring Persians and Arabs but also to the Europeans – and in particular to the Venetians – before the Portuguese came to know them[3].

In addition to the foregoing arguments, however, it should be noted that even discovery imparts no legal right save in the case of those things which were ownerless prior to the act of discovery[d]. But at the time when the Portuguese first came to the East Indies, the natives of that region – though they were in part idolaters, in part Mohammedans, and sunk in grievous sin – nevertheless enjoyed public and private ownership of their own property and possessions, an attribute which could not be taken from them without just cause[e]. This is the conclusion expounded by the Spaniard Victoria with irrefutable logic and in agreement with other authorities of the greatest renown.

Victoria[f] declares that 'Christians, whether laymen or clerics[4], may not deprive infidels of their civil power and sovereignty merely on the ground that the latter are infidels, unless they have been guilty of some other wrong'. For the factor of religious faith, as Thomas [Aquinas][g] rightly observes, does not cancel

---

[a] **L. 3. §. Neratius. in fine. ff. de acq. possess.**: D. 41, 2, 3, 3.
[b] **Lib. 1. epist. 1.**: [Horatius, Epistulae] I, 1 [45 f.].
[c] **Vide Plin. Nat. histor. lib. 6. c. 22**: Plinius, Naturalis historia, VI, 22 [24].
[d] **L. 3. ff. de acquir. rerum dom.**: D. 41, 1, 3.
[e] **Covar. in c. peccatum. §. 10, n. 2. et 4. et 5.**: Covarruvias in reg. Peccatum, ed. p. 505-507 (cf. Djbap, p.513-514).
[f] **De potest. civili parte 1. num. 9**: [Victoria,] De potestate civili, ed. p.132-133. In his quotation Grotius omits 'principes' before 'Christiani' and puts 'potestate civili' instead of 'huiusmodi potestate'.
[g] **2. 2. q. 10. art. 12.**: [Thomas Aquinas,] 2, 2, q. 10 art. 12 [read: art. 10], Summa, III, p. 44. The error was probably copied from Victoria, De Indis, I, 7, cf. next reference in Ml on p. 7; the Wright-edition, p. 226 n. 3, quotes q. 12 art. 2, where Thomas refers to q. 10 art. 10.

LIBERVM.

lit jus naturale aut humanum, ex quo dominia profecta sunt. Imo credere infideles non esse rerum suarum dominos, hæreticum est: & res ab illis possessas illis ob hoc ipsum eripere furtum est, & rapina, non minus quam si idem fiat Christianis. Recte igitur dicit Victoria non magis ista ex causa Hispanis jus in Indos quæsitum, quam Indis fuisset in Hispanos, si qui illorum priores in Hispaniam venissent. Neque vero sunt Indi Orientis amentes & insensati, sed ingeniosi & solertes, ita vt ne hinc quidem prætextus subijciendi possit desumi, qui tamen per se satis est manifestæ iniquitatis. Iam olim Plutarchus προφασιν πλεονεξιας fuisse dicit ἡμερῶσαι τὰ βαρβαρικὰ, improbam scilicet alieni cupiditatem hoc sibi velum obtendere, quod barbariem mansuefaciat. Et nunc etiam color ille redigendi in vitas gentes ad mores humaniores, qui Græcis olim & Alexandro usurpatus est, à Theologis omnibus, presertim Hispanis, improbus, atque impius censetur.

Vict. de Indis parte 1. n. 4. 5. 6. 7. & n. 19.

Vide Vasq. in præf. n. 5.

CAPVT III.
Lusitanos in Indos non habere ius dominij titulo donationis Pontificiæ.

SECVNDO si Pontificis Alexandri Sexti divisione vtentur, ante omnia illud attendendum est, volueritne Pontifex con-

the natural or human law from which ownership has been derived. On the contrary, it is heretical to hold that infidels are not the owners of the property that belongs to them and the act of snatching from them, on the sole ground of their lack of faith, those goods which have been taken into their possession, is an act of thievery and rapine no less than it would be if perpetrated against Christians[a]. Thus Victoria correctly maintains that the Spaniards acquired no greater right over the American Indians in consequence of that defect of faith, than the Indians would have possessed over the Spaniards if any of the former had been the first foreigners to come to Spain[1].

Furthermore, the Indians of the Orient are neither insane nor irrational[2], but clever and sagacious, so that not even in this respect can a pretext for their subjugation be found. For that matter, any such pretext is in itself clearly unjust. Long ago, Plutarch[3] pointed out that ἡμερῶσαι τὰ βαρβαρικά [the civilizing of barbarians] served as πρόφασις πλεονεξίας [a cloak for greed], or in other words, that shameless lust for another's property was wont to take cover under the excuse of introducing civilization into barbaric regions. Nowadays, even this pretext of bringing reluctant peoples to an acceptance of more refined customs – an explanation to which recourse was had in earlier times by the Greeks and by Alexander – is regarded in the judgement of all the theologians, and particularly in that of the Spaniards, as unjust and impious[b].

Chapter III

That the Portuguese have no right of dominion over the Indians by title of the Papal donation.

Secondly, if the Portuguese are basing their claim upon the apportionment made by Pope Alexander the Sixth, it will be necessary to take under consideration before everything else the question of

---

[a] **Vict. de Indis parte 1. n. 4. 5. 6. 7. et n. 19:** Victoria, De Indis, I, 4-7 and 19, ed. p. 222-226 and 229.
[b] **Vide Vasq. in praef. n. 5:** Vasquius, Controv., I, p. 4.

MARE

Vide Osorium, tentiones tantum Lusitanorum & Castellanorum dirimere, quod potuit sane, ut lectus inter illos arbiter, sicut & ipsi Reges jam ante inter se ea de re fœdera quædam pepigerant: & hoc si ita est, cum res inter alios acta sit, ad cæteras gentes non pertinebit: an vero prope singulos Mundi trientes duobus populis donare. Quod etsi voluisset, & potuisset Pontifex, non tamen continuo sequeretur domi- *Vide Inst. de rerum diviss. §. per tradit.* nos eorum locorum esse Lusitanos, cum donatio dominum non faciat, sed secuta traditio: quare & huic causæ possessio deberet accedere. Tum vero si quis jus ipsum sive divinum sive humanum scrutari volet, non autem ex commodo suo metiri, facile deprehendet donationem ejusmodi ut rei alienæ nullius esse momenti Disputationē de potestate Pontificis, hoc est Episcopi Romanæ Ecclesiæ, hic non aggrediar, nec quicquam ponam nisi ex hypothesi, hoc est quod confitentur homines inter eos eruditissimi, qui plurimum Pontificiæ tribuunt auctoritati: maxime Hispani: qui cum pro sua perspicacia *Luc. 12. 14. Iohan. 18. 36. Vict. de Indis f. 1. num. 25.* facile viderent Dominum Christum omne à se terrenum imperium abdicasse, mundi certe totius dominium, qua homo fuit, non habuisse, & si habuisset, nullis tamē argumentis astrui posse jus illud in Petrum, aut Romanam Ecclesiam Vicarii jure translatum: cum alias

Chapter III

whether or not the Pope was interested exclusively in settling the disputes between the Portuguese and the Castilians. This task he was of course empowered to discharge in his capacity as chosen arbiter between the two peoples[a], since the respective rulers themselves had previously concluded certain treaties on that very point. If we assume that the settlement of those disputes was the Pope's sole aim, we must infer that it was a thing done between others and therefore will not affect the rest of the peoples of the world. Or was it, instead, his intention to bestow almost a third of the whole earth upon each of the two nations above mentioned? Even in such circumstances – that is to say, if he had intended and had had the power to make such a donation – nevertheless, it would not necessarily follow that the Portuguese had become the owners of the Orient, since it is not the act of donation but the subsequent delivery that creates ownership[b]. Therefore, in order to give validity to such a claim, it would be necessary to add the title of actual possession to the title of donation.

Furthermore, anyone who chooses to make a thorough examination of the question of law, whether divine or human, weighing the matter independently of his personal interests, will readily discern that a donation of this kind, concerning as it does the property of others, is without effect[1]. I shall not enter here into any dispute as to the power pertaining to the Pope (in other words, to the Bishop of the Church of Rome); nor shall I make any assertion save on the basis of a hypothesis accepted by the most erudite of those men who attribute the highest possible degree of authority to the papal office, and among whom the Spaniards in particular[2] are included. With their characteristic acuteness, they have readily grasped these facts: that Christ the Lord renounced all earthly sovereignty[c]; that in his human form he certainly did not possess dominion over the entire world; and that if he had possessed such dominion, this sovereign right could not by any series of arguments be attributed to the Pope or transferred to the Church of Rome as his Vicarius[3]; because

---

[a] **Vide Osorium.**: Osorius, fol. 323 v.
[b] **Vide Instit. de rerum divis. §. per tradit.**: Inst. 2, 1, 40.
[c] **Luc. 12. 14. Iohan. 18. 36. Vict. de Indis, p. 1. num. 25.**: Lucas XII. 14; Johannes XVIII, 36; Victoria, De Indis, pars 1, num. 25 [= pars 2 num. 1], ed. p. 233-238.

LIBERVM.

alias etiam certum sit multa Christum habuisse in quæ Pontifex non successerit, interpretes affirmarunt (vtar ipsorum verbis) Pontificem non esse dominum civilem aut temporalem totius orbis. Imo etiam si quam talem potestatem in mundo haberet, eam tamen non recte exerciturum, cum spirituali sua jurisdictione contentus esse debeat, sæcularibus autem Principibus eam concedere nullo modo posse. Tum vero si quam habeat potestatem temporalem, eam habere, ut loquuntur, in ordine ad spiritualia. Quocirca nullam illi esse potestatem in populos infideles, ut qui ad Ecclesiam non pertineant. Vnde sequitur ex sententia Cajetani & Victoriæ & potioris partis tam Theologorum quam Canonistarum, non esse idoneum titulum adversus Indos vel quia Papa dederit provincias illas tanquam dominus absolute, vel quia non recognoscunt dominium Papæ: atque adeo ne Saracenos quidem isto titulo unquam spoliatos.

Vict. 16. n. 27.
Vide Vasq. c. 21. contro. ill. Turr. Crem. lib. 2. c. 113. Hugo 69. dist. cum ad Verum Bern. in 2. lib. ad Eug. Vict. de Ind. p. 1. n. 27. Cov. in c. pecca. §. 9. n. 7.
Matt. 20. 26. Iohan. 6. 15. Matt. 17. 27. Vict. ib. n. 28. Cov. de loco. 1. Cor. 5. in fine. Thom. 2. 2. 12. 2. Ayala li. 1. c. 2. n. 29. Vict. ibi. n. 30. Cov. d. loco Vide locū Cajetani infra Thom. 2. 2. q. 66. art. 8. Silv. de infid. §. 7. Inn. in c. quod super his de voto. Vict. n. 31.

CAPVT IV.

Lusitanos in Indos non habere ius dominii titulo belli.

His igitur sublatis cum manifestum sit, quod & Victoria scribit, Hispanos ad ter- *d. n. 31.*

in other respects it is also certain that Christ possessed many things to which the Pope did not fall heir[a], they [the erudite persons just mentioned] have boldly[1] asserted (and I use their own words), that the Pope is not the civil or temporal lord of the whole earth[b]; that even if the Pope did have worldly power of this kind, he would still not be right in exercising it, since he ought to be content with his spiritual jurisdiction[c]; that, in any case, he would in nowise be able to cede such power to secular princes[2,d]; that, moreover, if he does possess any temporal power, he possesses it, as the phrase goes, for spiritual ends[e]; and that, consequently, he has no power at all over infidel peoples, since they are not members of the Church[f].

Thus it follows from the opinions laid down by Cajetan[g] and by Victoria as well as from the preponderant authority of both theologians[h] and canonists[i], that there is no sound claim to be urged against the East Indians[j], either on the ground that the Pope as lord of the East Indian lands gave away this territory by an unrestricted act of donation, or on the ground that the inhabitants fail to acknowledge the papal dominion; and indeed, it is also clear that even the Saracens were never despoiled on such grounds.

Chapter IV

That the Portuguese have no right of dominion over the Indians by title of war.

Now that we have disposed of the pretexts just discussed, having plainly shown that (as Victoria[k] himself declares) the Hispanic peoples did not carry with them to

[99ʹ]

---

p. 503-504 (the references to Turrecremata, Huguccio and Bernardus were probably copied from Victoria, where the error in the reference to Huguccio –'69. dist.' instead of '96. dist.' – already appears).

[c] **Matt. 20. 26. Iohan. 6. 15. Matt. 17. 27:** Matthaeus 20, 26; Johannes 6, 15; Matthaeus 17, 27 [25-27].

[d] **Vict. ib. n. 28. Cov. de [read 'd.' (dicto) as the ms. has] loco:** Victoria, De Indis, pars 1, num. 28 [= pars 2, num. 4], ed. p. 241; Covarruvias, cited above (see note b). For the printer's error see Err. and note 2 on this page.

[e] **1. Cor. 5 in fine:** Ad Corinthos, I, 5 in fine.

[f] **Thom. 2. 2. 12. 2. Ayala li. 1. c. 2. n. 29. Vict. ibi n. 30. Cov. d. loco:** Thomas Aquinas, Summa, III, p. 50; Ayala, De iure belli, p. 35; Victoria, De Indis, pars 1, num. 30 [= pars 2, num. 6], ed. p. 243; Covarruvias, cited above (see note b).

[g] **Vide locum Caietani infra:** See the quotation from Caietanus below [see p. 11-12 of Ml]. Cf. also below, note j.

[h] **Thom. 2. 2. q. 66. art. 8. Silv. de infid. §. 7.:** Thomas Aquinas, Summa, III, p. 229-230; Sylvester Prierias, verbo Infidelitas, septimo, ed. p. 36 [§ 8]. Cf. below, note j.

[i] **Inn. in c. quod super his de voto:** Innocentius IV ad Decretal. III, 34, 8, ed. fol. 178. Cf. below note j.

[j] **Vict. n. 31:** Victoria, De Indis, pars 1, num. 31 [= pars 2, num. 7], ed. p. 243-245. (Victoria refers to the sources mentioned in notes g, h and i).

[k] **d. n. 31:** [Victoria,] in number 31, cited above, (see note j).

10 MARE

ras remotiores illas navigātes nullū jus secum attulisse occupādi eas provincias, unus duntaxat titulus belli restat, qui & ipse si justus esset, tamē ad dominiū proficere nō posset, nisi jure prædæ, hoc est post occupationem. Atqui tātum abest ut Lusitani eas res occupaverint, ut cū plerisq; gentibus quas Batavi accesserunt, bellū eo tempore nullū haberent. Et sic igitur nullū jus illis queri potuit: cum etiā si quas ab Indis pertulissent injurias, eas longa pace & amicis commerciis remisisse merito censeantur. Quanquam ne fuit quidem quod bello obtenderent. Nam qui Barbaros bello persequuntur, ut Americanos Hispani, duo solent prætexere, quod ab illis commercio arceātur, aut quod doctrinam veræ religionis illi nolint agnoscere. Et commercia quidem Lusitani ab Indis impetrarunt, ut hac in parte nihil habeant quod quærantur. Alter vero obtentus nihilo est justior, quam ille Græcorum in Barbaros, quo Boëtius respexit:

Vide Vasq. c. 24. contr. ill. Vict. p. 2. de Indis n. 10. Metr. 4. lib. 4. de consol.

An distant quia dissidentque mores,
Iniustas acies, & fera bella movent,
Alternisque volunt perire telis?
Non est iusta satis sævitiæ ratio.

2. 2. q. 10. art 8. c. de Iudæis dist. 45. c. qui sincera. eadē dist. Innoc. d. loco. Barto. ad l. 1. C. de pag. Covarr. ad c. peccatum

Ista autem & Thomæ & Concilij Toletani & Gregorii & Theologorum, Canonistarum, Iurisprudentiumque fere omnium conclusio est: Quantumcunque fides annuntiata sit Barbaris

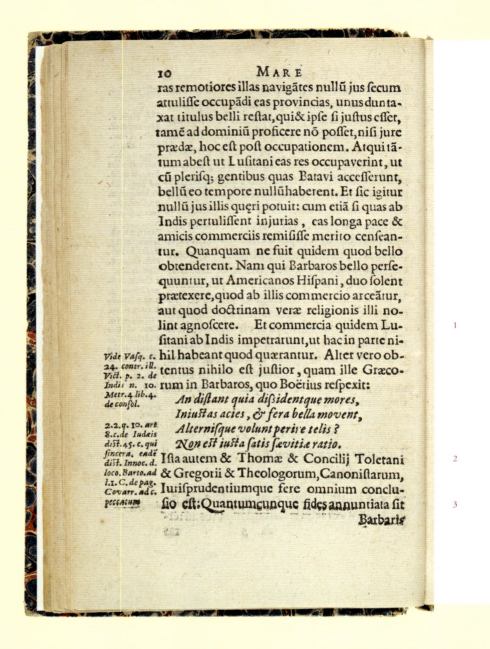

---

[1] After 'agnoscere' the ms. has an addition in the bottom margin which was later crossed out: 'sicut inter alia regnum amplissimum Peruanum hoc titulo armis quaesitum est, quod Rex Atabaliba Breviarium Romanum paginis sibi aliquot expositis quasi nullius usus librum proiecisset'. In the margin: 'v. Joh. Met. Praef. ad Osorium'; a reference to Johannes Metellus in his preface to Osorius, ed. fol. 12 v. The addition was probably written at the same time as the one on p. 12 which was not crossed out; the crossing out on p. 10 probably dates from the preparation for publication.

[2] In the margin of the ms. there is a separate reference to 'Matt. X, 23', which was probably written before the references of note c. In Ml it was put at the end of note c, preceded by 'argum.'; this probably meant that a general argument could (also) be taken from the text of Matthaeus. Hamaker puts the reference (in the form it has in the ms.) before the references of note c; Williams places it between the reference to Thomas and the one to Decretum Grat. Dist. 45, 5.

[3] The conclusion which follows – 'Quantumcunque ... bonis suis'– is, apart from the passage in parentheses, literally taken from Victoria, De Indis, pars 1 num. 41 [= pars 2, num. 15], ed. p. 252, not mentioned by Grotius. The references to Thomas, the Decretum Gratiani and Innocentius (see

Chapter IV

still more distant regions any right to take possession of the lands to which they sailed, there remains for consideration only one possible title, namely that based upon war. Such a title, even if it were in itself just, still could not create ownership save through the 'right of booty' (*jure praedae*), that is to say, only after 'occupation' (*occupatio*). But the Portuguese, far from occupying the lands in question, were not engaged at the time in any war with the majority of the peoples visited by the Dutch. Consequently, there was no right that they could claim; for even if they had suffered injuries of any sort at the hands of the East Indians, it could reasonably be assumed that those injuries had been forgiven, in view of the long period of peace and the friendly commercial relations that had been established.

As a matter of fact, there was no pretext that the Portuguese could offer for going to war, since anyone who makes war upon barbarians (as the Spaniards did upon the American Indians) is wont to advance one of two pretexts: either that he is prevented by the said barbarians from engaging in trade, or else that the latter refuse to accept[1] the doctrines of the true faith.

The Portuguese certainly did obtain rights of trade from the East Indians, so that they have no cause for complaint in this respect.

As for the other excuse, it would be quite as unjust[a] as the argument advanced by the Greeks against the barbarians, to which Boethius[b] refers in these terms:

> Do they wage savage frays and unjust wars,
> Seeking to perish by each other's swords,
> Because they dwell apart, with unlike ways?
> This is no just sufficient cause for rage.

Moreover[2], Thomas [Aquinas], the Council of Toledo, Gregory, and practically all of the theologians, canonists, and civilians[c] arrive at the following conclusion[3]: howsoever convincingly and fully the true faith may have been preached

---

note c) are also to be found in Victoria.

[a] **Vide Vasq. c. 24. contr. ill. Vict. p. 2. de Indis n. 10.:** See Vasquius, Controv. I, p. 220-222 [and] Victoria, De Indis, pars 2, num. 10, ed. p. 262-263.

[b] **Metr. 4. lib. de consol.:** [Boethius,] De consolatione philosophiae, IV, 4 [7 ff.].

[c] **2. 2. q. 10. art. 8. c. de Iudaeis dist. 45. c. qui sincerae. eadem dist. Innoc. d. loco. Barto. ad l. 1. C. de pag. Covarr. ad c. peccatum p. 2. §. 9 et 10. Ayala de iure belli lib. 1. c. 2. n. 28. argum. Matth. 10. 23.:** [Thomas Aquinas,] Summa, III, p. 42-43; Decretum Grat., Dist. 45, 5 (Concilium Toletanum) and 3 (Gregorius); Innocentius IV, cited above (see p. 9 note i); Bartolus on C. 1, 11, 1, ed. VII, fol. 25 r; Covarruvias in reg. Peccatum, ed. p. 499-507; Ayala, De iure belli, p. 34-35. A [further] argument [can be taken from] Matthaeus, X, 23. (In the ms. the reference to Thomas is separated from the rest).

LIBERVM.

Barbaris (nam de his qui subditi ante fuerunt Christianis Principibus, item de Apostatis alia est quæstio) probabiliter & sufficienter, & si noluerint eam respicere, non tamen licere hac ratione eos bello persequi, & spoliare bonis suis. Operæpretium est in hanc rem ipsa Cajetani verba describere: *Quidam*, ait, *infideles nec de iure nec de facto subsunt secundũ temporalem iurisdictionem Principibus Christianis, ut inveniuntur pagani, qui nunquam imperio Romano subditi fuerunt, terras habitantes, in quibus Christianum nunquam fuit nomen. Horũ namque domini, quamvis infideles, legitimi domini sunt, sive regali, sive politico regimine gubernantur: nec sunt propter infidelitatem à dominio suorum privati, quum dominium sit ex iure positivo, & infidelitas ex divino iure, quod non tollit ius positivum, ut superius in quæstione habitum est. Et de his nullam scio legem quoad temporalia. Contra hos nullus Rex, nullus Imperator, nec Ecclesia Romana potest movere bellum ad occupandas terras eorum, aut subijciendos illos temporaliter: quia nulla subest causa iusta belli, cum Iesus Christus Rex Regum, cui data est potestas in cœlo & in terra, miserit ad capiendam possessionem mundi, non milites armata militia, sed sanctos prædicatores, sicut oves inter lupos. Vnde nec in testamento veteri, ubi armata manu possessio erat capienda, terra infidelium*

p. 2. §. 9. & 10. Ayala de iure belli lib. 1. c. 2. n. 28. argum. Matth. 10. 23.

ad Sũ. Thom. 2. 2. q. 66. art. 8.

---

[1] 'ut inveniuntur': printer's error for 'ut si inveniuntur' (see ms. and text Caietanus). Hakluyt translates 'ut inveniuntur'.

[2] 'in quaestione': Grotius omits 'decima', referring to Thomas Aquinas, Summa, 2. 2. q. 10 (art. 2, ed., p. 37-38). It seems that this omission was never discovered by any editor or translator of Ml.

[3] 'his': Caietanus has 'istis'.

[4] 'subijciendos': printer's error for 'subjiciendos'; Caietanus has 'subiiciendum'.

Chapter IV

11

to barbarians (it is understood, of course, that quite a different question arises in the case of peoples previously subject to Christian princes, and likewise in the case of apostates), and even though the said barbarians may have refused to accept that faith, it is still not permissible to make war upon them or to deprive them of their goods merely on these grounds. It will be worth our while to quote in this connexion the exact words of Cajetan:

Some infidels (says Cajetan)[a] do not fall under the temporal jurisdiction of Christian princes either in law or in fact. Take as an example the case of pagans[1] who were never subjects of the Roman Empire, and who dwell in lands where the term 'Christian' was never heard. For surely the rulers of such persons are legitimate rulers, despite the fact that they are infidels and regardless of whether the government in question is a monarchical régime or a common-wealth; nor are they to be deprived of dominion over their own peoples on the ground of lack of faith, since dominion falls within the realm of positive law while lack of faith is a matter subject to divine law, and since the latter form of law does not abrogate the positive form, a point already established in the discussion of the [tenth] question[2]. Indeed, I do not know of any legal precept relative to such persons[3], in so far as temporal matters are concerned. No king, no emperor, not even the Church of Rome, is empowered to undertake war against them for the purpose of seizing their lands or reducing them[4] to temporal subjection. Such an attempt would be based upon no just cause of war; for the emissaries sent forth to take possession of the world, by Jesus Christ the King of Kings, unto whom power was given in heaven and on earth [Matthew, xxviii. 18], were not armed professional soldiers, but holy preachers, sheep in the midst of wolves [Matthew, x. 16; Luke, x. 3]. Thus I do not read in the Old Testament, in connection with the occasions on which it was necessary to seize possession by armed force, that war was ever declared against any nation of infidels

[100]

---

[a] ad. Sum. Thom. 2. 2. 4. (read 'q.'; see Err.) 66. art. 8: [Caietanus] on Thomas Aquinas, Summa, 2, 2, q. 66, art. 8, ed. III, p. 229-230 ('4' instead of 'q' is a printer's error, still found in the 20th and 21st century editions, although the 18th century editions had corrected it).

MARE

indictum lego bellum alicui propter hoc quod non erant fideles: sed quia nolebant dare transitum, vel quia eos offenderant, ut *Madianitæ*, vel ut recuperarent sua, divina largitate sibi concessa. Vnde GRAVISSIME PECCAREMVS, si fidem Christi Iesu per hanc viam ampliare contenderemus: nec essemus LEGITIMI DOMINI illorum: sed MAGNA LATROCINIA committeremus, & teneremur ad restitutionem, utpote INIVSTI DEBELLATORES AVT OCCVPATORES. *Mittendi essent ad hos prædicatores boni viri, qui verbo & exemplo converterent eos ad Deum: & non qui eos opprimant, spolient, scandalizent, subyciant, & duplo gehennæ filios faciant, more Pharisæorum.* Et in hanc formam audimus sæpe à Senatu in Hispania, & Theologis præcipue Dominicanis decretum fuisse, sola verbi prædicatione non bello Americanos ad fidem traducendos: libertatem etiam quæ illis eo nomine erepta esset, restitui debere, quod à Paulo tertio Pontifice, & Carolo Quinto Imperatore Hispaniarum Rege comprobatum dicitur. Omittimus jam Lusitanos in plerisque partibus religionem nihil promovere, ne operam quidem dare, cum soli lucro invigilent. Imo & illud ibi verum esse, quod de Hispanis in America Hispanus scripsit, non miracula, non signa audiri, non exempla vitæ religiosæ,

Vict. p. 1. §. 38.

---

[1] 'sed quia': Caietanus has 'sed vel quia'.
[2] 'Madianitae' (Caietanus has 'Madinitae'): for 'Midianites' see Liber iudicum, 6.
[3] Williams inserts the bracketed phrase with a reference to Matthaeus, XXIII, 15.
[4] 'Et in hanc formam ... comprobatum dicitur': addition in the top margin of the ms., with a reference (omitted in the edition) to 'Joh. Met. Praef. ad Osorium' (Johannes Metellus in his preface to Osorius, ed. fol. 15 v.); cf. the addition mentioned above, p. 10 note 1. Both additions seem to have been made when Grotius prepared the ms. for publication.

Chapter IV

on the ground that the latter did not profess the true faith. I find, instead, that the reason for such declarations of war was either[1] the unwillingness of the infidels to concede the right of passage, or the fact that they had attacked the faithful (as the Madianites[2] did, for example), or a desire on the part of the believers to recover their own property, bestowed upon them by divine bounty. Hence it follows that *we should be committing a very grave sin*, if we strove to extend by such means the realm of the faith of Jesus Christ. Moreover, this course of action would not make us *the legitimate masters* of the infidels; we should merely be committing *robbery on a large scale* and placing ourselves under an obligation to make restitution as *unjust conquerors or captors*. Men of integrity ought to be sent as preachers to these infidels, in order that unbelievers may be induced by teaching and by example to seek God; but men ought not to be sent with the purpose of oppressing, despoiling, offending and subduing them, and making them twofold more the children of hell [than the emissaries themselves][3], after the fashion of the Pharisees.

We are told, too[4], that pronouncements to precisely the same effect have frequently been issued by the Senate in Spain and by the theologians (especially the Dominicans), ruling that the American Indians should be converted to the faith not through war but solely through the preaching of the Word, and that the liberty taken from them on the pretext of conversion should be restored to them. This policy is said to have been approved by Pope Paul III and by the Emperor Charles V, King of the Spanish realms. For the rest, we shall not dwell here upon the fact that in most regions the Portuguese are in no sense advancing the cause of religion, nor even making any effort to do so, since they are intent only upon gain. Nor shall we pause to comment upon the further fact that one might truthfully apply to the Portuguese in the East Indies the observation made by a Spanish writer[a] regarding the Spaniards in America, namely: that no reports are received of miracles, portents, or examples of pious conduct,

---

[a] **Vict. p. 1. § 38.**: Victoria, De Indis, pars 1, num. 38 [= pars 2, num. 14], ed. p. 250. The quotation which follows in Grotius' text is practically literal.

LIBERVM.

religiosæ, quæ ad eandem fidem alios possent impellere, sed multa scandala, multa facinora, multas impietates. Quare cum & possessio & titulus deficiat possessionis, neque res ditionesque Indorum pro talibus haberi debeant quasi nullius ante fuissent, neq; cum illorum essent, alijs recte acquiri potuerint, sequitur Indorum populos, de quibus nos loquimur, Lusitanorum proprios non esse, sed liberos, & sui juris: de quo ipsi doctores Hispani non dubitant.[1]

Vict. in fine par. 2.1. relect. de Indis.

Caput V.

Mare ad Indos aut ius eo navigandi non esse proprium Lusitanorum titulo occupationis.

SI ergo in populos terrasque & ditiones Lusitani jus nullum quæsiverunt, videamus an mare & navigationem, aut mercaturam sui juris facere potuerint. De mari autem prima sit cōsideratio, quod cum passim in iure aut nullius, aut cōmune, aut publicū Iurisgentiū[2] dicatur, hæ voces quid significēt ita cōmodissime explicabitur, si Poëtas ab Hesiodo omnes, & Philosophos, & Iurisconsultos veteres imitati in tempora distinguamus, ea, quæ tempore forte haud longo, certa tamen ratione

---

[1] 'dubitant': after this word the ms. originally read 'cum de Americanis disputant' but these words were crossed out, probably when the ms. was prepared for publication; cf. van Ittersum, Preparing Mare liberum, p. 260 and p. 279 n. 83. The insertion (in the ms.) of the word 'ipsi' before 'doctores Hispani' might date from the same time.

[2] 'Iurisgentium': cf. Straumann, Is modern liberty ancient?, p. 68-69. I do not agree with his hypothesis (in n. 57) that 'in the manuscript the words *iuris gentium* look as if they originally read *iure gentium*, according to the law of nations, and were changed only later to the genitive'; this is not the case. But I agree with Straumann when he interprets 'iuris gentium' as 'a right of nations', comparing it with 'iuris mei'; cf. Grotius' *Defensio*, p. 348, quoted by Straumann, p. 68 n. 55. The Dutch translation of 1614 has: 'den volckeren publijk [toe te comen]'. This interpretation is confirmed by the passage below p. 18: 'Alia … sunt publica, hoc est populi propria'; cf. Feenstra (1996/2005), p. 183 n. 16 and p. 186. It should be noted that the manuscript and the editions of 1609, 1618 and 1633 have 'Iurisgentium' as one word; this seems to have been changed only from the 1667 edition onwards. For the terminology cf. D. 41, 3, 45 (Papinian), cited p. 39 note d.

such as might impel others to embrace the same faith, whereas, on the contrary, there are numerous reports of inducements to sin, criminal acts, and impiety.

Therefore, since the Portuguese lack both possession and title to possession, since the property and sovereign powers of the East Indians ought not to be regarded as things that had no owner prior to the advent of the Portuguese, and since that property and those powers - belonging as they did to the peoples of the Indies - could not rightly be acquired by other persons, it follows that the said peoples are not Portuguese chattels, but free men possessed of full social and civil rights [*sui iuris*]. On this point there is no doubt[1] among the Spanish Doctores themselves[a].

Chapter V

That the sea leading to the Indians or the right of navigation thereon does not belong exclusively to the Portuguese by title of possession.

Granting, then, that the Portuguese have not acquired any right over the East Indian peoples, lands or jurisdictions, let us ascertain whether or not the former have been able to bring the sea and matters of navigation, or the conduct of trade, under their own authority.

We shall consider first the question of the sea. As the sea is commonly described in [Roman] law as *res nullius*, as common property, or as public property according to the law of nations[2], the significance of these different terms will most fitly be explained if, in imitation of the method employed by all the poets since the days of Hesiod as well as by the philosophers and the old [Roman] jurists, we draw a chronological distinction between things which are perhaps not differentiated from one another by any considerable interval of time, but which do indeed

[100']

---

[a] **Vict. in fine par. 2. 1. relect. de Indis:**
Victoria at the end of pars 2 of the first relectio de Indis [i.e. De Indis, pars 1, num. 40 [= pars 2, num. 16], ed. p. 255].

ne & sui natura discreta sunt. Neque nobis vitio verti debet si in juris à natura procedentis explicatione auctoritate & verbis eorum utimur quos constat naturali judicio plurimum valuisse. Sciendum est igitur in primordijs vitæ humanæ aliud quam nunc est dominium, aliud communionem fuisse. Nam dominium nunc propri id significat, quod scilicet ita est alicujus ut alterius non sit eodem modo. Commune autem dicimus, cujus proprietas inter plures consortio quodam aut consensu collata est exclusis alijs. Linguarum paupertas coëgit voces easdem in re non eadem usurpare. Et sic ista nostri moris nomina ad jus illud pristinum similitudine quadam & imagine referuntur. Commune igitur tunc non aliud fuit quam quod simpliciter proprio opponitur: Dominium autem facultas non injusta utendi re communi, quem usum Scholasticis visum est facti non juris vocare, quia qui nunc in jure usus vocatur, proprium est quiddā, aut ut illorum more loquar, privative ad alios dicitur. Iure primo Gentium, quod & Naturale interdum dicitur, & quod Poëtæ alibi ætate aurea, alibi Saturni aut Iustitiæ regno depingunt, nihil proprium fuit: quod Cicero dixit: *Sunt autem privata nulla natura.* Et Horatius:

Vide Glos. & Castr. in l. ex hoc iure & c. jus nat. dist. I.

Vide Vasq. controv. usu frequ. c. I. num. 10. c. exijt qui seminat de Verb. sig. in 6. clem. exivide paradiso de verb. sign.

Nam

Chapter V

differ in certain underlying principles and by their very nature. Moreover[1], we ought not to be censured if, in our explanation of the law derived from nature, we avail ourselves of the authority and express statements of persons generally regarded as pre-eminent in natural powers of judgement.

Accordingly, it must be understood that, during the earliest epoch of man's history, ownership [*dominium*] and common property [*communio*] were concepts whose significance differed from that now ascribed to them[a]. For in the present age, the term 'ownership' connotes something peculiarly one's own[2], that is to say, something belonging to a given party in such a way that it cannot similarly belong to any other party; whereas the expression 'common property' is applied to something whose property has been assigned to several parties, in partnership (so to speak) or in mutual concord, to the exclusion of other parties. Owing to the poverty of human speech, however, it has become necessary to employ identical terms for concepts which are not identical. Consequently, because of a certain degree of similitude and by analogy, the above-mentioned expressions descriptive of our modern customs are applied to that other law, which existed in early times. Thus with reference to that early age, the term 'common' is nothing more nor less than the simple antonym of 'private' [*proprium*]; and the word 'ownership' denotes the power to make use rightfully of common property[b]. This [kind of] use the Scholastics choose to describe as a concept of fact but not of law[c]. For the right now connoted in law by the term 'use' [*usus*] is a certain propriety, or, in other words (if I may borrow from the phraseology of the Scholastics), 'use' carries with it a privative force with respect to all extraneous parties.

Under the primary law of nations, to which from time to time we also give the name of 'natural law', and which the poets represent in some passages as prevailing in the Golden Age while in other passages they assign it to the reign of Saturn or of Justice, there was no private property. In fact, we find this statement in the works of Cicero[3]: 'There is, however, no such thing as private property in the natural order'. Horace[4], too, wrote as follows:

---

[a] Vide Glos. et Castr. in l. ex hoc iure et c. ius nat. dist. 1: See the Gloss [of Accursius, verbis 'Dominia distincta'] and [Paulus] Castrensis in Dig. vet. on D. 1, 1, 5 (ed. I, fol. 5 ff.; cf. below, p. 53 note h) and [the text of] Decretum Grat. Dist. 1 [c. 7]. For details see Feenstra (1996/2005), p. 183 n. 18.

[b] Vide Vasq. controv. usu frequ. c. 1. num. 10.: Vasquius, Controv. II, p. 13-15; cf. Feenstra (1996/2005), p. 184 n. 19.

[c] c. exiit qui seminat de Verb. sig. in 6. clem. exivide [read: exivi de] paradiso de verb. sign.: Sextus 5, 12, 3; Clem. 5, 11, 1; cf. Feenstra (1996/2005), p. 184 n. 20.

LIBERVM. 15

Nam PROPRIÆ *telluris* HERVM NA-
TVRA *nec illum,*
Nec me nec quenquam statuit.

Neque enim potuit natura dominos distinguere. Hoc igitur significatu res omnes eo tempore communes fuisse dicimus, idem innuentes quod Poëtæ cum primos homines in medium quæsivisse, & Iustitiam casto federe res medias tenuisse dicunt: quod ut clarius explicent, negant eo tempore campos limite partitos, aut commercia fuisse ulla.

Avienus in Arat.

promiscua rura per agros
Præstiterant cunctis COMMVNIA *cuncta* VIDERI.

Recte additum est *videri* propter translationem ut diximus vocabuli. Communio autem ista ad usum referebatur:

Seneca Octavia.

pervium cunctis iter,
COMMVNIS VSVS *omnium rerum fuit.*

Cujus ratione dominium quoddam erat, sed universale, & indefinitum: Deus enim res omnes non huic aut illi dederat, sed humano generi, atque eo modo plures in solidum ciusdem rei domini esse non prohibebantur: quod si hodierna significatione sumamus dominium, contra omnem est rationem. Hoc
enim

Chapter V

15

> Nor he, nor I, nor any man, is made
> By Nature private owner of the soil.

For in the eyes of nature no distinctions of owners were discernible. In this sense, then, we say that all things were common property in those distant days, meaning just what the poets do when they declare that the men of earliest times made acquisitions on behalf of the community, and that the communal character of goods was maintained by justice in accordance with a sacred pact. In order to clarify this point, they explain that fields were not divided by boundary lines in that age, and that there were no commercial transactions.

[101]

> The mingled farms throughout the countryside
> Showed that all things *seemed common* to all men[a].

The word 'seemed' was properly included in these lines, in recognition of the changed meaning of the term 'common', to which we alluded above. This concept of common ownership had reference, of course, to the use of the things involved.

> ... To all the way was open;
> The *use* of all things was a *common* right[b].

Thus a certain form of ownership did exist, but it was ownership in a universal and indefinite sense. For God had given all things, not to this or that individual, but to the human race; and there was nothing to prevent a number of persons from being joint owners, in this fashion, of one and the same thing. But such a concept would be completely irrational if we were giving to the term 'ownership' its modern significance, involving

---

[a] **Avienus in Arat.:** Avienus on Aratus, Phaenomena [302 f.].
[b] **Seneca Octavia:** Seneca, Octavia [402 f.].

16 MARE.

enim proprietatem includit, quæ tunc erat penes neminem.

Aptissime autem illud dictum est:

Avienus.

> omnia rerum
> *Vsurpantis erant.*

Ad eam vero, quæ nunc est, dominiorum distinctionem non impetu quodam, sed paulatim ventum videtur, initium ejus monstrante Natura. Cum enim res sint nonnullæ, quarum usus in abusu consistit, aut quia conversæ in substantiam utentis nullū postea usum admittunt, aut quia utendo fiunt ad usum deteriores, in rebus prioris generis, ut cibo & potu, proprietas statim quædam ab usu nō sejuncta emicuit. Hoc enim est proprium esse, ita esse cujusquam ut & alterius esse non possit quod deinde ad res posterioris generis, vestes puta, & res mobiles alias aut se moventes ratione quadam productum est. Quod cum esset, ne res quidem immobiles omnes, agri puta, indivisi manere potuerunt: quanquam enim horum usus non simpliciter in abusu consistat, eorum tamen usus abusus cujusdam causa comparatus est, ut arva & arbusta cibi causa, pascua etiam vestium: omnium autem usibus promiscue sufficere non possunt. Repertæ proprietati lex posita est, quæ naturam imitaretur. Sicut enim initio per applicationem corporalem usus ille habebatur

ff. de usuf. ear. ver. quæ usu consf. Extrav. de verb. sign. ad conditorem & quia quorundā Thom. 2.2.78.

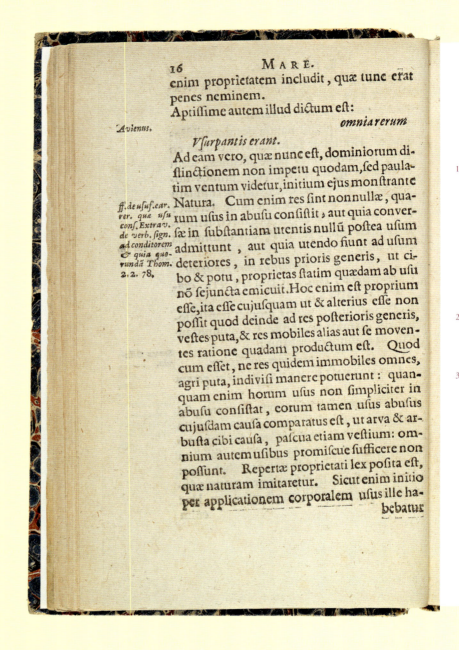

---

[1] 'dominiorum distinctionem': allusion to D. 1, 1, 5, cf. above, p. 14 note 5, cf. Feenstra (1996/2005), p. 184-185.

[2] 'possit quod': printer's error for 'possit: quod'; corrected in later editions (since 1633). Cf. Feenstra (1996/2005), p. 185 n. 26.

[3] 'indivisi': it would seem more correct to read 'indivisae' but the ms. also has 'indivisi'. Hamaker has corrected it tacitly into 'indivisae', just as later editions (since 1633).

Cf. Feenstra (1996/2005), p.185 n. 27.

Chapter V

16

propriety, an attribute which did not reside in any person during that epoch. In fact, it has been most aptly observed that,

> ... All things belonged to him
> Who put them to his use. . . .[a]

It is evident, however, that the present-day concept of distinction of ownerships[1] was the result, not of any sudden transition, but of a gradual process whose initial steps were taken under the guidance of nature herself. For there are some things which are consumed by use[b], either in the sense that they are converted into the very substance of the user and therefore admit of no further use, or else in the sense that they are rendered less fit for additional service by the fact that they have once been made to serve. Accordingly, it very soon became apparent, in regard to articles of the first class (for example, food and drink), that a certain form of private ownership was inseparable from use. For the essential characteristic of private property is the fact that it belongs to a given individual in such a way as to be incapable of belonging to somebody else as well. This basic concept[2] was later extended by a logical process to include articles of the second class, such as clothing and various other things capable of being moved or of moving themselves. Because of these developments, it was not even possible for all immovable things (fields, for instance) to remain unapportioned[3], since the use of such things, while it does not consist directly in their consumption, is nevertheless acquired [in some cases] with purposes of consumption (as it is when arable lands and orchards are used with a view to obtaining food, or pastures for [animals intended to provide] clothing), and since there are not enough immovable goods to suffice for indiscriminate use by all persons.

The recognition of the existence of private property led to the establishment of a law on the matter, and this law was patterned after nature's plan. For just as it was through a physical act of attachment that originally was acquired that kind of use,

[101′]

---

[a] **Avienus:** Avienus [ibid. 301 f.].
[b] **ff. de usuf. ear. rer. quae usu cons. Extrav. de verb. sign. ad conditorem et quia quorundam Thom. 2. 2. 78 [ms.: 78, 1]:** D. 7, 5; Extravag. Ioan. XXII, 14, 3 and 5; Thomas Aquinas, Summa, III, p. 257-259 at p. 258. Cf. Feenstra (1996/2005), p. 185 n. 25.

LIBERVM.   17

bebatur, unde proprietatem primum ortam diximus, ita simili applicatione res proprias cuiusque fieri placuit. Hæc est quæ dicitur occupatio, voce accommodatissima ad eas res quæ ante in medio positæ fuerant: quo Seneca Tragicus alludit.

IN MEDIO *est scelus* POSITVM OCCVPANTI. *Sen. Thyeste.*

[1] Et Philosophus: *Equestria* OMNIVM *Equitum Romanorū sunt: in illis tamen locus meus sit* PROPRIVS *quē* OCCVPAVI. Hinc Quintilianus dicit, quod omnibus nascitur industriæ esse præmium, & Tullius, factas esse veteri occupatione res eorum qui quondam in vacua venerant. Occupatio autem hæc in his rebus quæ possessioni renituntur, ut sunt feræ bestiæ, perpetua esse debet, in alijs sufficit, corpore cœptam possessionem animo retineri. Occupatio in mobilibus est apprehensio, in immobilibus instructio aut limitatio: unde Hermogenianus cum dominia distincta di- [2] cit, adddit, agris terminos positos, ædificia collocata. Hic rerum status à Poëtis indicatur. *Sen. Ben. lib. 7. c. 12. Decl. 13. De off. 1. L. ex hoc iure ff. de Iust. & iure.*

Tum laqueis captare feras, & fallere visco Inventum: *Virg. 1. Georg.*
Tum primum subiere domos.
COMMVNEMQVE PRIVS, *ceu lumina solis & auræ* *Ovid. in Metam.*

B   Caussus

---

[1] 'Et philosophus ... *occupavi*' and the reference to Seneca, De beneficiis, VII, 12, are additions in the top margin of the ms., probably dating from the preparation of the ms. for publication; cf. van Ittersum, The wise man, at note 45, and id., Dating the manuscript, p. 138.

[2] 'adddit': printing error for 'addit'.

Chapter V

which (as we have observed) was the very source of private property, so it was agreed that through similar acts of attachment the goods should be acquired in private property by each individual. This is the process known as 'occupation' [*occupatio*], a particularly appropriate term in connexion with those goods which were formerly at the disposal of the community. Seneca[a] has in mind that very process, when he says, in one of his tragedies:

> *A common opportunity* for crime
> Awaits the one who first shall *grasp* the chance [*occupanti*].

Again[1], speaking as a philosopher, he[b] makes this statement: 'The equestrian rows of seats belong to *all* the Roman knights; yet the place that I have *occupied* in those rows becomes my *own*'. Similarly, Quintilian[c] notes that certain things created for all, become the reward of the industrious. Cicero[d], too, declares that some goods are acquired, in consequence of long occupancy, as the property of those who came upon them before they had been taken into anyone's possession. This occupancy, [or tenure,] must be continuous, however, in the case of things that resist possession, such as wild beasts. In other cases, the only requisite is that the status of possession initiated by a physical act shall be continued mentally. With respect to movables, moreover, occupancy implies physical seizure [*apprehensio*]; with respect to immovables, it implies some activity involving construction or the definition of boundaries. It is for this reason that Hermogenianus[e], [in listing certain effects of the law of nations,] mentions immediately after 'determination of property rights', these two items: 'establishment of boundaries for lands' and 'erection of buildings'. The same stage in the development of private property is described by the poets. [Virgil[f] wrote:]

> 'Twas then men learned to capture beasts with snares,
> To practise trickery with birdlime, too.

[In the works of Ovid[g], we find the following passages:]

> Then first were *houses* sought by humankind.
> . . . .
> Surveyors marked with careful, long-drawn lines,
> *The bound'ries* for the soil which *hitherto*
> Had been a *common* good like sun and air.

---

[a] **Sen. Thyeste.:** Seneca, Thyestes [203-204].
[b] **Sen. Ben. lib. 7. c. 12.:** Seneca, De beneficiis, VII, 12.
[c] **Decl. 13.:** [Quintilianus,] Declamationes, XIII [8].
[d] **De off. 1.:** [Tullius = Cicero,] De officiis [I, 7, 21].
[e] **L. ex hoc iure ff. de Iust. et iure.:** D. 1, 1, 5.
[f] **Virg. 1. Georg.:** Vergilius, Georgica, I [139-140].
[g] **Ovid. in Metam.:** Ovidius, Metamorphoses, I [121, 135 f.]. [The last line of the Latin text is printed on p. 18].

MARE

Cautus humũ longo signavit LIMITE *messor.*
Celebratur post hæc, ut Hermogenianus indicat, commercium, cujus gratia

Ovid.   *Fluctibus ignotis insultavere carinæ.*

Eodem autem tempore & respublicæ institui cœperunt : Atque ita earum quæ à prima communione divulsa erant duo facta sunt genera. Alia enim sunt publica, hoc est populi propria (quæ est gemina istius vocis significatio) alia mere privata, hoc est singulorum. Occupatio autem publica eodem modo fit, quo privata. Seneca: *Fines Atheniensium, aut Campanorum vocamus, quos deinde inter se vicini privata terminatione distinguũt.* Gens enim unaquæque

De benef. 7. 4.

Seneca Octav.   PARTITA FINES *regna constituit, novas*

Extruxit VRBES.

Offic. 1.   Hoc modo dicit Cicero agrum Arpinatem Arpinatum dici, Tusculanum Tusculanorum: *similisque est*, inquit, *privatarum possessionum descriptio, ex quo quia suum cuiusque sit, eorum quæ natura fuerant* COMMVNIA, *quod cuique obtigit, id quisque teneat.* Contra autem Thucydides eam terram quæ in divisione populo nulli obvenit, ἀόριςον, hoc est indefinitam, & limitibus nullis circumscriptam vocat. Ex his quæ hactenus dicta sunt duo intelligi possunt. Prius est, eas res quæ quam

Lib. 1.

Vide Duar. in tit. de rerum div. & qual.

1, 2

3

4

---

[1] 'ceperunt': in the ms. follows 'de quarum origine alibi dictum est' with a marginal reference 'In c. 2'. For obvious reasons this was crossed out when the ms. was prepared for publication. The reference is to chapter 2 of Djp, where indeed a passage on this subject occurs on fol. 10 v (see Williams, p. 19-20). Hamaker should have inserted the reference in his edition (p. 217).

[2] 'earum': read 'eorum', see ms.

[3] 'gemina': printer's error for 'genuina', see Err.

[4] 'Seneca: *Fines ... distinguunt*' and the reference to De beneficiis VII, 4, are additions in the top margin of the ms., probably dating from the preparation of the ms. for publication; cf. van Ittersum, The wise man, at note 176, and id., Dating the manuscript, p. 138.

Chapter V

18

At a subsequent stage in the evolution of property, as Hermogenianus indicates [in the above-mentioned list], commerce began to be widely practised; and for the sake of commerce, so Ovid[a] tells us,

> The keels of ships leapt over unknown waves.

During the same period, moreover, the establishment of states was first undertaken[1].

Accordingly, we find that those things[2] which were wrested from the original domain of common ownership have been divided into two categories. For some are now public property, or in other words, they are owned by the people, which is the true[3] meaning of the expression 'public property'; and others are strictly private property, that is to say, they belong to individuals.

[102]

Nevertheless, public occupation is achieved by the same method as private occupation. Seneca[4, b] makes this observation: 'We designate as "territory of the Athenians", or "territory of the Campanians", lands which the inhabitants in their turn divide among themselves by fixing private boundaries'. For every individual nation

> Established kingdoms *marked with bound'ry lines*
> And *built* new cities. . . .[c]

In like manner, Cicero[d] notes that the territory of Arpinum is said to belong to the people of Arpinum, and that of Tusculum to the Tusculans. To this he adds the following comment: '. . . and the apportionment of private property is similar. Accordingly, since each individual's part of those things which nature gave as *common property* becomes his own, let each person retain possession of that which has fallen to his lot'. On the other hand, lands that did not fall into the possession of any nation in the process of apportionment, are called by Thucydides[e] ἀόριστον, that is to say, 'undefined' regions, marked by no fixed limits.

From the foregoing discussion, two inferences may be drawn. The first runs[f] as follows: those things which

---

[a] **Ovid.**: Ovidius [Metamorphoses, I, 134]. Cf. Williams, p. 230 n. 1.
[b] **De benef. 7. 4.**: [Seneca,] De beneficiis, VII, 4.
[c] **Seneca Octav.**: Seneca, Octavia [420 f.].
[d] **Offic. 1**: [Cicero, De officiis [I, 7, 21].
[e] **Lib. 1**: [Thucydides,] I [139].
[f] **Vide Duar. in tit. [ff] de rerum div. et qual.**: Duarenus on D. 1, 8, ed. p. 15. 'ff' is an addition above the line in the ms.; was the omission in the ed. a printer's error, an error by the copyist or might there be another explanation? Strictly speaking the addition is not necessary: cf. p. 40 note b, where, in a similar reference, 'ff' does not figure. See Introduction, note 112.

LIBERVM

occupari non possunt, aut occupatæ nunquam sunt, nullius proprias esse posse: quia omnis proprietas ab occupatione coeperit. Alterum vero, eas res omnes, quæ ita à natura comparatæ sunt, ut aliquo utente nihilominus alijs quibusvis ad usum promiscue sufficiant, eius hodieque conditionis esse, & perpetuo esse debere cujus fuerant cùm primum a natura proditę sunt. Hoc Cicero voluit: *Ac latissime quidem patens hominibus inter ipsos omnibus inter omnes societas hæc est, in qua omnium rerum, quas ad communem usum natura genuit, est servanda communitas.* Sunt autem omnes res hujus generis, in quibus sine detrimento alterius alteri commodari potest. Hinc illud esse dicit Cicero: *Non prohibere aqua profluente.* Nam aqua profluens qua talis, non qua flumen est, inter communia omnium à Iurisconsultis refertur: & à Poëta:

Quid prohibetis AQVAS? VSVS COMMVNIS *aquarum est.*

Nec Solem PROPRIVM NATVRA *nec* AËRA *fecit,*

Nec tenues VNDAS. *in* PVBLICA *munera veni.*

Dicit hæc non esse natura propria, sicut Vlpianus natura omnibus patere, tùm quia primum à natura prodita sunt, & in nullius adhuc dominium pervenerunt (ut loquitur

B 2 Nera-

offic. 1.

Ovid. lib. 6. Metam.

L. venditor ff. com. præd.

Chapter V

are incapable of being occupied, or which never have been occupied, cannot be the private property of any owner, since all property has its origin as such in occupation. The second inference may be stated thus: all those things which have been so constituted by nature that, even when used by a specific individual, they nevertheless suffice for general use by other persons without discrimination, retain to-day and should retain for all time that status which characterized them when first they sprang from nature. Cicero[a] upheld this principle, when he wrote: 'Herein, to be sure, lies the most comprehensive of the bonds uniting men to men and all to all; and in observance thereof, our common participation in all things produced by nature for mankind's common use should be maintained'.

Now, the category thus defined includes everything capable of serving the convenience of a given person without detriment to the interests of any other person; and this concept (according to Cicero[1]) is the source of the maxim, 'Deny to no one the water that flows by'. For running water, considered as such and not as a stream, is classed by the [Roman] jurists among the things that are common to all. Ovid[b] adopts the same classification in the following lines:

> Why would you withhold *water* from my lips?
> *The use* of water is a *common* right.
> Nor sun nor air nor water's gentle *flow*
> Are *private* things by *natural* design.
> The gifts I seek are *public* property.

Thus Ovid contends that the goods above mentioned are not private possessions according to nature's plan; just as Ulpian[c] declares that by the said plan they are free to all. For, in the first place, they proceeded originally from nature and have not yet been placed under the ownership of anyone (as

[102′]

---

[a] **Offic. 1.:** [Cicero,] De officiis, I [XVI, 51].
[b] **Ovid. lib. 6. Metam.:** Ovidius, Metamorphoses, VI [349 ff.].
[c] **L. venditor. ff. com. praed.:** D. 8, 4, 13.

20 MARE

L. quod in littore. ff. de acq. rer. dom.
loco citato.
Vide Comi. comm. civ. lib. 3. c. 2. Donell. lib. 4. c. 2.
L. ult. de usucap.

Neratius) tum quia ut Cicero dicit, à natura ad usum communem genita videntur. Publica autem vocat tralatitia significatione, non quæ ad populum aliquem, sed quæ ad societatem humanam pertinent, quæ publica Iurisgentium in Legibus vocantur: hoc est communia omnium, propria nullius. Hujus generis est Aër, duplici ratione, tum quia occupari non potest, tum quia usum promiscuum hominibus debet. Et eisdem de causis commune est omnium Maris Elementum, infinitum scilicet ita, ut possideri non queat, & omnium usibus accommodatum: sive navigationem respicimus, sive etiam piscaturam.

L. Arist. de rer. div.

Cujus autem juris est mare, ejusdem sunt si qua mare alijs usibus eripiendo sua fecit, ut arenæ maris, quarum pars terris continua littus dicitur. Recte igitur Cicero: *quid tam* COMMVNE *quam* MARE *fluctuantibus,* LITTVS *eiectis?* Etiam Virgilius auram, undam, littus cunctis patere dicit. Hæc igitur sunt illa quæ Romani vocant communia omnium jure naturali, aut quod idem esse diximus, publica jurisgentium, sicut & usum eorum modo communem, modo publicum vocant. Quanquam vero etiam ea nullius esse, quod ad proprietatem attinet, recte dicantur, multum tamen differunt ab his quæ nullius sunt, & communi usui attributa non sunt,[1]

loco citato. Iust. de rer. div. §. & quidem naturali, & §. littorum. ff. de rer. div. l. 1. & L. 2. & L. Aristo. eod. tit. L. quod in Littore. L. quavis. de acq. rer. dom. L. si quis me, de Iniur. L. littora. Ne quid in loco pub. cum. L. seq.

---

[1] [Cicero, Pro Sexto Roscio Amerino, XXVI, 72].

[a] **L. quod in littore ff. de acq. rer. dom.:** D. 41, 1, 14.

[b] **loco citato:** [Cicero,] as cited [De officiis, I, XVI, 51].

[c] **Vide Comi. [printer's error for 'Conn.'] comm. civ. lib. 3. c. 2. Donell. lib. 4. c. 2:** See Connanus, Commentaria iuris civilis, ed. fol. 152v-158r; Donellus, Commentaria de iure civili, ed. I, p. 230-233 at p. 232. It should be noted that the printer's error 'Comi.' was not corrected in any of the 17th century editions and even led Magoffin to suppose that Philippe de Comines was meant (an interpretation taken over by Wright and some later translations!). However, the 1712, 1720, 1735 and 1773 editions had already corrected the error.

[d] **L. ult. de usucap.:** D. 41, 3, 45 (this text was the last of the title 41, 3 in a number of

Chapter V

Neratius[a] points out); and in the second place, it is evident (as Cicero[b] observes) that nature produced them for our common use[c]. Ovid, however, using a transferred meaning, calls public not those things which pertain to a particular nation, but those which pertain to the whole society of mankind, which by the [Roman] laws are called 'public by the law of nations'[d]: that is common to all, proper to none. Air falls into this class for two reasons: first, because it is not possible for air to be made subject to occupation; secondly, because all men have a common right to the use of air. For the same reasons, the sea is an element common to all, since it is so vast that no one could possibly take possession of it, and since it is fitted for use by all, with reference to purposes of navigation and to purposes of fishing, as well. Furthermore, the right that exists in regard to the sea exists likewise in regard to anything that the latter has diverted from other uses and made its own[e], such as the sands of the sea, of which the portion merging into the land is called the shore. Therefore, Cicero[1] is justified in asking, 'What is so *common* . . . as is the sea to those who are tossed by the waves, or the *shore* to castaways?' Similarly, Virgil[f] asserts that the air, the water, and the shore are freely accessible to everyone.

These, then, are the things described by the Romans[g] as common to all by natural law, or as public according to the law of nations, which (according to the foregoing discussion) is another way of expressing the same concept. In like manner, the Romans sometimes describe the use of such things as common, while at other times they refer to it as public.

Nevertheless, even though the said things are correctly called *no man's* in so far as private ownership is concerned, they are very different from those which are no man's and are not assigned for common use:

---

old editions; Grotius (or his source) must have used one of these. Cf. below, p. 25 note a, where the reference is corrected in the ms.

[e] **L. Arist. de rer. div.**: D. 1, 8, 10.

[f] **loco citato**: [Virgilius] as cited [above]. The ms. has 'loco s[upra] citato.' The reference should be linked to 'Virgilius' and not to 'Cicero', as almost all editions (since 1633) and translations do. An exception is the German translation (Boschan, p. 44 n. 18), where the reference is linked to 'Virgilius'

and interpreted as indicating the quotation in chapter 1 (see above p. 3 note b). This could indeed explain why the ms. had '*supra citato*'; the source of the quotation from Cicero (cf. note 1), for that matter, does not occur anywhere else in Ml.

[g] **Inst. de rer. div. §. et quidem naturali, et §. littorum. ff. de rer. div. l. 1 et L. 2 et L. Aristo. eod. tit. L. quod in Littore L. quamvis. de acq. rer. dom. L. si quis me** [read: l. iniuriarum § si quis me]**, de Iniur.**

L. Littora. Ne quid in loco pub. cum L. seq.: Inst. 2, 1, 1 and Inst. 2, 1, 5, D. 1, 8, 1 and D. 1, 8, 2 and D. 1, 8, 10, D. 41, 1, 14, D. 41, 1, 50, D. 47, 10, 13, 7 [cf. below, p. 25], D. 43, 8, 3 with D. 43, 8, 4.

LIBERVM. 21

ut feræ, pisces, aves: nam ista si quis occupet, in jus proprium transire possunt, illa vero totius humanitatis consensu proprietati in perpetuũ excepta sunt propter usum, qui cum sit omnium, nõ magis omnibus ab uno eripi potest, quam à te mihi quod meum est. Hoc est quod Cicero dicit inter prima esse Iustitiæ *off. 1.* munera, rebus communibus pro communibus uti. Scholastici dicerent esse communia alia affirmative, alia privative. Distinctio hæc non modo Iurisprudentibus usitata est, sed vulgi etiam confessionem exprimit: unde apud Athenæum convivator mare commune esse dicit, at pisces capientium fieri. Et in Plautina Rudente servato dicenti, *Mare quidem commune certo est omnibus*, assentit piscator, addenti autem *In mari inventum est, commune est*, recte occurrit:

*Meum quod rete atque hami nacti sunt,
meum potiſsimum est.*

Mare igitur proprium omnino alicujus fieri non potest, quia natura commune hoc esse non permittit, sed jubet; imo ne littus quidem: nisi quod hæc addenda est interpretatio, *Vide Don. E.* ut si quid earum rerum per naturam occupa- *4. c. 2.* ri possit, id eatenus occupatis fiat, quatenus ea occupatione usus ille promiscuus non læditur. Quod merito receptum est: nam cum ita se habet, cessat utraque exceptio per quam

B 3   QVE-

e.g. wild beasts, fish, and birds. Items belonging to the latter class can be made subject to private ownership, provided that someone does take possession of them; whereas items falling within the former class have been rendered forever exempt from such ownership by the unanimous agreement of mankind, in view of the fact that the right to use them, pertaining as it does to all men, can no more be taken from humanity as a whole by one individual than my property can be taken from me by you. Among the prime functions of justice Cicero[a] lists this very task of leading men to make use of common possessions for common interests. The Scholastics would say that the one class is common in a positive sense, and the other, in a privative sense. This distinction is not only familiar to the jurists, but also representative of the popular belief.

Thus Athenaeus[1] depicts the master of the feast as maintaining that the sea is common property, whereas fish become the property of the persons who catch them. And again, in Plautus' play entitled *The Rope*[2], the fisherman assents when the young slave[3] says,

> The sea's most certainly common to all;

but when the slave adds,

> 'Tis common property, found in the sea,

the fisherman justly objects,

> Whatever is caught by my net and hook
> Is mine in the truest sense. . . .

It is, then, quite impossible for the sea to be made the private property[b] of any individual; for nature does not merely permit, but rather commands, that the sea shall be held in common. Furthermore, not even the shore can become private property.

These statements should be qualified, however, by the addition of an interpretative comment, to the following effect: if any part of the things in question is susceptible of occupancy in accordance with nature's plan, that part may become the property of the person occupying it, in so far as is possible without impeding its common use. This principle is rightly accepted. For, under such circumstances, there is no longer any occasion to apply either of the two restrictive norms above-mentioned,

---

[a] **off. 1.:** [Cicero,] De officiis I [VII, 20].
[b] **Vide Don. L. 4. c. 2.:** See Donellus, Commentaria de iure civili, I, p. 230-233, at p. 232.

MARE.

eveniſſe diximus, ne omnia in jus proprium transcriberentur. Quoniam igitur inædificatio species est occupationis, in littore licet ædificare, si id fieri potest sine cæterorum incommodo, ut Pomponius loquitur: quod ex Scævola explicabimus, niſi usus publicus, hoc est communis impediretur. Et qui ædificaverit, soli dominus fiet: quia id solum nec ullius proprium, nec ad usum communem necessarium fuit. est igitur occupantis: sed non diutius quam durat occupatio, quia reluctari mare possessioni videtur; exemplo feræ, quæ si in naturalem se libertatem receperit, non ultra captoris est, ita & littus postliminio mari cedit. Quicquid autem privatum fieri occupando, idem & publicum, hoc est populi proprium poſſe ostendimus. Sic littus Imperii Romani finibus inclusum, Populi Romani eſſe Celsus existimat: quod si ita est, minime mirandũ est, eundẽ Populũ subditis suis occupandi littoris modũ per Principẽ aut Prętorẽ potuisse cõcedere. Cęterũ & hęc occupatio nõ minus quã privata ita restringenda est, ne ulterius porrigatur, quã ut salvus sit usus Iurisgẽtium. Nemo igitur potest à Populo Romano ad littus maris accedere prohiberi, & retia siccare, & alia facere, quæ semel omnes homines in perpetuum sibi licere voluerunt. Maris autem natura hoc differt à littore, quod mare

Inst. de rer. div. §. litt. l. viparum. §. 1. ff. de rer. div. l. fluminum. ff. de damno inf. L. quamvis de acq. rer. dom. L. in littore. Ne quid in loco pub. L. Aristo. de rerum div. L. quod in littore. de acq. rer. dom.

d. L. littora ne quid in loco publ. Donell. lib. 4. c. 2. & c. 9. l. L. quamvis de acq. rer. dom. L. 2. in princ. & §. merito. & §. Si quis à Principe. Ne quid in loco pub. L. Nemo igitur. ff. de rer. divis. Vide. d. L. littora. ff. Ne quid in loco publ.

niſi

Chapter V

which prohibit the transfer of certain things to the realm of private rights. Consequently, since the erection of buildings upon a given site constitutes a form of occupation, it will be permissible to erect buildings upon the shore[a] subject to the condition (expressly laid down by Pomponius[b]) that one must be able to do so without inconveniencing other persons. Following Scaevola[c], we shall interpret this condition as meaning that the public use (that is to say, the common use) of the shore may not be impeded. Moreover, the person who constructs the building will become the owner of the site, since the latter was not previously the private property of any individual, nor was it needed for the common use. Accordingly, it belongs to the person who occupies it, but only for the duration of such occupation[d]. For the sea would seem to resist possession, after the fashion of a wild beast which is no longer the property of its captor once it has regained its natural liberty. In precisely this fashion, the shore returns to the sea, under the principle of postliminium.

We have also shown that anything capable of becoming private property through the process of occupation, is likewise capable of becoming public property, or in other words, property of the people.

Thus Celsus held that the shore included within the limits of the Roman Empire belonged to the Roman People[e]; and if this contention was correct, it was not at all strange that the said People, acting through its prince or praetor, was able to allow its subjects a certain form of occupation in regard to the shore[f]. This kind of occupation, however, no less than the private form, should be subject to the restriction that it must not extend to a point where it will infringe upon the uses for which the law of nations provides. Accordingly, no one could be prevented by the Roman People from approaching the shore of the sea[g], spreading his nets there to dry, and performing other acts which – as mankind had willed once and for all – were to be forever permissible to all men[h].

The sea, on the other hand, differs by nature from the shore, in that the former

---

[a] Inst. de rer. div. §. litt. l. riparum. §. 1 ff. de rer. div. l. fluminum. ff. de damno inf.: Inst. 2, 1, 5, D. 1, 8, 5, 1, D. 39, 2, 24 [pr.].
[b] L. quamvis de acq. rer. dom.: D. 41, 1, 50.
[c] L. in littore. Ne quid in loco pub.: D. 43, 8, 4.
[d] L. Aristo. de rerum div. L. quod in littore. de acq. rer. dom.: D. 1, 8, 10, D. 41, 1, 14.
[e] d. L. littora ne quid in loco publ. Donell. lib. 4. c. 2. et c. 9.: D. 43, 8, 3 (already cited), Donellus, Commentaria de iure civili, I p. 230-233 and 246-247.
[f] d. L. quamvis de acq. rer. dom. L. 2. in princ. et §. merito. et §. Si quis a Principe. Ne quid in loco pub.: D. 41, 1, 50 (already cited), D. 43, 8, 2 pr., D. 43, 8, 2, 10, D. 43, 8, 2, 16.
[g] L. Nemo igitur. ff. de rer. divis.: D. 1, 8, 4.
[h] Vide d. L. Littora. ff. Ne quid in loco publ.: See D. 43, 8, 3 (already cited).

nisi exigua sui parte nec inædificari facile, nec includi potest: & ut posset, hoc ipsum tamen vix contingeret, sine usus promiscui impedimento. Si quid tamen exiguum ita occupari potest, id occupanti conceditur. Hyperbole est igitur

 Contracta pisces æquora sentiunt   Horat.
 Iactis in altum molibus.

Nam Celsus jactas in mare pilas ejus esse dicit qui jecerit. Sed id non concedendum si deterior maris usus eo modo futurus sit. Et Ulpianus eum qui molem in mare jacit, ita tuendū dicit si nemo damnū sentiat. Nam si cui hæc res nocitura sit, Interdictum utique, Ne quid in loco publico fiat competiturum. Vt & Labeo, si quid tale in mare struatur, Interdictum vult competere, Ne quid in Mari, quo portus, statio, iterve navigiis deterius sit, fiat. Quæ autem navigationis eadem piscatus habenda est ratio, ut communis maneat omnibus. Neque tamen peccabit si quis in maris diverticulo piscandi locum sibi palis circumsepiat, atque ita privatum faciat: sicut Lucullus exciso apud Neapolim monte ad villam suam maria admisit. Et hujus generis, puto fuisse piscinas maritimas quarum Varro & Columellam eminerunt. Nec Martialis alio spectavit, cum de Formiano Apollinaris loquitur.

margin notes: d.L. littora. L. 2. ne quid in loco publ. §. Advers. L. 1. §. si in mare. ff. de fluminibus. Plin. lib. 10. c. 54.

B 4   Si

Chapter V

(save for a very small portion thereof) cannot easily be built upon nor enclosed; and furthermore, even if this were not the case, the sea could hardly be so employed without hindrance to its common use. Nevertheless, if some tiny part of it does prove susceptible of such occupation, that part is conceded to the occupant. Thus Horace[a] was exaggerating when he wrote:

> The fishes note the sea's diminished breadth
> When piers are laid that jut into the deep.

Certainly Celsus[b] maintains that piles driven into the sea are the property of him who placed them there, although the same authority adds that no such concession should be made if the structure in question is an impediment to the subsequent use of the sea. Ulpian[c] likewise declares that this protection must be extended to the rights of the person who has constructed a foundation in the sea provided that no damage to anyone else results therefrom, whereas the interdict prohibiting the erection of a building in any public place will undoubtedly be applicable if the structure is likely to conflict with the interests of another person. Similarly, Labeo holds that if any structure of this kind is erected in the sea[d], recourse may properly be had to the interdict forbidding the construction therein of 'anything whereby a harbour, a roadstead, or the course of navigation might be rendered less satisfactory'.

The principle applicable in regard to navigation – namely, that the activity in question shall remain open to all – should also be applied in connexion with fishing. No transgression will have been committed, however, if someone fences in a fishing-pool for himself in some small portion of the sea, surrounding it with stakes and thus turning the spot into private property, just as Lucullus brought the sea to his own villa by cutting through a mountain near Naples[e]. I suppose, indeed, that the marine fish-ponds mentioned by Varro[1] and by Columella[2] were of this nature.

---

[a] Horat.: [Horatius, Odae, III, 1, 33 f.].
[b] d. L. littora: D. 43, 8, 3 (already cited).
[c] L. 2. ne quid in loco publ. § Advers.: D. 43, 8, 2, 8.
[d] L. 1. §. si in mare. [read: mari.] ff. de fluminibus.: D. 43, 12, 1, 17.
[e] Plin. lib. 10. c. 54.: Plinius, Naturalis historia, X, 54 [X, 80, 170].

24 MARE

Lib. 10. Epigr. 30.

Si quando NEREVS sentit Aeoli regnum.
Ridet procellas tuta de SVO mensa.

De Nabut. c. 3.

Et Ambrosius: *Inducis mare intra prædia tua ne desint belluæ.* Hinc apparere potest quæ mens Pauli fuerit, cum dicit, si maris proprium jus ad aliquem pertineat, Vti possidetis interdictum ei competere. Esse quidem hoc Interdictum ad privatas causas comparatum, non autem ad publicas, (in quibus etiam ea comprehenduntur quæ jure gentium communi facere possumus) sed hic jam agi de jure fruendo quod ex causa privata contingat, non publica, sive communi. Nam teste Marciano, quicquid occupatum est & occupari potuit, id jam non est jurisgentium, sicut est mare. Exempli causa, si quis Lucullum aut Apollinarem in privato suo, quatenus diverticulum maris incluserant, piscari prohibuisset, dandum illis interdictum Paulus putavit, non solum injuriarum actionem, ob causam scilicet privatæ possessionis. Imo in diverticulo maris, sicut in diverticulo fluminis, si locum talem occuparim, ibique piscatus sim, maxime si animum privatim possidendi plurium annorum continuatione testatus fuerim, alterum eodem jure uti prohibebo: ut ex Marciano colligimus, non aliter quam in lacu qui mei dominii est. Quod verum quamdiu durat

L. sane si maris. ff. de iniuriis.

L. nemo igitur. ff. de rer. div.

L. si quisquā. de diverf. & temp. præscr.

[1]

[2, 3]

---

[1] 'Nam teste Marciano ... sicut est mare' and the reference (note d): addition in the bottom margin of the ms. (fol. 103 v).

[2] 'ut ex Marciano colligimus': reference to D. 44, 3, 7 (note e), not to D. 1, 8, 4 (note d), which is an addition in the bottom margin of the ms. (see above, note 1).

[3] 'non aliter quam in lacu qui mei dominii est': addition in the top margin of the ms. (fol. 104 r), which adds a reference to 'l. Iniuriarum § ult. ff. de Iniuriis' (D. 47, 10, 13, 7). This text is cited twice below, p. 25 in notes b and c, but in another context.

Chapter V

24

Martial[a] too, in his description of Apollinaris' villa at Formiae, referred to the same device as follows:

> Whene'er the deep doth feel the Wind God's sway,
> Apollinaris' table mocks the storm,
> Securely stocked with produce of its own.

Yet again, we find this comment in the works of Ambrose[b]: 'You bring the very sea into your estates, so that there may be no lack of fish'.

The foregoing remarks will serve to clarify the meaning of Paulus in the passage where he says[c] that if a given individual possesses a private right to any part of the sea, he will be entitled to use the interdict for the possession of land (*Uti possidetis*) [in the event that he is hindered from exercising the said right]. Paulus adds that this device was of course intended for use in private suits, and not in those of a public nature (among which are included the suits that may be brought in accordance with the common law of nations); but he holds that the case which he describes would relate to the enjoyment of a right based on a private – rather than on a public, or common – title. For[1] (as the testimony of Marcianus[d] indicates) whatever has been subjected to occupancy and was properly susceptible of such subjection, no longer comes under the law of nations as the sea does. For example, if any person had prevented Lucullus or Apollinaris from fishing in one of the private preserves that they had constructed by enclosing a small portion of the sea, then, in the opinion of Paulus, the owner of the preserve would have been entitled to avail himself of the interdict [*Uti possidetis*] and not merely to bring an action for damages, that is to say [he is entitled to the interdict] on grounds of private possession. Indeed, even in the case of a small inlet of the sea, just as in the case of a river-fork[e], if I have taken over the locality as an occupant, if I have fished there, and above all if by pursuing this course over a period of many years I have formally proclaimed my intention of establishing private possession of the inlet, then I may prohibit other persons from enjoying the same rights (a conclusion drawn from the statement of Marcianus[2]), precisely as[3] I might do so with respect to a lake forming part of my own domain. This rule holds good for the duration

[104]

---

[a] **Lib. 10. Epigr. 30.**: [Martialis,] Epigrammata X, 30 [19-20].
[b] **De Nabuts.** (read 'Nabuthe'.) **c. 3**: [Ambrosius,] De Nabuthe, III [12].
[c] **L. sane si maris. ff. de iniuriis.**: D. 47, 10, 14.
[d] **L. nemo igitur. ff. de rer. div.**: D, 1, 8, 4.
[e] **L. si quisquam, de divers. et temp. praescr.**: D. 44, 3, 7.

LIBERVM.

rat occupatio, quemadmodum in littore *L. præscriptio.* antea diximus. Extra diverticulum idem non *ff.de usucap.* erit, ne scilicet communis usus impediatur. Ante ædes igitur meas aut prætorium ut pi- *L. iniuria-* scari aliquem prohibeant usurpatum quidem *rum. §. ultim.* est, sed nullo jure, adeo quidem ut Vlpianus *d. L. iniuria-* comtemta ea usurpatione si quis prohibeatur *rum §. si quis* injuriarum dicat agi posse. Hoc Imperator *Novell. 56.* Leo (cujus Legibus non utimur) contra juris rationem mutavit, Voluitque προϑύρα, hoc est vestibula maritima eorum esse propria, qui oram habitarent, ibique eos jus piscandi habere: quod tamen ita procedere vo- *Novella Leo* luit, ut septis quibusdā remoratorijs quas ἐπο- *102. 103. 104.* χάς Greci vocāt, locus ille occuparetur: existi- *Vide Cuiac.* mans nimirum non fore ut quis exiguam *14. obs. 1.* mari portionem alteri invideret qui ipse toto mari ad piscandum admitteretur. Certe ut quis magnam maris partem, etiamsi possit, publicis utilitatibus eripiat, non tolerandæ est improbitatis: in quam merito Vir Sanctus in- *Ambr. Lib. 5.* vehitur. SPATIA MARIS *sibi vindicant* *Hex. c. 10.* IVRE MANCIPII, *pisciumque iura sicut vernaculorum conditione sibi servitij subiecta commemorant. Iste inquit,* SINVS *maris meus est: ille alterius. Dividunt elementa sibi potentes.* Est igitur Mare in numero earum *Donnell. li.* rerum quæ in commercio non sunt, hoc est, *4. c. 6.* quæ proprij juris fieri non possunt. Unde se-

B 5 quuntur

Chapter V

of my occupation, even as we have already shown that it does in regard to the shore[a].

If the region involved exceeds the limits proper to a small inlet, the said rule will not be applicable, for it might interfere with the common use of that region[b]. Thus it has been assumed that I may prohibit[1] fishing by any other person in front of my dwelling or country-seat, but the assumption lacks any legal basis. In fact, it is so gravely lacking in this respect that Ulpian[c], in rejecting it, declares that anyone who is made the object of such a prohibition may bring an action for damages. The Emperor Leo[d] (whose laws we do not observe) changed this ruling, in defiance of the underlying legal principles, and maintained that πρόθυρα, or coastal waters 'opening out upon' the sea, were the private property of the persons dwelling along the shore, to whom he also assigned the fishing rights attached to such waters. He laid down one condition, however, for the applicability of his own ruling, namely, that the site in question should be brought under occupation by means of certain structures which would block it off and which the Greeks called ἐποχαί [checks, i.e. breakwaters][e]. Leo doubtless assumed that no person would begrudge another a tiny portion of the sea[2] as long as he himself had access to [practically] all of its waters for fishing. Certainly it would be intolerably wicked for any individual to cut off a large part of the sea from public use, even if he were able to do so. Such wickedness is deservedly assailed by the Holy Man[f], in the following terms: 'They claim *whole tracts of the sea* for themselves *by right of formal acquisition*; and they remind us that rights over fishing, in precisely the same fashion as those over homeborn slaves, are subject to their will under conditions of servitude. "This *curve of the sea*", says one, "is mine; that curve belongs to someone else". The mighty divide the very elements among themselves'.

In short, the sea is included among those things which are not articles of commerce[g], that is to say, the things that cannot become part of anyone's private domain. Hence it follows[3],

---

[a] **L. praescriptio. ff. de usucap.**: D. 41, 3, 45 (the ms. corrects 'l. ult.' into 'l. praescriptio', cf. above p. 20 note d).

[b] **L. iniuriarum. §. ultim. ff. de iniuriis.**: D. 47, 10, 13, 7.

[c] **d. L. iniuriarum §. si quis me.**: D. 47, 10, 13, 7, already cited (see note b, where the § is called 'ultima').

[d] **Novell. 56.**: [Imperator Leo], Nov. Leonis [Const.] 56. This allegation was omitted in all editions from 1633 onwards; the edition 1618 corrupted it into 'Novell. 59'.

[e] **Novella Leo 102. 103. 104. Vide Cuiac. 14. obs. 1.**: Nov. Leonis [Const.] 102, 103, 104; Cuiacius, Observationes, 14 [1], ed. col. 325-327. Grotius should have added in the first place a reference to Leo's Nov. [Const.] 57, where the ἐποχαί (checks, i.e. breakwaters) are mentioned, see Williams. Such a reference occurs in the text of Cuiacius.

[f] **Ambr. Lib. 5. Hex. c. 10.**: Ambrosius, Hexaemeron, V, 10 [27]. Cf. also below, p. 61 note d.

[g] **Donnell. lib. 4. c. 6.**: Donellus, Commentaria de iure civili, ed. I, p. 241-242, at p. 241.

quitur si proprie loquamur, nullam Maris partem in territorio populi alicujus posse censeri. Quod ipsum Placentinus sensisse videtur, cū dixit, Mare ita esse commune, ut in nullius dominio sit nisi solius Dei : & Ioannes Faber, cū mare cesserit relictum in suo jure, & esse primęvo, quo omnia erāt communia. Alioquin nihil differrent quę sunt omniumcommunia ab his quę publica proprie dicuntur, ut mare à flumine. Flumen populus occupare potuit, ut inclusum finibus suis, mare non potuit. Territoria autē sunt ex occupationibus populorū, ut privata dominia ex occupationibus singulorū. Vidit hoc Celsus, qui clare satis distinguit inter littora, quę Populus Romanus occupare potuit, ita tamē ut usui communi nō noceretur, & mare quodpristinā naturā retinuit. Nec ulla lex diversum indicat. Quę vero leges à cōtrarię sententię auctoribus citantur, aut de insulis loquuntur, quas clarū est occupari potuisse, aut de portu qui non communis est, sed proprie publicus. Qui vero dicunt mare aliquod esse Imperij Romani, dictū suum ita interpretantur, ut dicant jus illud in mare ultra protectionem & jurisdictionem non procedere: quod illi jus à proprietate distinguūt: nec forte satis animadvertunt idipsum quod Populus Romanus classes praesidio navigantium disponere potuit, & deprehensos in mari piratas

Marginalia:
Ioh. Faber ad d. §. Litt orū. inst. de rerum divis. adde DD. ad l. actionis. ff. ad l. Rhodiam.

L. littora. Ne quid in loco pub.

Vide L. insule. ff. de iudicijs. Vide L. Cæsar ff. de public. Gloss. in L. quædam. de rerum divis. & in d. L. littora. & in §. 1. Inst. de rer. divis. Bal. in d. l. quædam.

---

[1] 'si proprie': the ms. changes this into 'si recte et proprie' (addition as in note 3 above, p. 25; also mentioned by Van Ittersum).

[2] 'Quod ipsum Placentinus … communia': this passage is an addition in the ms., probably made when he started to use Rodericus Zuarius, Consilium I de usu maris (see below, p. 27 note a, and p. 36 note c). The mention of Placentinus and Johannes Faber (see note a) was probably copied from Zuarius, Cons. I, num. 9 (ed. p. 856), who renders Faber's opinion in practically the same words as Grotius (Faber, in his turn, probably took the reference to Placentinus from the commentaries of Jacques de Révigny and Pierre de Belleperche who agreed with Placentinus' opinion); cf. also Introduction note 166.

[3] 'cesserit': printer's error for 'asserit', see Err. Hakluyt translates 'cesserit' ('when the sea shall depart').

Chapter V

to speak strictly[1], that no part of the sea may be regarded as pertaining to the domain of any given nation. Placentinus[2] would seem to have been aware of this fact when he said that the sea was common to all in such a degree that no being save God alone could possess ownership over it. Apparently, too, Johannes Faber[a] was sensible of the same fact when he asserted[3] that the sea had been left in its own right, and in that primeval state in which all things had been held in common.

If this were not the case, there would be no difference between things common to all, such as the sea, and things designated as public in the strict sense of the term, such as rivers. It was possible for a particular nation to take possession of a river, as of something enclosed within its own boundaries, but it was not possible to take possession of the sea in the same way. The dominion of a nation over its territories, however, must be the result of occupation by that nation, just as private ownership results from occupation by individuals. This truth was perceived by Celsus[b], who drew a very clear distinction between the shores of the sea, which the Roman nation was empowered to occupy (though only subject to the condition that the common use of the shores should not be impeded by that act), and the sea itself, which retained its pristine nature unimpaired. Nor is there any law that points to a contrary doctrine. The laws cited by writers who have held a contrary view, relate in point of fact either to islands[c], which are clearly susceptible of occupation, or to harbours[d], which (properly speaking) are not common, but public. Furthermore, those authorities[e] who maintained that some sea belonged to the Roman Empire, interpreted their own statement in such a way as to restrict that Roman right over the sea to functions of protection and jurisdiction, distinguishing that right from ownership. Perhaps, too, the said authorities paid insufficient heed to the fact that it was

[104']

---

[a] **Ioh. Faber ad d. §. Littorum. inst. de rerum divis. adde DD. ad l. ἀξιαροῖς ff. ad. l. Rhodiam.**: Johannes Faber on Inst. 2, 1, 5 (cited above), ed. fol. 29 v. Add the Doctores on D. 14, 2, 9.
[b] **L. littora. quid in loco pub.**: D. 43, 8, 3.
[c] **Vide L. insulae. ff. de iudiciis.**: D. 5, 1, 9.
[d] **Vide L. Caesar ff. de public.**: D. 39, 4, 15.
[e] **Gloss. in L. quaedam. de rerum divis. et in d. L. littora. et in §. 1. Inst. de rer. divis. Bal. in d. l. quaedam.**: Glosses [of Accursius] on D. 1, 8, 2 [verbo 'Litora'], and on D. 43, 8, 3 (already cited) [verbo 'Arbitror'] and on Inst. 2, 1, 1 [verbis 'et per hoc']. Baldus on D. 1, 8, 2 (already cited), ed. fol. 46 v. In the ms. the reference to Baldus is not at the end, but just after 'Gl. in l. quaedam ff. de rer. divis.': 'et ibi Bal.' Grotius probably did not consult an edition of the commentary of Baldus nor even an edition of the Corpus iuris with the Accursian Gloss (in some editions of the Corpus iuris the text of Baldus is added to the gloss 'Litora' on D. 1, 8, 2), but copied the reference from Zuarius, Consilium I (cf. above note 2), num. 9, ed. p. 855.

LIBERVM. 27

gatas punire, non ex proprio, sed ex communi jure accidisse, quod & aliæ liberę gentes in mari habent. Illud interim fatemur, potuisse inter gentes aliquas convenire, ut capti in maris hac vel illa parte, hujus aut illius reipublicæ judicium subirent, atque ita ad commoditatem distinguendæ jurisdictionis in mari fines describi, quod ipsos quidem eam sibi legem ferentes obligat, ut alios populos non item: neque locum alicujus proprium facit, sed in personas contrahentium jus constituit. Quæ distinctio ut naturali rationi consentanea est, ita Vlpiani responso quodam comprobatur, qui rogatus an duorum prædiorum maritimorum dominus, alteri eorum quod venderet servitutem potuisset imponere, ne inde in certo maris loco piscari liceret, respondet rem quidem ipsam, mare scilicet, servitute nulla affici potuisse, quia per naturam hoc omnibus pateret, sed cum bona fides contractus legem venditionis servari exposceret, personas possidentium & in jus eorum succedentium per istam legem obligari. Verum est loqui Iurisconsultum de prædijs privatis, & lege privata, sed in territorio & lege populorum eadem hic est ratio, quia populi respectu totius generis humani privatorum locum obtinent. Similiter reditus qui in piscationes maritimas constituti.

Bal. in c. in princ. in 2. col. Quib-mod. feud. amitt. adde L. unic. C. de class. lib. 11. & Ang. in l. sane. ff. de injur.

L. Venditor fundi. Com. præd. adde L. caveri. eod. tit.

c. quæ sunt Regalia in Feudis.

Chapter V

not in virtue of a private right, but through a common maritime right possessed by other free nations also, that the Roman People were authorized to distribute fleets for the protection of sailors, and to punish pirates captured at sea.

On the other hand, we admit that it was possible for agreements to be drawn up between specific nations, stipulating that persons captured upon the sea in this or that particular region should be subject to judgement by this or that particular state; and we furthermore admit that, in this sense, boundaries upon the seas were indeed defined, for convenience in distinguishing the different areas of jurisdiction[a]. Such an arrangement is binding, to be sure, upon the parties who have imposed a legal agreement of this kind upon themselves; but[1] it is not binding in like manner upon other peoples, nor does it convert an area thus delimited into the private property of any possessor, for it merely establishes rights between the contracting parties.

This distinction, which is in conformity with natural reason, derives further confirmation from a reply made on a certain occasion by Ulpian[b], when the jurist was asked whether the owner of two maritime estates had possessed the power to impose upon one of them, which he was selling, a servitude involving a prohibition against fishing from that estate in a certain part of the sea. Ulpian answered that the actual object concerned – namely, the sea – could not be subjected to a servitude, since it was by nature open to all; but he added that the factor of good faith implicit in the contract, demanded the observance of a condition attaching to the sale, so that the parties actually in possession and those succeeding to the right of possession were personally bound by the said condition. It is true that Ulpian was referring to private estates and to private law; but the same principle is equally applicable to the present discussion concerning the territories and laws of nations, since nations in their relation to the whole of mankind occupy the position of private individuals.

Similarly[c], the revenues which are levied on maritime fisheries

---

[a] Bal. in c. [ms.: c. 1.] in princ. in 2. col. Quib. mod. feud. amitt. adde L. unic. C. de class. lib. 11 et Ang. in l. sane ff. de iniur.: Baldus in Feud., LF I, 16 [,1], 2nd col., ed. fol. 15[v]; add C. 11, 13 (12), 1, and Angelus de Ubaldis on D. 47, 10, 14, ed. fol. 152v-153v. Grotius probably did not consult editions of the commentaries by Baldus and Angelus, but copied the references from Rodericus Zuarius, Consilium I de usu maris (see below, p. 36 note c), who gives them in num. 1 and 3 (ed. p. 851 and 852), the first with the specification '2. colum.'.

[b] L. Venditor fundi. Com. praed. adde L. caveri. eod. tit.: D. 8, 4, 13; add D. 8, 4, 3.

[c] c. quae sunt [read 'sint' as the ms. has] Regalia in Feudis.: LF II, 56.

stituti Regalium numero censentur¹, non rem, hoc est mare, aut piscationem, sed personas obligant. Quare subditi, in quos legem ferendi potestas Reipublicæ aut Principi ex consensu competit, ad onera ista compelli forte poterunt: sed exteris jus piscandi ubique immune esse debet, ne servitus imponatur mari quod servire non potest. Non enim maris eadem quæ fluminis ratio est: quod cum sit publicum, id est populi, jus etiam in eo piscandi a populo aut Principe concedi aut locari potest, ita ut ei qui conduxit etiam interdictum Veteres dederint, de loco publico fruendo, addita conditione, si is cui locandi jus fuerit, fruendum alicui locaverit: quæ conditio in mari evenire non potest. Cæterum qui ipsam piscationem numerant inter Regalia, ne quidē illū locum quem interpretabantur satis inspexerunt. quod Iserniam & Alvarotum non latuit. Demonstratum est nec populo nec privato cuipiam jus aliquod proprium in ipsum mare (nam diverticulum excepimus) competere posse, cum occupationem nec natura, nec usus publici ratio permittat. Hujus autem rei causa instituta fuerat hæc disputatio, ut appareret Lusitanos mare quo ad Indos navigatur sui juris non fecisse. Nam utraque ratio quæ proprietatem impedit, in hac causa est quam in cæteris omnibus

c. quæ sint Regalia. in Feudis.

Vide Balbum de præscr. 4. parte 5. part. princ. qu. 6. n. 4.

d. l. iuriarum §. si quis me. vers. conductori ff. de iniur. ff. de loco publ. fruendo.

Ad d. locum. Quæ sint Regalia.

---

[1] 'Alvarotum': from the ed. 1618 onwards all editions have the printer's error 'Alvotum' (cf. Bensly, p. 116) which has been the source of a false identification by Magoffin and his followers, see Introduction, section 10.

and are regarded as belonging to the *regalia*[a], do not bind the object of the levies (namely, the sea or the particular fishery in question) but the persons concerned. Accordingly, subjects, over whom the state or prince exercises a legislative power by consent can perhaps be compelled to these burdens, but, in so far as foreigners are concerned, fishing rights should everywhere be exempt from any charges, lest a servitude be imposed upon the sea, which cannot properly be subjected to any servitude. For, in the case of the sea, the basic principle involved is not the same as it would be in the case of a river[b], since the latter has a public character (that is to say, it is the property of the nation), so that even the right to fish therein may be conceded or leased by the nation or by the prince. In fact, the *veteres*[c] [the Roman jurists from the second and first century BC.] interpreted this right in such a way as to grant the lessee recourse to an interdict regarding the use of a public place (*de loco publico fruendo*), subject to the following condition: 'provided that the privilege of using that place, shall have been leased to the party in question by one who has the right of leasing it'[d]. This condition could not be met in cases involving the sea. For the rest, those persons who include fishing itself among the perquisites of the Crown have paid insufficient attention to the very passage which they themselves cite, an error that has not escaped the notice of [Andreas of] Isernia and Alvarotus[1,e].

We have shown it to be impossible that any right of property over the sea itself (for we made an exception in regard to small forks of the sea), should pertain to any nation or private individual, since occupation of the sea is impermissible both in the natural order and for reasons of public utility. This disputation was undertaken for the purpose of making it clear that the Portuguese have not established a right of property over that part of the sea which one traverses in sailing to the East Indies. For both of the factors impeding property are infinitely more cogent in this particular case than in any of the others mentioned. What constitutes merely a difficulty in those other cases is

---

[a] c. quae sint Regalia. in Feudis.: LF II, 56.
[b] **Vide Balbum de praescr. 4. parte 5. part. princ. qu. 6 n. 4.**: See Balbus, De praescr., ed. p. 470.
[c] d. l. iuriarum [read 'iniuriarum' as the ms. has] §. si quis me. vers. conductori ff. de iniur.: D. 47, 10, 13, 7 (already cited), in the phrase 'conductori autem veteres interdictum dederunt [etc.]'.
[d] ff. de loco publ. fruendo.: D. 43, 9 [,1].
[e] **Ad d. locum. Quae sint Regalia.**: [Andreas de Isernia and Iacobus Alvarotus] on the passage already cited, LF II, 56. Grotius probably did not consult these two authors; he might have taken over these references from Rodericus Zuarius, Consilium I de usu maris (see below, p. 36 note c), who gives them in num. 11 (ed. p. 857). The text of Andreas de Isernia, Super feudis, can be found in ed. fol. 115 v, at no. 5, on the words Redditus piscatorum; the text of Alvarotus, Super feudis, in ed. fol. 134r-135r, on 135 r, at nos. [6 and] 7.

nibus infinito efficacior. Quod in alijs difficile videtur, in hac omnino fieri non potest: quod in alijs iniquum judicamus, in hac summe barbarum est, atque inhumanum. Non de mari interiore hic agimus, quod terris undique infusum alicubi etiam fluminis latitudinem non excedit, de quo tamen satis constat locutos Romanos juris consultos, cum nobiles illas adversus privatam avaritiam sententias ediderunt[1]: de Oceano quæritur, quem immensum, infinitum, rerum parentem, cœlo conterminum antiquitas vocat: cujus perpetuo humore non fontes tantum & flumina & maria, sed nubes, sed ipsa quodammodo sidera pasci veteres crediderunt: qui denique per reciprocas æstuum vices terram hanc humani generis sedem ambiens, neque teneri, neque includi potest, & possidet verius quam possidetur. In hoc autem Oceano non de sinu aut freto, nec de omni quidem eo quod è littore conspici potest controversia est. Vindicant sibi Lusitani quicquid duos Orbes interjacet, tantis spatijs discretos, ut plurimis sæculis famam sui non potuerint transmittere. Quod si Castellanorum, qui in eadem sunt causa, portio accedat, parvo minus omnis Oceanus duobus populis mancipatus est, alijs tot gentibus ad Septentrionum redactis angustias: multumque

---

[1] 'nobiles … sententias': the ms. adds in the margin 'supra allegatas'.

Chapter V

in the present instance an absolute impossibility; and what we condemned as an injustice in a different connexion is in this instance utterly barbarous and even inhuman.

We are not treating here of an inner sea which washes against the land on all sides and is in some places no wider than a mere river; but it is quite certain that the Roman jurists were referring to just such a concept in the above-mentioned celebrated opinions[1] opposing private avarice. The subject of our discussion is the Ocean, which was described in olden times as immense, infinite, the father of created things, and bounded only by the heavens; the Ocean, whose never-failing waters fed not only upon the springs and rivers and seas, according to the ancient belief, but upon the clouds, also, and in a certain measure upon the stars themselves; in fine, that Ocean which encompasses the terrestrial home of mankind with the ebb and flow of its tides, and which cannot be held nor enclosed, being itself the possessor rather than the possessed.

In this Ocean the question at issue is not limited to some bay or strait, nor even to the entire expanse of its waters visible from the shore. On the contrary, the Portuguese claim for themselves the whole tract lying between two parts of the world which are separated by spaces so vast that in the course of many centuries those two regions were not able to make themselves known to each other. Indeed, if the share of the Spaniards (who join in the same claim) is added to the share demanded by the Portuguese, very nearly the entire Ocean will have been delivered into the hands of two peoples, while all the remaining nations will find themselves restricted to the narrow waters of the north. Thus nature will have been sorely deceived;

que deceptâ est Natura, quæ cum Elementum illud omnibus circumfudit, omnibus etiam suffecturū credidit. In tanto mari si quis usu promiscuo solum sibi imperiū & ditionē exciperet, tamen immodicę dominationis affectator haberetur: si quis piscatu arceret alios, insanę cupiditatis notam nō effugeret. At qui etiam navigatū impedit, quo nihil ipsi perit, de eo quid statuemus? Si quis ab igni qui totus suus est, ignem capere, lumen suo de lumine, alterū prohiberet, legē hunc humanę societatis reū peragerē: quia vis ea est istius naturæ.

Ennius. *Vt nihilominus ipsi luceat, cum illi accenderit.*
Cic. de off. 1. Quid ni enim quādo sine detrimento suo potest, alteri cōmunicet, in ijs quæ sunt accipiēti utilia, dāti nō molesta? Hęcsūt quę Philosophi
Sen. lib. 3. c. 28. nō alienis tantū, sed & ingratis præstari volūt. Quæ vero in rebus privatis invidia est, eadē in re communi nō potest nō esse immanitas. Improbissimū enim hoc est, quod naturæ instituto, consensu gentiū, meū non minus quā tuū est, id te ita intercipere, ut ne usum quidē mihi concedas, quo concesso nihilō minus id tuū sit, quā antea fuit. Tū vero etiā qui alienis in-cūbant, aut communia intercipiūt, certa quadam possessione se tuētur. Quia enim prima, ut diximus, occupatio res proprias fecit, iccirco imaginem quandam dominii pręsert quamvis injusta detentio. At Lusitani num sicuti terras

solemus,

[1]

[2]

---

[1] 'Haec sunt quae Philosophi ... volunt' and the reference to Seneca, De beneficiis, III, 28, are additions in the top margin of the ms., probably dating from the preparation of the ms. for publication; cf. van Ittersum, Dating the manuscript, p. 138, who does not mention this passage specifically.

[2] 'incumbant': printer's error for 'incubant', see ms. (edd. 1633 ff. have the wrong emendation 'incumbunt').

Chapter V

for when she encompassed all peoples with this watery element, she believed that it would likewise suffice for all. If anyone in so great a sea should cut off from the common domain, and reserve to himself, nothing more than sovereignty and dominion, he would nevertheless be regarded as a seeker after immoderate power; if he should forbid others to fish therein, he would not escape the stigma of monstrous cupidity; but what shall we say of one who obstructs even navigation upon those waters, despite the fact that he himself would suffer no loss in consequence of such navigation?

If the sole owner of a fire forbade another to take fire therefrom, or to take light from his light, I should prosecute him to the bitter end as a criminal under the law of human society. For the force of this nature [just mentioned] is such [that]:

His own light shines no less when he hath lit
Another's lamp therefrom. . . .[a]

Why, then, since it is possible to do so without injury to oneself, should one not bestow upon another a share in those things which will be useful to the recipient and whose bestowal will not harm the giver[b]? It is to goods of this kind[1] that the philosophers[c] refer, when they maintain that certain benefits should be accorded not merely to foreigners but even to ingrates.

Furthermore, that attitude which comes under the head of jealousy when it relates to private possessions, must be characterized as savagery when common property is involved. For it is the height of wickedness that a thing which is no less mine than yours by natural dispensation and by the common consent of nations, should be appropriated by you in such exclusive fashion that you deny me even its use, although that concession would render the property appropriated in nowise less your own than it was, previously.

Then, too, it should be noted that even those persons who fasten upon[2] the possessions of others, or take for themselves exclusively property that is common to all, defend themselves on the ground that a certain form of possession has been established by them. For the institution of private property arose from original occupation, as we have already indicated; and consequently, detention of a given thing, even though it be unjust detention, produces in a sense a semblance of ownership.

But have the Portuguese people

---

[a] **Ennius.**: Ennius [in Cicero, De officiis, I [16, 52]].
[b] **Cic. de off. 1.**: Cicero, De officiis, I [16, 52].
[c] **Sen. lib. 3. c. 28.**: Seneca, [De beneficiis] III, 28.

LIBERVM. 31

solemus, sic mare illud impositis praesidijs ita undique cinxerunt, ut in ipsorum manu esset quos vellent excludere? An vero tantum hoc abest, ut ipsi etiam, cum adversus alios populos mundum dividunt, non ullis limitibus aut natura, aut manu positis, sed imaginaria quadam linea se tueantur? quod si recipitur & dimensio talis ad possidendum valet, jamdudu nobis Geometrae terras, Astronomi etiam, coelum eriperent. Vbi hic igitur est ista, sine qua nulla dominia coeperunt, corporis ad corpus adjunctio? Nimirum apparet in nulla re verius dici posse, quod Doctores nostri prodiderunt, Mare cum sit incomprehensibile, non minus quam aër, nullius populi bonis potuisse applicari. Si vero ante alios navigasse, & viam quodammodo aperuisse, hoc vocant occupare, quid esse potest magis ridiculum? Nam cum nulla pars sit maris, in quam non aliquis primus ingressus sit, sequetur omnem navigatione ab aliquo esse occupatā. Ita undique excludimur. Quin & illi qui Terrarum Orbem circumvecti sunt, totum sibi Oceanū acquisivisse dicēdi erūt. Sed nemo nescit navē per mare transeuntē non plus juris quā vestigii relinquere. Verū etiam quod sibi sumunt neminem ante ipsos cum Oceanum navigasse, id minime verum est. Magna enim pars ejus de quo agitur maris ambitu,

Iohann. Faber ad §. litt- torum.

Mauritanię,

---

[1] 'alios populos'; the ms. has put this instead of 'Castellanos' (crossed out). This correction is no doubt connected with the crossing out mentioned in note 2.

[2] 'tueantur?': the ms. has, in the bottom margin of fol. 106 r, an addition which has been crossed out: 'ita Castellanos triginta et sex gradibus, quos appellant, ab Hesperidum insulis distans linea ortivis locis prohibet: Angli intra Solstitii aestivi circulum quondam inclusi'. The crossing out might date from preparing the manuscript for publication.

[3] 'Doctores nostri': the ms. has put these words instead of 'Johannes Faber et alii' (cf. above p. 26 note 2 and note a). This correction may have resulted from the reference mentioned below, p. 35 note 1.

[4] 'verum est': the ms. has, in the bottom margin of fol. 106 v, an addition which has been crossed out: 'atque adeo ut plerisque aliis ita et hac ratione multo est speciosior Castellanorum causa, qui Americam petiverunt, quantum sciri potest nunquam antea tentato itinere. Unde et in ipso Pontificis Diplomate diserte exprimitur de *mari nunquam navigato* et *insulis incognitis*: additque [instead of 'unde colligit', crossed out] Pontifex nemini se ius quaesitum auferre, quod hic dici non potest' (in the margin, to be linked with 'Pontificis diplomate'): 'Dato 4 Non. Maii 1493'. See for this removed passage van Ittersum,

Chapter V

encompassed that expanse of ocean with fortifications erected on all sides, as we are wont to do when tracts of land are seized, in such fashion that they have acquired the power to exclude whomsoever they will? Or is this so far from being the case that the Portuguese, in apportioning the world to the disadvantage of other peoples[1], have failed even to defend their claim by marking out boundaries (whether natural or artificial), relying instead upon an imaginary line[2]? If this claim is to be recognized, and if such a method of measurement suffices to constitute valid possession, the geometers must have taken the earth from us long since, just as the astronomers must also have taken the heavens. Where, then, in the present case, do we encounter that factor of corporeal attachment without which ownership has never been established? Surely it must be obvious that no conceivable case could better illustrate the truth of the doctrine propounded by our Doctores[3,a], namely: that the sea, since it is as incapable of being seized as the air, cannot have been attached to the possessions of any particular nation.

If, on the other hand, the Portuguese describe as 'occupation' the acts of navigating at an earlier date than other peoples and of more or less opening the way, what contention could be more absurd? For there is no part of the sea upon which someone has not been the first to enter, so that it would necessarily follow from such a contention that every navigable region had been 'occupied' by some voyager. Thus we should be excluded from all parts of the sea. Indeed, it would even be necessary to admit that the [earliest] circumnavigators of the globe had acquired for themselves the whole Ocean! But no one is ignorant of the fact that a ship sailing over the sea no more leaves behind itself a right than it leaves a permanent track. In any case, the claim put forward by the Portuguese – namely, that no one had sailed over the aforesaid tracts of the Ocean before they themselves did so – is by no means true[4]. For a large part of the waters in question, in the neighbourhood of

---

Mare liberum in the West Indies?, p. 78 (facsimile) and p. 80 (note 64 on p. 93), and id., Preparing Mare liberum, p. 260.

[a] **Iohann. Faber ad §. littorum.**: Johannes Faber on Inst. 2, 1, 5, ed. fol. 29 v.

32 MARE

Ex Plin.lib. 2.c.69.&lib. 6.c.31.&Melæ lib.3.

Mauritaniæ jam olim navigata est: ulterior & in orientem vergens Victorijs Magni Alexandri lustrata est, usque in Arabicum sinum. Olim autem hanc navigationem Gaditanis percognitam fuisse, multa argumento sunt. Cajo Cæsare Augusti filio in Arabico sinu res gerente signa navium ex Hispaniensibus naufragiis agnita. Et quod Cælius Antipater tradidit, uidisse se qui ex Hispania in Æthiopiam commercii gratia navigasset: Etiam Arabibus, si verum est, quod Cornelius Nepos testatus est, Eudoxum quendam sua ætate cum Lathyrum Regem Alexandriæ fugeret, Arabico sinu egressum Gades usque pervectum. Pœnos autem, qui re maritima plurimum valuerunt, eum Oceanum non ignorasse longe clarissimum est, cum Hanno Cathaginis potentia florente circumvectus a Gadibus ad finem Arabiæ, præternavigato scilicet promontorio quod nunc Bonæ Spei dicitur, (Vetus videtur nomen Hesperion ceras fuisse) omne id iter, situmque littoris & insularum scripto complexus sit, testatusque ad ultimum non mare sibi, sed commeatum defuisse. Ab Arabico autem sinu ad Indiam, Indicique Oceani insulas, & auream usque Chersonesum, quam esse Iapanem credunt plerique, etiam re Romana florente navigari solitum, *Lib.6.c.23.* iter à Plinio descriptum, legationes ab Indis ad

[1]

[2]

---

[1] The interruption of the Latin phrase 'Ab Arabico ... satis ostendunt' on p. 32 and p. 33 of the 1609 edition could not be followed in the translation (just as Williams could not follow the interruption of the Latin text of the manuscript, see the page numbers in the margin). To compare the Latin and the English text the reader will have to look at the two different pages, as well as for the notes.

[2] See p. 33.

Chapter V

Mauritania, was navigated in quite ancient times[a]; and a more distant portion of those same waters, lying toward the East, was traversed as far as the Arabian Gulf in the course of the victories won by Alexander the Great. There are, moreover, many indications that the people of Cadiz were formerly well acquainted with this navigable area: for example, when Gaius Caesar, the [adopted] son of Augustus, was in command over the Arabian Gulf, figureheads of ships were found and recognized as remnants of wrecked Spanish vessels; and the statement made by Caelius Antipater to the effect that he had seen a man who had voyaged from Spain to Ethiopia on a commercial mission. These very waters were known to the Arabs, also, if we may accept as true the account given by Cornelius Nepos, in which it is related that one of his contemporaries, a certain Eudoxus, sailed from the Arabian Gulf as far as Cadiz while fleeing from Lathyrus the King of Alexandria. Again, it is absolutely certain that the Carthaginians, who enjoyed great maritime power, did not long remain in ignorance regarding that part of the Ocean. For Hanno, in the days when Carthage was mighty, made the voyage from Cadiz to the borders of Arabia (that is to say, by sailing around the promontory that is now known as the Cape of Good Hope, although the ancient name appears to have been Hesperion Ceras ['The Western Horn']); and he included in his record a description of the entire route, specifying the position of the coast and of the various islands, and stating that at the farthest point reached the sea had not ended but his supplies were indeed coming to an end. Furthermore[1], the route described by Pliny[b], the embassies dispatched by the East Indians

---

[a] Ex Plin. lib. 2. c. 69. et lib. 6. c. 31. et Mela lib. 3.: Plinius, Naturalis historia, II, 69 [67], VI, 31, and Mela, III [9].
[b] Lib. 6. c. 23.: [Plinius, Naturalis historia], VI, 23 [24].

LIBERVM. 33

ad Augustum, ad Claudium etiam ex Taprobane insula, deinde gesta Trajani & tabulæ Ptolemæi satis ostendunt. Iam suo tempore Strabo Alexandrinorum mercatorum classem *Lib.2.& 17.* ex Arabico sinu, ut Æthiopiæ ultima, ita & Indiæ petijsse testatur, cum olim paucis navibus id auderetur. Inde magna populo Romano vectigalia. Addit Plinius impositis sagittariorum cohortibus piratarum metu navigatum: *loco cit. & lib. 12, c, 19.* solamque Indiam quingenties sestertium, si Arabiam addas & Seres, millies annis omnibus Romano Imperio ademisse: & merces centuplicato venditas. Et hæc quidem vetera satis arguunt primos non fuisse Lusitanos. In singulis autem sui partibus Oceanus ille & tunc cum eum Lusitani ingressi sunt, & nunquam non cognitus fuit. Mauri enim, Æthiopes, Arabes, Persæ, Indi eam maris partem cujus ipsi accolæ sunt, nescire neutiquam potuerunt. Mentiuntur ergo qui se mare illud invenisse jactant. Quid igitur, dicet aliquis, parumne videtur, quod Lusitani intermissam multis forte sæculis navigationem primi repararunt, &, quod negari non potest, Europeis gentibus ignotam ostenderunt, magno suo labore, sumtu, periculo? Imo vero si in hoc incubuerunt ut quod soli reperissent id omnibus monstrarent, quis adeo est amens, qui non plurimum se illis debere profiteatur? Eandem

C

---

[1] 'Taprobane': in this context to be translated as 'Ceylon' (and not as 'Sumatra', cf. above p. 4 n. 1); see Williams, p. 241 n. 1 and p. 5 n. 1.

[2] 'et auream usque Chersonesum, quam esse Iapanem credunt plerique' [Latin text on p. 32]: cf. the commentary of Williams, p. 241 n. 2, stating 'Chersonesus Aurea, the 'Golden Peninsula', is usually regarded as the ancient name for Malacca (cf. note 1, p. 186, *supra*). It should be noted, moreover, that Grotius himself does not expressly approve the identification of this region with Japan'.

[3] 'Iam suo tempore Strabo ... et merces centuplicato venditas' and the references to Strabo and Plinius are additions in the top margin of the ms., fol. 107 r, probably dating from the preparation of the ms. for publication; cf. van Ittersum, Dating the manuscript, p. 140 (and id., Preparing Mare liberum, p. 262-263).

Chapter V

to Augustus as well as those sent from the island of Taprobane[1] to Claudius, and subsequently the recorded deeds of Trajan and the writings of Ptolemy, have made it sufficiently evident that navigation was customary at the height of Rome's power also, from the Gulf of Arabia to India, to the islands of the Indian Ocean, and even to the Golden Chersonese, which many persons identify with Japan[2]. Indeed[3], as early as the age of Strabo[a], according to his own testimony, a fleet belonging to Alexandrian merchants set sail from the Arabian Gulf in search of the farthest regions both of Ethiopia and of India, although few ships dared to attempt that voyage in ancient times. The Roman people derived rich revenue from these sources. Pliny[b] adds that companies of archers were attached to the ships, owing to fear of pirates; that every year India alone drew from the Roman Empire fifty million sesterces, or – if Arabia and China were also to be taken into account – that the sum received from the Empire amounted to one hundred million sesterces; and that the merchandise from those regions was sold for a hundred times as much. These examples recorded by antiquity certainly afford sufficient proof that the Portuguese were not the first [navigators of the waters above mentioned].

For that matter, each separate part of this oceanic tract was known before the Portuguese entered upon it; nor was there ever a time when those parts were unknown. For surely the Moors, the Ethiopians, the Arabs, the Persians, and the East Indians could not have been unacquainted with the seas near which they themselves dwelt. Therefore, those persons are lying who now boast of having discovered the seas in question.

Well, then (someone will ask), does it seem a trifling matter that the Portuguese were the first to restore to use a navigable area which had lain neglected for perhaps many centuries, and that they undeniably brought this region – at the cost of tremendous labour, expense, and peril on their own part – to the attention of the European nations not acquainted with it? By no means! If this was the purpose they cherished – namely, to point out to all the tract which they had rediscovered by their own unaided efforts – who will be so insensate as to withhold acknowledgement of the great debt that he owes to them? For

---

[a] Lib. 2. et 17.: [Strabo,] Geographica, II [5, 12] and XVII.
[b] loco cit. et lib. 12. c. 19: [Plinius] cited above (p. 32, note b) and XII, 19 [18].

dem enim gratiã, laudemq; & gloriã immortalem illi promeruerint, qua omnes contenti fuerunt rerum magnarũ inventores, quotquot scilicet non sibi, sed humano generi prodesse studuerunt. Sin Lusitanis suus ante oculos quæstus fuit, lucrum quod semper maximum est in prævertendis negotiationibus, illis sufficere debuit. Et scimus itinera prima proventus interdum quater decuplos, aut etiam uberiores dedisse: quibus factum ut inops diu populus ad repentinas divitias subito prorumperet, tanto luxus apparatu, quantus vix beatissimis gentibus in supremo progressæ diu fortunæ fastigio fuit. Si vero eidem in hoc præiverunt, ne quisquam sequeretur, gratiam non merentur, cum lucrum suum respexerint. lucrum autem suum dicere non possunt, cum eripiant alienum. Neque enim illud certum est nisi ivissent eo Lusitani iturum fuisse neminem. Adventabant enim tempora, quibus ut artes pene omnes, ita & terrarum & marium situs clarius in dies noscebantur. Excitassent vetera, quæ modo retulimus, exempla, & si non uno impetu omnia patuissent, at paulatim promota velis fuissent littora, alio semper aliud monstrante. Factum denique fuisset, quod fieri potuisse Lusitani docuerunt, cum multi essent populi non minus flagrantes mercaturæ & rerum externarum studio.

Chapter V

in that event the Portuguese will have earned the same gratitude, praise, and undying glory with which all great discoverers have been content, whenever their discoveries were made in a zealous attempt to benefit not themselves but humanity.

If, on the other hand, the Portuguese acted with a view to their own enrichment, they should have been satisfied with the profits acquired; for in enterprises of this kind the greatest gain always falls to the earliest entrants. In fact, we know that the first Portuguese voyage yielded profits amounting in some in stances to forty times the sum invested or even to larger returns; and we also know that, in consequence of these returns, a people who had long dwelt in poverty, suddenly burst into unlooked-for wealth and into such lavish pomp and luxury as had hardly been attained by the most prosperous nations at the very peak of ever-increasing good fortune.

Finally, if the Portuguese led the way into this enterprise with the intention of preventing all others from following in their footsteps, they deserve no gratitude, since they were mindful of their own profit [exclusively].

Yet they cannot properly speak of such profit as their 'own', inasmuch as they are snatching away something that belongs to others. For it has not been proven that no one else would have sought out the regions in question if the Portuguese had failed to do so. Indeed, the time was drawing on apace when the location of lands and seas, as well as almost every other aspect of art and science, was to become better known, day by day. The above-mentioned examples set in ancient times would in any case have excited interest; and even if those distant shores had not been laid open at a single stroke, at least they would have been revealed gradually in the course of different voyages, with each succeeding discovery pointing the way to another. In short, the achievement whose feasibility was demonstrated by the Portuguese would have been accomplished even without that people, since there were in existence many nations no less aflame with zeal for commerce and for enterprise in foreign lands.

studio. Venetis qui multa jam Indiæ didicerant, cætera inquirere promtum fuit. Gallorum Brittonum indefessa sedulitas, Anglorum audacia cœpto non defuisset. Ipsi Batavi multo magis desperata agressi sunt. Nulla igitur æquitatis ratio, ne probabilis quidem ulla sententia a Lusitanis stat.   Omnes enim qui mare volunt imperio alicujus subijci posse, id ei attribuunt qui proximos portus & circumjacentia littora in ditione habet. At Lusitani in illo immenso littorum tractu paucis exceptis præsidijs nihil habent quod suum possint dicere.   Deinde vero etiam qui Mari imperaret nihil tamen posset ex usu communi deminuere, sicut Populus Romanus arcere neminem potuit, quo minus in littore Imperii Romani cuncta faceret, quæ jure gentium permittebantur. Et si quicquam eorum prohibere posset, puta piscaturam qua dici quodammodo potest pisces exhauriri, at navigationem non posset, per quam mari nihil perit. Cui rei argumentum est longe certissimum, quod ex Doctorum sententia ante retulimus, etiam in terra, quæ cum populis, tum hominibus singulis in proprietatem attributa est, iter tamen certe inerme & innoxium, nullius gentis hominibus juste negari: sicut & potum ex flumine. Ratio apparet, quia cum unius rei naturaliter usus essent diversi, eum duntaxat

Gloss. in c. ibi peric. §. porro super verbo territorio De elect. in sexto & ibi Can. Gloss. in c. licet. ff. de Ferijs.

L. nemo igitur ff. de ver. divis. adde Alber. Gentilem de iure belli lib. 1. c. 19. sub finem.

[1] 'quod ex Doctorum sententia ante retulimus': the ms. has a reference in the margin: 'hoc capite' ('in this chapter', for Djp this means chapter XII, for Ml it is chapter V); cf. above p. 26 note a and p. 31 note 3.

Chapter V

The Venetians, who had already learned a great deal about India, were eagerly disposed to seek after further knowledge. The unflagging assiduity of the Breton French, and the audacity of the English, would not have left the task unfinished. The Dutch themselves have undertaken ventures far more desperate.

Thus the contention of the Portuguese is supported neither by any argument based upon equity nor even by any probable opinion [of an authority]. For every authority[a] who does hold that the sea can be made subject to individual sovereignty, attributes such sovereignty to him who has dominion over the closest ports and neighbouring shores. But on all the vast extent of coast to which we have referred, the Portuguese can point to no possession aside from a few fortified posts, which they may call their own.

Furthermore, even if a given person did possess sovereignty over the sea, he would still lack authority to diminish its common usefulness, just as the Roman People lacked authority to prevent the commission, on shores belonging to the Roman Empire, of any act whatsoever that was permissible under the law of nations[b]. Yet again, even if it were possible to prohibit some particular act of this kind, such as fishing (for it may be maintained that the supply of fish is, in a sense, exhaustible), it would in any case be impossible to prohibit navigation, through which the sea loses nothing. By far the most conclusive evidence in support of this point is what we have already reported above [in this chapter[1]] from the opinion of the Doctores: even in the case of land that has been assigned as private property, whether to nations or to single individuals, it is nevertheless unjust to deny the right of passage (that is to say, of course, unarmed and innocent passage) to men of any nation, precisely as it is unjust to deny them the right of drinking from a stream. The reason underlying this opinion is clear. For it would seem that, because nature has designed a given thing for

---

[a] Gloss. in c. ibi peric. [read 'in c. ubi peric.' as the ms. has] §. porro super verbo territorio De elect. in sexto et ibi Can. Gloss. in c. licet. ff. [this 'ff' is an error, occurring also in the ms.; it should be deleted] de Feriis.: Gloss 'territorio' on VI, 1, 6, 3, 2 and canonists thereon; Gloss 'ecclesiis' on X. 2, 9, 3. Grotius took over the two references from Zuarius, Consilium I de usu maris (see below p. 36 note c), num. 1 and 2. In Zuarius' text there is nothing which could explain the error 'ff'; Magoffin wrongly supposes that the Digest title 'De feriis' is meant and that 'l. solet' (D. 2, 12, 3) should be read instead of 'c. licet'.

[b] L. nemo igitur ff. de rer. divis. adde Alber. Gentilem de iure belli lib. I. c. 19. sub finem: D. 1, 8, 4; Gentilis, De iure belli, I, 19, ed. p. 148-149.

MARE

gentes divisisse inter se videntur, qui sine proprietate commode haberi non potest, contra autem eum recepisse, per quem domini conditio deterior non esset futura. Omnes igitur vident eum qui alterum navigare prohibeat nullo jure defendi, cum eundem etiam injuriarum teneri Vlpianus dixerit: alij autem etiam interdictum utile[1] prohibito competere existimaverint. Et sic Batavorum intentio communi jure nititur, cum fateantur omnes permissum cuilibet in mari navigare etiam a nullo Principe impetrata licentia: quod Legibus[2] Hispanicis diserte expressum est.[3]

l. 2. §. si quis in mari. ff. Ne quid in loco publ. Gloss. ad L. 1. ut in flumine publ. Bal. in L. item lapilli. 3. col. ff. de rer. divis. Rodericus Zuarius Hispanus in consilio 1. de usu maris. 3. partit. tit. 28. L. 10. & 12.

CAPVT VI.
Mare aut ius navigandi proprium non esse Lusitanorum titulo donationis Pontificiæ.

DONATIO Pontificis Alexandri, quæ a Lusitanis mare aut jus navigandi solis sibi vindicantibus, cum inventionis deficiat titulus, secundo loco adduci potest, satis ex ijs quæ ante dicta sunt vanitatis convincitur. Donatio enim nullum habet momentum in rebus extra commercium positis. Quare cum mare aut jus in eo navigandi proprium nulli hominum esse possit, sequitur neque dari a Pontifice

---

[1] 'interdictum utile': i.e. an adaptation of the interdictum 'Ut in flumine publico navigare liceat', dealt with in D. 43, 14, 1 pr.
[2] 'quod legibus': the ms. has 'quod et legibus'.
[3] In the 1633 edition, followed by all editions up to that of 1773, notes c and d were put together, an error resulting in a misinterpretation of the text of note d, see Introduction, note 135.

more than one use, the nations have apportioned among themselves the use which cannot properly be exercised apart from private ownership, while retaining [for the whole of mankind], on the other hand, the use whose exercise would not lead to impairment of the owner's status.

It is, then, a universally recognized fact, that he who prohibits another to navigate is supported by no law. In fact, Ulpian[a] declares that the person who issues such a prohibition is even liable with an *actio iniuriarum*; other jurists, however, have held that also an *interdictum utile*[1] is available to the person who has been prohibited[b]. Thus the Dutch plea rests upon the common [civil] law, since it is admitted by all that navigation of the seas is open to any person whatsoever, even when permission to navigate them has not been obtained from any ruler[c]. Indeed, this principle is expressly set forth in the laws[2] of Spain[d].

Chapter VI

That the sea or the right of navigation thereon does not belong to the Portuguese by title of Papal donation.

The donation of Pope Alexander, which may be adduced by the Portuguese as a second argument in defence of their attempt to claim the sea or the right of navigation for themselves alone (since the title of discovery fails them), is quite clearly revealed, in the light of the foregoing observations, as a vain and empty pretext. For a donation has no weight in regard to things that do not fall within the sphere of commerce; and therefore, since neither the sea nor the right of navigation thereon can be the private property of any man, it follows that such gifts could not have been bestowed by

---

[a] L. 2. §. si quis in mari. ff. Ne quid in loco publ.: D. 43, 8, 2, 9.
[b] Gloss. ad L. 1. ut in flumine publ.: [Accursian] Gloss 'interdicam' on D. 43, 14, 1 pr. Cf. below p. 65 note b.
[c] Bal. in L. item lapilli. 3. col. ff. de rer. divis. Rodericus Zuarius in consilio 1. de usu maris.: Baldus on D. 1, 8, 3, ed. fol. 46 r; Rodericus Zuarius, consilium I de usu maris, num. 13, ed. p. 858. Grotius probably did not consult an edition of the commentary by Baldus but copied the reference from Zuarius, who gives the specification '3. col.'.
[d] 3. partit. tit. 28. L. 10. et 12.: [Legibus Hispanicis = Siete Partidas] 3, 28, 3 [!] and 6 [!], ed. III, fol. 155v-156v. In the 1633 edition, followed by all editions up to that of 1773, notes c and d were put together, an error resulting in a misinterpretation of the text of note d, see Introduction, note 135. was taken over from Zuarius, no. 14 at p. 859, where indeed the nos. '3, 28, 10' and '3, 28, 12' occur, but followed by incipits corresponding with the nos. 3, 28, 3 and 6 of the Lopez-edition, Salamanca 1555 (which I used). The text of no. 14 also cites a third 'lex', numbered as '3, 28, 6'; according to the incipit 3, 28, 11 is meant (ed. III, fol. 157 v). Williams notices the error but refers only to 3, 28, 3. See Introduction, notes 171 ff.

Pontifice, neque a Lusitanis accipi potuisse. Præterea cum supra relatū sit ex omniū sani iudicij hominum sententia Papam non esse dominum temporalem totius orbis, ne Maris quidem esse satis intelligitur: quanquam et si id concederetur, tamen jus annexum Pontificatui in Regem aliquem aut populum pro parte nulla transferri debuisset. Sicut nec Imperator posset Imperij provincias in suos usus cōvertere aut pro suo arbitrio alienare. Illud saltem nemo negaturus est, cui aliquid sit frontis, cum jus disponendi in temporalibus Pontifici nemo concedat, nisi forte quantum ejus rerum spiritualium necessitas requirit, ista autem de quibus nunc agimus, mare scilicet & jus navigandi, lucrum & quęstum merum, non pietatis negotium respiciant, sequi nullam hac in re fuisse illius potestatem. Quid quod ne Principes quidem, hoc est domini temporales possunt ullo modo a navigatione aliquē prohibere, cum si quod habent jus in mari id sit tantum iurisdictionis ac protectionis? Etiam illud notissimū est apud omnes, ad ea facieda quę cū lege Naturæ pugnāt, nullam esse Papæ auctoritatem. Pugnat autem cum lege Naturæ, ut mare aut ejus usum quisquam habeat sibi proprium, ut jam satis demonstravimus. Cum denique jus suum auferre alicui Papa minime possit, quæ erit fa-

Vict. loco cita-to. n. 26.

Silv. in Verba Papa, n. 16.

Chapter VI

the Pope nor received by the Portuguese.

Moreover, in view of our earlier assertion (based upon the expressed opinion of particularly sagacious authorities) that the Pope is not the temporal lord of the whole earth, it will be quite readily understood that, similarly, he is not the temporal lord of the sea. But even if this form of dominion were conceded to him, it would still have been proper that a right attaching to the Pontificate should in no part be transferred to any king or nation; just as the Emperor could not convert the provinces of the Empire to his own uses, nor alienate them in accordance with some whim of his own[a]. In any case, only an utterly shameless person will deny the validity of the following argument: since no one concedes to the Pope the right to make rulings in temporal matters, save perhaps in so far as such intervention is required by some necessity derived from his spiritual functions, and since, moreover, the matters now under discussion – that is to say, the sea and the right of navigation – are being considered solely from the standpoint of profit and gain, not in connexion with any pious enterprise, it follows that in regard to the present question the papal power was null and void.

Then, too, what answer is there to the objection that even princes – in other words, temporal lords – are in no sense empowered to prohibit any person from navigation? For if such princes possess a right over the sea, it is merely a right of jurisdiction and protection.

Furthermore, it is a universally recognized principle, that the Pope has no authority to commit acts repugnant to the law of nature[b]; and we have already demonstrated quite clearly that it is repugnant to the law of nature for any person to possess the sea, or the use thereof, as private property.

Finally, since the Pope has no power whatsoever to deprive any man of his rights,

---

[a] **Vict. loco citato n. 26.:** Victoria, cited above [= De Indis, pars 1] num. 26 [= pars 2 num. 2], ed. p. 238-240. The ms. reads 'ubi supra' instead of 'loco citato'; the passage 'sicut nec Imperator ... alienare' (to which the reference is linked) is an addition in the ms.

[b] **Silv. in Verbo Papa, n. 16.:** Sylvester Prierias, verbo Papa, decimosexto, ed. p. 268-269 [§ 16].

MARE

cti istius defensio, si tot populos immerentes, indemnatos, innoxios ab eo iure quod ad ipsos non minus quam ad Hispanos pertinebat uno verbo voluit excludere? Aut igitur dicendum est nullam esse vim ejusmodi pronuntiationis, aut quod non minus credibile est, eum Pontificis animum fuisse, ut Castellanorum & Lusitanorum inter se certamini intercessum voluerit, aliorum autem juri nihil diminutum.

CAPVT VII.

Mare aut ius navigandi proprium non esse Lusitanorum titulo præscriptionis aut cōsuetudinis.

VLTIMVM iniquitatis patrocinium in præscriptione solet esse aut consuetudine. Et huc igitur Lusitani se conferunt: sed utrumque illis præsidium certissima juris ratio præcludit. Nam præscriptio a Iure est civili[1], unde locum habere non potest inter Reges, aut inter populos liberos: multo autem minus vbi jus naturæ aut gentium resistit, quod jure civili semper validius est. Quin & ipsa lex civilis præscriptionem hic impedit. Vsucapi enim aut præscriptione acquiri prohibentur, quæ in bonis esse non possunt, deinde

Vasq. c. 51.

Vide Do el. lib. 5. com. c. 22. & seq. L. sed Celsus. ff. de contrah. emnt. L. usucapionem. ff. de usucap.

what defence can be offered for his conduct, if we assume that he intended to exclude by a mere word a multitude of nations – undeserving of such treatment, not condemned for any fault, harmful to no one – from a right which belonged to them no less than to the Iberian peoples?

Therefore, we must conclude either that the proclamation, interpreted in the manner suggested, was without force, or else (and this alternative is no less credible) that the Pope's intention was based upon a desire to intervene in the dispute between the Spaniards and the Portuguese without diminishing in the least degree the rights of other persons.

Chapter VII

That the sea or the right of navigation thereon does not belong to the Portuguese by title of prescription or custom.

As a last resort, injustice is frequently defended on grounds of prescription or of custom. Accordingly, the Portuguese seek also to defend themselves upon these grounds; but irrefutable legal arguments prevent them from finding support in either concept.

For prescription is rooted in civil law [positive law][1]. Therefore, it is not applicable between kings or between free peoples[a], and far less can it have force in opposition to the law of nature, or [primary] law of nations, which is always stronger than civil law. Nay, even civil law itself presents an obstacle to prescription in the case under discussion[b]. For it prohibits acquisition by usucapion or by prescription in regard to those things which cannot be included under the head of property,

[109]

---

[a] **Vasq. c. 51.:** Vasquius, [lib. II], cap. 51 [num. 23 and 28], ed. Controv. I, p. 419 and 420.

[b] **Vide Donel. lib. 5. com. c. 22. et seq. L. sed Celsus. ff. de contrah. empt. L. usucapionem. ff. de usucap.:** Donellus, Commentaria de iure civili, ed. I, p. 395-398; D. 18, 1, 6, D. 41, 3, 9. In the ms. the reference to Donellus is separated from the one to the two texts of the Digest but there seems to be no special reason for this separation.

LIBERVM. 39

inde quæ possideri vel quasi possideri nequeunt, & quorum alienatio prohibita est. Hæc autem omnia de mari & usu maris vere dicuntur. Et cum publicæ res hoc est populi alicujus nulla temporis possessione quæri posse dicantur, sive ob rei naturam, sive ob eorum privilegium adversus quos præscriptio ista procederet, quāto iustius humano generi quam uni populo id beneficium dandum fuit in rebus communibus? Et hoc est quod Papinianus scriptum reliquit, prescriptionem longæ possessionis ad obtinenda loca jurisgentium publica concedi non solere : eiusque rei exemplum dat in littore, cujus pars imposito ædificio occupata fuerat: nam eo diruto, & alterius ędificio in eodem loco postea exstructo exceptionē opponi nō posse : quod deinde similitudine rei publicæ illustrat: nam & si quis in fluminis diverticulo pluribus annis piscatus sit, postea, interrupta scilicet piscatione, alterum eodem jure prohibere non posse. Apparet igitur Angelum & qui cum Angelo dixerunt Venetis & Ianuensibus per præscriptionem jus aliquod in sinum maris suo littori præjacentem acquiri potuisse, aut falli, aut fallere, quod sane Iurisconsultis nimium est frequens, cum sanctæ professionis auctoritatem, non ad rationes & leges, sed ad gratiam conferunt potentiorum. Nam Martiani quidem

L. sine. ff. eod. & sine poss. de Reg. iur. in 6. L. alienationis. ff. de verb. sig. L. si fundum. ff. de fundo dotal. L. præscriptio. C. de oper. publ. L. diligenter. C. de Aquæductu. L. viam. ff. de via publ. L. ult. ff. de usucap.

Cons. 289. Thema tale est: inter cætera capitula pacis

C 4

Chapter VII

and also in regard to those which are not susceptible of possession nor of quasi possession[a], or which cannot be alienated[b]; and all of these characteristics are correctly ascribed the to sea and to the use thereof.

Again, since it is maintained that public things (in other words, things belonging to a given nation) cannot be [privately] acquired as a result of possession over any period of time[c], howsoever long, either because of the nature of the things involved or because of some prerogative pertaining to those persons against whom the prescription should proceed, how much more justly was that benefit to be given in common things to mankind than to one people! In fact, this is precisely the principle laid down in the writings of Papinian[d], in the following terms: 'Prescription based upon long possession is not usually conceded to have force for the acquisition of places that are public according to the law of nations'. Papinian mentions the seashore by way of illustration, referring to a hypothetical case in which a part of the shore has been occupied through the construction of a building on that spot; for if, in such a case, the said building should be demolished and another, belonging to a different person, should afterwards be erected on the same site, no exception could be opposed. He adds another illustration, based upon analogy with public [i.e. national] possessions, as follows: if a given person has fished for years in some small river fork, even then (assuming, of course, that there has been a subsequent interruption of this activity), he will not be empowered to prohibit another person from enjoying the same right.

Thus it seems that Angelus[e], and those who have agreed with Angelus in saying that the Venetians and the Genoese were able to acquire through prescription a certain right over the maritime gulf adjacent to their shores, are either mistaken or guilty of deliberate deceit, as is all too often the case with jurists when they exercise the authority of their sacred profession, not in the interests of law and reason, but for the gratification of those in power. For the reply

[109ʹ]

---

[a] L. sine. ff. eod. c. sine poss. de Reg. iur. in 6.: D. 43, 3, 25, Sextus 5, ult., 3.

[b] L. alienationis ff. de verb. sig. L. si fundum. ff. de fundo dotal.: D. 50, 16, 28, D. 23, 5, 16.

[c] L. praescriptio. C. de oper. publ. L. diligenter. C. de Aquaeductu. L. viam. ff. de via publ.: C. 8, 11 (12), 6, C. 11, 43 (42), 9, D. 43, 11, 2.

[d] L. ult. ff. de usucap.: D. 41, 3, 45 (cf. above p. 20 note d).

[e] Cons. 289. Thema tale est: inter caetera capitula pacis: [Angelus de Ubaldis], Consilia, num. 290 [!], ed. fol. 205v-207r. – 'Thema tale est: inter caetera capitula pacis' is the incipit of the consilium (not 'Grotius' note' as supposed by Armitage, p. 40 n. 6). Grotius literally copied the reference from Balbus, De praescr., p. 471, who has 'Cons. 289' for what in the ed. 1575 (which was available to me) is Cons. 290. In a 1476 edition, mentioned in Gentili, De iure belli (Italian edition), p. 132 n. 57, the consilium 'Thema tale est' indeed has the number 289 and Balbus must have used an old edition. Incidentally, in the ed. 1618 of MI '289' was changed into '286', probably by a printer's error; all later editions have copied this error!

MARE

L. si quisquā. ff. de divers. & temp. præscript.

dem responsum, de quo & ante egimus, si recte cum Papiniani verbis comparetur, non aliam accipere potest interpretationem, quam eam quæ & Iohanni olim & Bartolo probata est, & nunc a doctis omnibus recipitur: ut scilicet jus prohibendi procedat quamdiu durat occupatio: non autem si ea omissa sit: omissa enim non prodest, nec si per mille annos fuisset continuata, ut recte animadvertit Castrensis. Et quamvis hoc voluisset Martianus, quod minime credendus est cogitasse, in quo loco occupatio conceditur, in eodem præscriptionem concedi, tamen absurdum erat quod de flumine publico dictum erat ad Mare commune, & quod de diverticulo ad sinum proferre, cum hæc præscriptio usum quæ est Iuregentium communis, impeditura sit, illa autem publico usui non admodum noceat. Alterum autem Angeli argumentum quod ex aquæ ductu sumitur, eodem Castrensi monstrante, ut a quæstione alienissimum, ab omnibus merito exploditur. Falsum igitur est talem præscriptionem etiam eo tempore gigni, cujus initium omnem memoriam excedat. Vbi enim lex omnem omnino tollit præscriptionem, ne istud quidem tempus admittitur, hoc est, ut Felinus loquitur, materia impræscriptibilis tempore immemoriali non sit præscriptibilis. Fatetur hæc vera esse Balbus: sed

Duar. de usu-cap. c. 3. Cuiac. ad d. l. ult. de usuc. Donell. Com. lib. 5. c. 22. in d. l. ultima. n. 4. per l. quod in littore. ff. de acq. per. dom.

Ex l. usum aquæ C. de Aquæd. lib. 11. confer cum l. Diligenter eod. tit. & cum l. hoc iure. §. Ductus aquæ. ff. de Aqua quot. & æst.

ad c. accedentes. de præscrip.

---

[1] 'de quo et ante egimus': see above, p. 24 note e.

[2] 'eam quae et Iohanni olim et Bartolo probata est': Johannes Bassianus in gloss 'prohibet' on D. 44, 3, 7; Bartolus on the same text, ed. V, fol. 158 r. Both references were probably taken over from Cuiacius (cf. note b).

of Marcianus[a] (to which we have referred in a previous context[1], also), if duly coupled with the words of Papinian, is certainly susceptible of no other interpretation than the one approved in former times by Johannes and by Bartolus[2], and accepted now by all learned authorities[b]. This interpretation runs as follows: the right to impose the prohibition in question is valid while the occupation continues, but not if it has ceased; for (as Castrensis[c] correctly observes) once such an interruption occurs, occupation loses its force, though it may have continued previously throughout a thousand years. Moreover, even if Marcianus had meant to say that a prescriptive title is conceded wherever occupation is conceded (although one can scarcely believe that he entertained such an opinion), it would still be absurd to apply a statement regarding a public river to the common sea, or one regarding a small river fork to a gulf; for prescription affecting the sea or a gulf would impede the use of something that is common property by the law of nations, whereas in the other cases mentioned prescription would result in no great impediment to public use. The other argument of Angelus, drawn from [texts on an] aqueduct[d], is rightly rejected by all on the ground that it is (as that same Castrensis points out) entirely extraneous to the question.

Therefore, it is not true that prescription of the kind suggested could also come into being by a lapse of time whose beginning lies beyond every record of memory. For that matter, in cases where the law absolutely does away with all prescription, not even such a lapse of time is accepted as a pertinent factor; that is to say (if we may borrow the explanation of Felinus[e]), an object which is imprescriptible does not become prescriptible merely because of the passage of time immemorial. Balbus

---

[a] L. si quisquam. ff. de divers. et temp. praescript.: D. 44, 3, 7.

[b] Duar. de usucap. c. 3. Cuiac. ad d. l. ult. de usuc. Donell. Com. lib. 5. c. 22.: Duarenus on D. 41, 3, caput 3, ed. p. 659-660, at p.660; Cuiacius in Pand., on D. 41, 3, 45, ed. col. 282-283; Donellus, Commentaria de iure civili, I, p. 395-397 (citing D. 41, 3, 45 as 'l. praescriptio sive ultima').

[c] in d. l. ultima. n. 4. per. [read 'per' as the ms. has] l. quod in littore. ff. de acq. rer. dom.: [(Paulus) Castrensis] on D. 41, 3, 45, cited above [p. 39, note d], num. 4 (ed. I, fol. 69 v); an argument is to be found in D. 41, 1, 14.

[d] Ex l. usum aquae C. de Aquaed. lib. 11. confer cum l. Diligenter eod. tit. et cum l. hoc iure. §. Ductus aquae. ff. de Aqua quot. et aest.: C. 11, 43 (42), 4; compare with C. 11, 43 (42), 9 and with D. 43, 20, 3, 4.

[e] ad c. accedentes, de praescript.: [Felinus (Sandeus)] on X. 2, 26, 11, ed. pars tertia, col. 248-259, at col. 253-254 (in § 6).

LIBERVM. 41

sed Angeli sententiam receptam dicit hac ratione, quia tempus extra memoriam positum idem valere creditur privilegio, cum titulus aptissimus ex tali tempore presumatur. Apparet hinc non aliud illos sensisse, quam si pars aliqua reipublicæ, puta Imperij Romani, supra omnem memoriam usa esset tali jure, ei dandam præscriptionem hoc colore, quasi Principis concessio præijsset. Quare cum nemo sit dominus totius generis humani, qui jus illud adversus homines omnes homini aut populo alicui potuisset concedere, sublato illo colore, necesse est etiam præscriptionem interimi. Et sic ex illorum etiam sententia inter Reges aut populos liberos prodesse nihil potest lapsus infiniti temporis. Vanissimū autem & illud est quod Angelus docuit, etiamsi ad dominium præscriptio proficere non potest, tamen dandam esse possidenti exceptionem. Nam Papinianus disertis verbis exceptionem negat: & aliter non potuit sentire cum ipsius sæculo præscriptio nihil esset aliud quam exceptio. Verum igitur est quod & leges Hispanicæ exprimunt in his rebus quæ communi hominum usui sunt attributæ, nullius omnino temporis præscriptionem procedere, cujus definitionis illa præter cæteras ratio reddi potest, quod qui re communi utitur, ut communi uti

Depræsc. 4. par. 5. part. princip. q. 6. n. 8.

d. l. ultima.

Par. 3. tit. 29. l. 7. in c. Placa. Rod. Znarius, d. consf. n. 4.

C 5 videtur,

Chapter VII

grants the truth of these observations[a], but explains that the opinion of Angelus has been accepted, for the reason that a lapse of time extending beyond the limits of memory is regarded as having the same force as a legal grant of special privilege, in that a thoroughly satisfactory title is to be inferred therefrom.

On the basis of the foregoing comments, it is apparent that the opinion of the authorities cited was nothing more nor less than this: if any part of a state (for example, some part of the Roman Empire) had exercised a right of the kind in question, at a time antedating all the annals of memory, a prescriptive title would have been conceded to the said part on that pretext, just as if a grant had previously been made by the prince. By the same token, since no person is the master of all mankind and therefore capable of having granted such a right to any particular man or nation as opposed to the whole human race, and since the said pretext is thus destroyed, it necessarily follows that the corresponding prescriptive title is also destroyed. Therefore, even according to the opinion held by those same authorities, the lapse of unmeasured time cannot avail to establish such a title in the relations between kings or free peoples.

Furthermore, Angelus propounded a thoroughly foolish doctrine when he maintained that even if prescription could not serve to produce ownership, nevertheless, an exception should be given to a possessor. For Papinian[b] distinctly denies the existence of such exceptions; nor would it have been possible for him to take a different stand, since prescription itself, in his day, was nothing else but an exception.

Thus it is true, which also the Spanish laws[c] express, that prescription, upon whatsoever interval of time it may be based, is not applicable in regard to those things which have been assigned to all mankind for its common use. One argument among others which support this assertion may be set forth as follows: he who makes use of a common thing is obviously

---

[a] De praesc. 4. par. 5 part. princip. q. 6. n. 8.: [Balbus], ed. p. 472-473.
[b] d. l. ultima: D. 41, 3, 45, cited above (p. 39, note 3).
[c] Par. 3. tit. 29. l. 7. inc. Placa. Rod. Zuarius, d. cons. n. 4.: [Leges Hispanicae = Siete Partidas,] 3, 29, 7 (incipit 'Placa'), ed. fol. 166v-167r; Rodericus Zuarius, in his consilium cited above [Consilium I de usu maris, see p. 36 note c], num. 4, ed. p. 853. The reference to the Siete Partidas was probably taken over from Zuarius.

videtur, non autem jure proprio, & ita præscribere non magis quam fructuarius potest
vitio possessionis. Altera hæc etiam non con-*[1]*
temnenda est, quod in præscriptione temporis
cujus memoria non extat, quamvis titulus &
bona fides præsumantur, tamen si reipsa appa-
reat titulum omnino nullum dari posse, & sic
manifesta sit fides mala, quæ in populo maxime quasi uno corpore perpetua esse censetur, ex duplici defectu præscriptio corruit. Tertia vero, quia res hæc est meræ facultatis, quæ
non præscribitur, ut infra demonstrabimus.*[2]*
Sed nullus est finis argutiarum. Inventi sunt
qui in hoc argumento a præscriptione consuetudinem distinguerent, ut illa scilicet ex-
clusi, ad hanc confugerent. Discrimen autem
quod hic statuunt sane ridiculum est: Ex præscriptione ajunt jus unius quod ab eo aufertur
alteri applicari: sed cum aliquod jus ita alicui
applicatur ut alteri non auferatur, tum dici
consuetudinem: quasi vero cum jus navigandi quod communiter ad omnes pertinet exclusis alijs ab uno usurpatur, non necesse sit
omnibus perire quantum uni accedit. Errori
huic ansam dederunt Pauli verba non recte
accepta, qui cum de jure proprio maris ad aliquem pertinente loqueretur, fieri hoc posse
dixit Accursius per privilegium aut consuetudinem: quod additamētum ad Iuriscon-
sulti

Marginalia:
- Fachin. lib. 8. c. 26. & c. 33. Covar. de præscr. parte 2. §. 2. n. 8. & §. 8. n. 5. & 6.
- Fachi. lib. 8. c. 28.
- Aret. in rubr. ff. de rer. divis. alleg. Balbus. d. loco n. 2. Vide Vasq. contr. ill. c. 29. n. 38.
- ad d. l. sane.

---

[1] 'Altera haec … ut infra demonstrabimus' (with the references in the margin) is an addition in the ms., at the bottom of the page. Grotius probably made it when he gained access to the work of Fachinaeus.

[2] 'demonstrabimus': see below, chapter XI.

Chapter VII

using it as common and not in his proper right, so that, because of imperfect possession, he can no more prescribe than a usufructuary. A second argument[1], too, is worthy of consideration[a]: that in a prescription based upon a lapse of time extending beyond the limits of memory, even though the existence of a title and good faith is presumed, nevertheless, if the facts of a particular case clearly show that absolutely no title can be granted and if the existence of bad faith is correspondingly evident (bad faith being regarded as permanent especially in the case of a nation; considered as one body) the prescription fails because of this twofold defect. Yet again, a third argument[b] lies in the fact[c], that the thing consists in a mere faculty which (as we shall presently show[2]) does not allow of prescription.

There is, however, no end to the subtleties advanced in disputing this point. Some persons have been known to draw a distinction in this connexion between prescription and custom, with a view, of course, to taking refuge in the latter concept if they are cut off from the former. But the distinction set up by them is indeed absurd. They assert[c] that by prescription a right previously pertaining to one individual and subsequently taken from him is assigned to another person, whereas when a certain right is assigned a given individual without first taking it from another person this is called custom[d]. As if when the right of navigation (originally bestowed upon all men in common) is usurped by one claimant to the exclusion of the rest, it does not necessarily follow that whatever is gained by that one is lost to mankind as a whole!

The way was prepared for this error by a misinterpretation of the words of Paulus. Although Paulus was discussing a private right to [any part of] the sea pertaining to a specific person, Accursius[e] claimed that the situation discussed in that passage could be brought about through privilege or through custom. This addition to the text of the jurist

---

[a] **Fachin. lib. 8. c. 26. et c. 33. Covar. de praescr. parte 2. §. 2. [read §. 3?] n. 8. et §. 8. n. 5. et 6.**: Fachinaeus, Controv., ed. II, p. 192-193 and p. 194-195; Covarruvias in reg. Possessor malae fidei, ed. p. 414 (probably p. 418-419 [= § 3 n. 8] was meant) and p. 434-435.

[b] **Fachi. lib. 8. c. 28.**: Fachinaeus, Controv., ed. II, p. 201- 203.

[c] **Aret. in rubr. ff. [read 'Inst.'] de rer. divis. alleg. Balbus. d. loco n. 2.**: [Angelus] Aretinus on the rubrica of Inst. 2, 1 [ed., fol. 58 v] to whom Balbus, cited above (p. 41 note a) at num. 2 [ed. p. 469] refers. The error 'ff.' for 'Inst.' (also occurring in the ms.) was copied from Balbus. Williams, p. 248, corrected the error but Armitage, p. 42 n. 17, neglects this correction. For confusions between Angelus (de Gambilionibus) Aretinus and Angelus de Ubaldis (Perusinus) see Introduction, section 10.

[d] **Vide Vasq. contr. ill. c. 29. n. 38. [read 'c. 89. n. 38.']**: Vasquius, Controv. I, p. 755. The error also occurs in the ms. and has been maintained in all later editions; it was, however, corrected by Boschan, p. 65 n. 2.

[e] **ad. d. l. sane.**: [Accursius] on D. 47, 10, 14, cited above (p. 24 and 27), i.e. gloss 'Pertineat'.

sulti textum nullo modo accedens mali potius conjectoris esse videtur quam boni interpretis. Mens Pauli supra explicata est. Cæterum illi si vel sola Vlpiani verba, quæ paulo ante præcedunt, satis considerassent, longe aliud dicturi erant. Fatetur enim ut quis ante ædes meas piscari prohibeatur, esse quidem usurpatum: hoc est receptum consuetudine: sed nullo iure: ideoque injuriarum actionem prohibito non denegandam. Contemnit igitur hunc morem, & usurpationem vocat, ut & inter Christianos Doctores Ambrosius. Et merito. Quid enim clarius quam non valere consuetudinem, quæ juri naturæ, aut gentium ex adverso opponitur? Consuetudo enim species est juris positivi, quod legi perpetuæ obrogare non potest. Est autem lex illa perpetua ut Mare omnibus usu commune sit. Quod autem in præscriptione diximus, idem in consuetudine verum est, si quis eorum qui diversum tradiderunt sensus excutiat, non aliud reperturum, quam consuetudinem privilegio æquiparari. Atqui adversus genus humanum concedendi privilegium nemo habet potestatem: quare inter diversas respublicas consuetudo ista vim nō habet. Verum omnem hanc questionem diligentissime tractavit Vasquius, decus illud Hispaniæ, cujus nec in explorando jure

in d. L. iniuriarum. §. ult.

Vide Gloss. eod. loco.

l. de offic. 28. Gentil. lib. I. c. 19. Sub finem.

auth. ut nulli iudici. §. 1. c. cum tanto de consuet.

Chapter VII

is in no sense concordant with it, and would seem to have been contributed by a poor guesser rather than by a good interpreter. We have already explained[1] what Paulus had in mind. Moreover, if those persons who misinterpret his statement had even considered with sufficient care nothing more than the words of Ulpian[a] in the passage placed just before the one in question, they would have dealt with the matter in an entirely different fashion. For Ulpian admits that the practice to forbid anyone to fish in front of my dwelling exists by usurpation – that is to say by custom[b] – but is not authorized by any law, so that the person on whom the prohibition was imposed should be allowed to bring an action for injury.

Thus Ulpian rejects the practice of imposing such prohibitions, describing it as 'usurpation'; and, among the Christian authorities, Ambrose[c] does likewise. Are they not right in so doing? For what could be clearer than the fact that a custom diametrically opposed to the law of nature, or to the law of nations, is not valid[d]? Custom is a form of positive law, and positive law cannot derogate from perpetual law. But that law is perpetual that the use of the sea should be common to all. Furthermore, what we have said in discussing prescription is likewise true with respect to custom: any inquiry into the opinions of those authorities who hold an opposing view will certainly show that they place custom on the same level as privilege; yet no one has the power to grant a privilege unfavourable to the interests of the human race; and therefore, the custom above mentioned has no force where the relations between different states are involved.

As a matter of fact, this entire question has been quite thoroughly discussed by Vasquius, the pride of Spain, a jurist who in no instance leaves

---

[a] **in d. l. iniuriarum. §. ult.:** [Ulpianus] in D. 47, 10, 13, 7.
[b] **Vide Glos. eod. loco:** Accursian gloss 'Usurpatum' on D. 47, 10, 13, 7.
[c] **1. de offic. 28. Gentil. lib. 1. c. 19. Sub finem.:** [Ambrosius,] De officiis, I, 28 [132]; Gentilis, De iure belli, I, 19, ed. p. 148 [refers also to Ambrosius; Grotius probably copied this reference from Gentili].
[d] **auth. ut nulli iudici.** [ms.: iud.] **§. 1. c. cum tanto de consuet.:** Nov. 134, 1 (= Authenticum 9, 17, 1); Decretal. 1, 4, 11.

44 MARE

controv. ill. c. 89. n. 12. & seq.

jure subtilitatem, nec in docendo libertatem unquam desideres. Is igitur posita Thesi Loca publica & jure gentium communia præscribi non posse, quam multis firmat auctoribus: exceptiones deinde subjungit ab Angelo & alijs confictas, quas supra retulimus. Hæc autem examinaturus recte judicat istarum rerum veritatem pendere a vera juris tam naturæ quam gentium cognitione. Ius enim naturæ cum a divina veniat providentia, esse immutabile. Hujus autem juris naturalis partem esse jus gentium, primævum quod dicitur, diversum a jure gentium secundario sive positivo: quorum posterius mutari potest. Nam si qui mores cum jure gentium primævo repugnent, hi non humani sunt, ipso judice, sed FERINI, corruptelæ & abusus, non leges & usus. Itaque nullo tempore præscribi potuerunt, nulla lata lege justificari, nullo multarum etiam gentium consensu, hospitio, & exercitatione stabiliri, quod exemplis aliquot, & Alphonsi Castrensis Theologi Hispani testimonio confirmat. *Ex quibus apparet*, inquit, *quam suspecta sit sententia eorum, quos supra retulimus, existimantium Genuenses aut etiam Venetos posse non iniuria prohibere alios navigare per Gulfum aut pelagus sui maris, quasi æquora ipsa præscripserint. id quod non solum est contra leges: sed etiam est contra ipsum*

de potestate legis poenalis. lib. 2. c. 14. p. 572.

all. L. quod in littore. ff. de acq. rer. dom. l. fin. in princ. ff. de usucap.

---

[1] 'Is igitur ... testimonio confirmat'. The 22 lines which separate the mention of Vasquius and the beginning of the long verbatim quotation (cf. below, note 2) are a paraphrase of what Vasquius says in nos. 12-29 (ed. p. 749-752), in particular of no. 28, where he gives a number of examples, taken from Alphonsus de Castro, De potestate legis poenalis, lib. 2, c. 14, cited with the page number 572. Grotius copied 'p. 572' but apparently he had not seen an edition of Castro at all. For details see Beaufort, p. 208 ff. Apparently '572' is a printing error in the 1599 edition of Vasquius: the 1564 edition has 'quingentesima sexagesimaprima' and the 1572 edition 'quingentesima sexagesima secunda'. This reference must have been taken from one of the two Lyonese editions 1556 of Castro's work; other early editions do not have page but folio numbering. According to the inventory of his books made in 1620 Grotius possessed a copy of Castro's work. As Rabbie, p. 128-129, has shown, this copy must have been a Lyons 1556 edition (which, however, came into his possession only shortly before 1620).

[2] The beginning of this long verbatim quotation from Vasquius, Controv. I, can be found on page 752 no. 30 (this reference is added in pencil in the ms., probably by Hamaker, cf. his edition p. 237 n. 1); the end is on p. 754, in the middle of no. 35.

Chapter VII

anything to be desired in the keenness of his investigation of law nor in the candour with which he expounds it[a]. Vasquius, then[1], having laid down a thesis which he confirms by citing many authorities – namely, the thesis that public places and such as are common by the law of nations cannot be made the objects of prescription – appends to this statement certain exceptions formulated by Angelus and by others, which we have already mentioned. Before undertaking an examination of these exceptions, however, he rightly observes that the truth in regard to such matters rests upon a true conception of both the law of nature and the law of nations. For Vasquius argues that the law of nature, since it proceeds from Divine Providence, is immutable; and that the primary law of nations (which is regarded as different from the secondary or positive law of nations, the latter being susceptible to change whereas the former is immutable) constitutes a part of that natural law. For if there are certain customs incompatible with the primary law of nations, they are customs proper not to human beings (in the opinion of that same jurist) but to *wild beasts*; neither do they represent law and usage, but rather, corruption and abuse; and therefore, they cannot be prescribed as the result of any interval of time whatsoever, they cannot be justified by the establishment of any law, nor can they be definitively confirmed by agreement, acceptance, and practice even on the part of many nations. Vasquius strengthens this argument by citing several examples together with the testimony of the Spanish theologian, Alfonso de Castro[b].

In the light of these observations (says Vasquius[2]), we clearly perceive the questionable nature of the opinion held by the above-mentioned persons who believe that the Genoese or even the Venetians can, lawfully, prohibit others from navigating the gulf or the open spaces of their respective seas, as if to claim by prescription the very surface of the waters. Such conduct would be contrary not only to the [Roman] laws[c] but even

---

[a] controv. ill. c. 89. n. 12. et seq.: [Vasquius], Controv. I, p. 749 ff.
[b] [Alphonsi Castrensis] de potestate legis poenalis. lib. 2. c. 14. p. 572.: Alphonsus de Castro, fol. 238 v (cf. above, note 1, and cf. below, p. 49 note c).
[c] all. L. quod in littore. ff. de acq. rer. dom. l. fin. in princ. ff. de usucap. [p. 45:] §. flumina, verbo omnibus. Inst. de rer. divis. l. si quisquam. ff. de diversis et temp. praescr. l. sane si maris. ff. de iniuriis.: [Vasquius] refers to D. 41, 1, 14, D. 41, 3, 45 pr. [!], Inst. 2, 1, 2 at the word Omnibus, D. 44, 3, 7, D. 47, 10, 14. (Vasquius cites D. 41, 3, 45 as 'l. fin.', cf. above, p. 20 note d).

LIBERVM. 45

ius naturæ, aut gentium primævum, quod mutari non posse diximus. Quod sit contra illud ius constat, quia non solum maria aut æquora eo iure communia erant, sed etiam reliquæ omnes res immobiles. Et licet ab eo iure postea recessum fuerit ex parte, puta quoad dominium & proprietatem terrarum, quarum dominium iure Naturæ commune, distinctum & divisum, sicque ab illa communione segregatum fuit: tamen diversum fuit & est in dominio maris, quod ab origine Mundi, ad hodiernum usque diem est fuitque semper in communi, nulla ex ex parte immutatum, ut est notum. Et quamvis ex LVSITANIS magnam turbam sæpe audiverim in hac esse opinione ut eorum Rex ita præscripserit navigationem INDICI Occidentalis (forte Orientalis)[1] eiusdemque VASTISSIMI MARIS, ita ut reliquis gentibus æquora illa transfretare non liceat, & ex nostrismet HISPANIS VVLGVS in eadem opinione fere esse videtur[2], ut per VASTISSIMVM IMMENSVMQVE PONTVM ad Indorum regiones quas potentissimi Reges nostri[3] subegerunt reliquis mortalium navigare, præterquam Hispanis ius minime sit, quasi ab eis id ius præscriptum fuerit, tamen istorum omnium non minus INSANÆ sunt opiniones, quam eorum qui quoad Genuenses & Venetos in eodem fere SOMNIO esse adsolent, quas sen-

Marginalia:
§. flumina, verbo omnibus. Inst. de rer. divis. l. si quisquam. ff. de diversis & temp. præscr. l. sane si maris. ff. de iniuriis.

all. l. ex hoc iure. ff. de inst. & iure. §. ius gentium, & §. ius autem gent. Inst. de Iure natur.

---

[1] '(forte Orientalis)' was added by Grotius.
[2] 'videtur' is a printing error for 'videatur', see ms. and Vasquius; cf. also *Defensio*, p. 333.
[3] The ms. and Vasquius read 'reges nostri Hispaniarum'; cf. also *Defensio*, p. 333.

Chapter VII

to the law of nature itself, or the primary law of nations, which we have already characterized as immutable. The fact that it would conflict with the former, is perfectly evident: for not only the seas and the surface thereof, but also all other immovable things, were common property according to the said law. Moreover, even though that law was in later times partially abandoned – for example, in so far as ownership and property rights over lands were concerned, since ownership over lands, though common under the law of nature, was subjected to a process of differentiation and division which removed it from that community[a] – nevertheless, ownership of the seas was and still is a different matter. For the seas, from the beginning of the world down to the present day, are and have always been common property, unvaryingly and without exception, as is well known. To be sure, I have often heard that a great many *Portuguese* hold the opinion that their King has established a prescriptive right over navigation upon the seas of the West (perhaps [an error for] 'East')[1] *Indies* as well as upon that same *vast Ocean*, with the result that other peoples are not permitted to sail across those waters; and apparently[2] *the common people* of our own country, Spain, cherish much the same belief – namely, that navigation upon *the vast and boundless deep* to the regions of the Indians subjugated by our mighty rulers, the sovereigns of the Spanish realms[3], constitutes a right by no means open to any mortal other than the Spaniards, as if this right was acquired by the latter through prescription. But the opinions of all these persons are no less *wildly erroneous* than the opinions of those who are wont to embrace a very similar *delusion* in regard to the Genoese and the Venetians.

---

[a] [To be attached to 'fuit' on line 9:] all. l. ex hoc iure. ff. de inst. [read 'iust.' as the ms. has] et iure. §. ius gentium, et §. ius autem gent. Inst. de Iure natur.: [Vasquius] refers to D. 1, 1, 5, Inst. 1, 2, 1 [at the words 'ius gentium'], Inst. 1, 2, 2 [at the words 'ius autem gentium'].

46 MARE.

sententias INEPTIRE vel ex eo dilucidius apparet, quod istarum rationum singulæ contra seipsas nequeunt præscribere: hoc est, non respublica Venetiarum contra semetipsam, non respublica Genuensium contra semetipsam, non Regnum Hispanicum contra semetipsum, non Regnum Lusitanicum contra semetipsum. Esse enim debet differentia inter agentem & patientem. Contra reliquas vero nationes longe minus præscribere possunt, quia ius præscriptionum est mere civile, ut fuse ostendimus supra. Ergo tale ius cessat cum agitur inter Principes vel populos, superiorem non recognoscentes in temporalibus. Iura enim mere civilia cuiuscunque regionis, quoad exteros populos, nationes, vel etiam homines singulos, non magis sunt in consideratione, quam si re vera non esset tale ius, aut nunquam fuisset, & ad ius commune gentium primævum vel secundarium recurrendum est, eoque utendum, quo iure talem maris præscriptionem & usurpationem admissam non fuisse satis constat. Facit, nam & hodie usus aquarum communis est, non secus quam erat ab origine Mundi. Ergo & in æquoribus & aquis nullum ius est aut esse potest humano generi, præterquam quoad usum communem. Præterea de iure naturali & divino est illud præceptum, ut Quod tibi non vis alteri non facias. Vnde cum navigatio nemini possit esse nociva, nisi ipsi naviganti, par est ut nemini

Marginal note: Alit. l. sequitur. §. si viâ. ff. de usucap. §. si itaq; inst. de act. Vt dictis iurib. & l. cum filio ubi multa per Bartol. & Ias. ff. de legat. I. Part. I. in pr. q. 3. & 4.

---

[1] 'rationum' is a printing error for 'nationum' (Err.).
[2] 'Hispanicum' is probably a printing error for 'Hispanorum', see ms. and Vasquius.
[3] 'Lusitanicum' is probably a printing error for 'Lusitanorum', see ms. and Vasquius.
[4] Instead of 'sunt' Vasquius has 'est' which is probably a printing error.
[5] Instead of 'nunquam' the ms. and Vasquius read 'unquam'.
[6] Vasquius adds 'ergo, etc.'.
[7] Grotius omits two quotations from Ovidius occurring in Vasquius' text.
[8] Instead of 'Ergo et' Vasquius has only 'Ergo'.

Chapter VII

The *absurdity* of all such beliefs is rendered still more manifest by the fact that the individual nations[1] involved are not able to set up prescriptions against themselves: that is to say, the Republic of Venice cannot set up a prescription against itself, the Republic of Genoa labours under a like disability as regards its own case, and the same is true of the Kingdoms of Spain[2] and Portugal[3], respectively[a]. For the agent and the passive party must be different entities[b]. On the other hand, these nations are far less able to employ prescription against other peoples, inasmuch as the law of prescriptions is merely civil law, a point fully brought out by us in an earlier passage[c]. Thus the said law does not apply when the interested parties are all princes or peoples who recognize no superior in temporal matters. For the strictly civil laws of a given region have[4] no more bearing on the issue in so far as foreign peoples, states, or even individuals are concerned, than they would if those laws did not actually exist or had never[5] existed. In dealing with such foreign entities, the common law of nations, either in its primary or in its secondary phase, must be consulted and applied; and it is a sufficiently well-established fact that the said law has not authorized such maritime prescription and usurpation[6]. This argument is decisive for even today the use of waters constitutes a common right just as it always did, since the beginning of the world[7]. Accordingly[8], in cases involving the sea or other waters, men do not and cannot possess any right other than that which relates to common use. Moreover, both natural law and divine law uphold that famous precept: 'Do ye not unto others what ye would not have others do unto you'. Therefore, since navigation cannot prove injurious save perhaps to the navigator himself, it is fitting

---

[a] All. l. sequitur. §. si viam. ff. de usucap. §. si [read: 'sic' as the ms. has] itaque inst. de act.: [Vasquius] referring to D. 41, 3, 4, 27, Inst. 4, 6, 14.

[b] Ut dictis iurib. et l. cum filio ubi multa per Bartol. et Ias. ff. de legat. I.: As in the aforementioned texts (cited in note a) and D. 30, 11 discussed at length by Bartolus, in Dig. IV, fol. 6v-7v, and Jason de Maino in Dig. IV, fol. 24 v [nos. 15 ff.] (these allegations were also copied from Vasquius, who places them as a separate reference after 'patientem'; the fusion of notes a and b is probably a printer's error, see ms. and Vasquius).

[c] Part. I. in pr. q. 3 et 4.: reference copied from Vasquius; probably the beginning of Vasquius, Controv. I, c. 51, is meant, ed. I, p. 415 ff.

LIBERVM. 47

ut nemini poſsit, aut debeat impediri, ne in re ſui natura libera, ſibique minime noxia navigantium libertatem impediat, & lædat contra dictum præceptum & contra regulam. præſertim cum omnia intelligantur eſſe permiſſa, quæ non reperiuntur expreſsim prohibita. Quinimo non ſolum contra ius naturale eſſet, velle impedire talem navigationem, ſed etiam tenemur contrarium facere, hoc eſt, prodeſſe iis quibus poſſumus, cum id ſine damno noſtro fieri poteſt. Quod cum multis auctoritatibus tam divinis quam humanis cōfirmaſſet, ſubjungit poſtea: *Ex ſuperioribus etiam apparet ſuſpectam eſſe ſententiam Iohannis Fabri, Angeli, Baldi, & Franciſci Balbi; quos ſupra retulimus, exiſtimantium loca iuris gentium communia, & ſi acquiri non poſsint præſcriptione, poſſe tamen acquiri conſuetudine, quod omnino* FALSVM *eſt, eaque traditio* COECA *&* NVBILA *eſt* OMNIQVE RATIONIS LVMINE CARENS, *legemque verbis non rebus imponens. In exemplis enim de Mari Hiſpanorum,* LVSITANORVM, *Venetorum, Genuenſium, & reliquorum, conſtat conſuetudine ius tale navigandi, & alios navigare prohibendi non magis acquiri quam præſcriptione. Vtroque enim caſu ut apparet, eadem eſt ratio. Et quia per iura & rationes ſupra relatas id eſſet*

contra

l. libertas. ff. de ſtatu hom. §. libertas. Inſt. de Iure perſ. l. 1. & 2. ff. de homine lib. exh. l. 1. §. quæ onerandæ. ff. Quar. rer. act. n. d. l. ſi quando. §. illud. verb. aſtringendos. C. de inoffic. teſt. L. nec-non. §. quod eis. ff. ex quib. cauſ. ma. l. ſuper ſtatuas. C. de religioſis.

Contra l. 2. cum vulgatis. C. comm. de leg.

l. illud. ff. ad l. Aquil.

---

[1] 'nemini' is a printing error for 'a nemine', see the ms. and Vasquius.
[2] After 'libera' Vasquius has 'et permissa'.
[3] After 'navigationem' Vasquius has 'praetextu praescriptionis, cum impedienti id minime prosit, et impedito noceat'; in the ms. 'praetextus ... possit' was taken over, 'et impedito noceat' was omitted (Hamaker, p. 239, adds it without putting [ ]).
[4] After 'potest' Grotius omits 22 lines of Vasquius' text (being the second half of no. 35) and continues with the text of no. 36. Williams, in a marginal note on p. 252, suggests that '36' was written by Grotius himself in the margin of the ms.; it is, however, written in pencil in a modern hand, probably by Hamaker.
[5] After 'ratio' Vasquius adds 'ergo, etc.'.

Chapter VII

that this activity can nor should be denied by anybody[1], lest in a matter whose very nature implies free[2] participation and which is in no sense harmful to himself, he hinders and obstructs the liberty of navigators, transgressing the aforesaid precept and the established rule[a]. Our argument is strengthened by the principle that all activities against which no express prohibition is found to exist, are understood to be permitted[b]. Indeed, it is not enough to say that an attempt to prevent such navigation[3] would be contrary to natural law, for we are also under a positive obligation to pursue the opposite course, that is to say, an obligation to benefit all persons whom we can benefit without consequent injury to ourselves.

After citing numerous authorities, both divine and human, in support of the foregoing argument, Vasquius[4] adds this statement:

Thus we also clearly perceive the questionable nature of the opinion held by certain authors already cited, namely, Johannes Faber, Angelus, Baldus and Franciscus Balbus. For these authorities believe that places which are common property under the law of nations can be acquired through custom, even if they cannot be acquired through prescription. This contention is altogether *false*; and the doctrine implicit therein is *vague, obscure, completely cut off from the light of reason* and aimed at the establishment of a law upon a foundation of words, not facts[c]. For examples relating to the seas of the Spaniards, *Portuguese*, Venetians, Genoese, and other peoples clearly indicate that such a right to navigate and to prohibit navigation by others, can no more be acquired through custom than it can through prescription. For obviously, the principles involved are the same in both cases[5,d]: the laws and arguments adduced above show that acquisition of this right would be

---

[a] l. libertas. ff. de statu. hom. §. libertas. Inst. de Iure pers. l. 1. et 2. ff. de homine lib. exh. l. I. §. quae onerandae. ff. Quarum rer. act. n. d. l. si quando. §. illud. verb. astringendos. C. de inoffic. test.: D. 1, 5, 4, Inst. 1, 3, 1, D. 43, 29, 1 and 2, D. 44, 5, 1, 5, C. 3, 28, 35, 1 at the word 'adstringendos' (allegations copied from Vasquius).

[b] L. necnon. §. quod eis. ff. ex quibus caus. ma. l. super statuas. C. de religiosis: D. 4, 6, 28, 2, C. 3, 44, 7 (these allegations, as those of note a, were copied from Vasquius, who places them as a separate reference after 'prohibita'; the fusion of notes a and b is probably a printing error, see ms. and Vasquius).

[c] Contra l. 2. cum vulgatis. C. comm. de leg.: against C. 6, 43, 2 with the usual commentaries (reference copied from Vasquius).

[d] l. illud. ff. ad l. Aquil.: D. 9, 2, 32 (allegation copied from Vasquius).

MARE

contra naturalem æquitatem, nec ullam induceret utilitatem, sed solam læsionem, sicque ut lege expressa introduci non possent, ita etiam nec lege tacita, qualis est consuetudo. Et tempore id non iustificaretur, sed potius deterius & iniurius indies fieret. Ostendit deinde ex prima terrarum occupatione posse populo ut venandi jus ita piscandi in suo flumine competere, & postquam illa semel ab antiqua communione separata sunt, ita ut particularem applicationem admittant, præscriptione temporis ejus, cujus initij memoria non extet, quasi tacita populi concessione acquiri posse. Hoc autem per præscriptionem contingere, non per consuetudinem, quia solius acquirentis conditio melior fiat, reliquorum vero deterior. Et cum tria enumerasset quæ requirūtur, ut jus propriū in flumine piscandi præscribatur: *Quid autem*, subdit, *quoad mare? Et in eo magis est quod etiam concursus istorum trium non sufficeret ad acquirendum ius. Ratio differentiæ inter mare ex una parte, & terrā & flumina ex altera, quia illo casu ut olim ita & hodie, & semper, tam quoad piscandum quam quoad navigandum mansit integrum ius gentium primævum, neque unquam fuit a communione hominum separatum, & alicui vel aliquibus applicatum. Posteriore autem casu, nempe in terra vel fluminibus aliud fuit, ut iam disseruimus. Sed quare ius gentium secunda-*

e. Erit autem lex 4. dist. l. 1. & 2. ff. de legib. L. de quib. cum seq. ff. de legib.
6. fin, depræscr.

Chapter VII

contrary to natural equity, and would produce no benefit but only injury, so that, just as such acquisition could not be expressly authorized by any precept of express law[a], it would likewise be impossible to authorize that same development on the basis of any tacit law, such as custom[b]; and furthermore, the said development would not be justified by the passage of time, but would on the contrary grow daily less valid and more unjust[1,c].

Vasquius then proceeds to demonstrate that, from the time when lands first began to be occupied, it was possible for a particular people to possess the right of fishing in their own streams just as they possessed the right of hunting [in their own territory]; and he also shows that, after these rights had once been separated from the ancient community of rights in such a way as to admit of their assignment to specific individuals, it was possible for them to be acquired by the said individuals through prescription based upon the lapse of time immemorial, as if through a tacit concession on the part of the nation. In addition, however, Vasquius stresses the point that such a result would be brought about through prescription and not through custom, inasmuch as only the status of the party making the acquisition is improved, while the status of the remaining parties is impaired. Again, after enumerating the three requisites for establishment by prescription of a private right over the fishing in a given stream, the same writer[2] adds:

And what shall we say in regard to the sea? In this connexion, indeed, the better opinion is that even the conjunction of the three requisites above mentioned would not suffice for the acquisition of such a right. The reason for the distinction made between the sea, on the one hand, and lands or streams, on the other hand, is this: in cases involving the sea, just as in earlier epochs, today and for all time the right conferred by the primary law of nations in regard both to fishing and to navigation remains intact, nor has it ever been separated from the community of men and attached to one or more specific individuals; whereas in cases coming under the latter head (that is to say, in those which relate to lands or streams), the course of events was different, as we have already explained. But why

[a] c. Erit autem lex 4. dist. l. 1. et 2. ff. de legib.: Decretum Grat. Dist. 4, 2; D. 1, 3, 1 and 2 (copied from Vasquius).
[b] L. de quib. cum seq. ff. de legib.: D. 1, 3, 32 ff. (this allegation, as those of note a, was copied from Vasquius, who places it as a separate reference after 'consuetudo'; the fusion of notes a and b is probably a printing error, see ms. and Vasquius).
[c] c. fin. de praescr.: Decretal. 2, 26, 20 (copied from Vasquius).

LIBERVM. 49

secundarium, ut eam separatione quoad terras & flumina facit, quoad mare facere desiit? responde, quia illo casu expediebat ita fieri: hoc autem casu non expediebat. Constat enim quod si multi venentur, aut piscentur in terra vel flumine, facile nemus feris, & flumen piscibus evacuatum redditur, id quod in mari non est. Item fluminum navigatio facile deterior sit & impeditur per ædificia, quod in mari non est. Item per aquæductus facile evacuatur flumen: non ita in mari. ergo in utroque non est par ratio. Nec ad rem pertinet quod supra diximus, communem esse usum aquarum, fontium etiam & fluminum. Nam intelligitur quoad bibendum & similia, quæ fluminis dominium aut ius habenti vel minime vel levissime nocent. Minima enim in consideratione non sunt. Pro nostris sententiis facit, quia iniqua nullo tempore præscribuntur. & ideo lex iniqua nullo tempore præscribitur, aut iustificatur. Mox: Et quæ sunt impræscriptibilia ex legis dispositione, nec per mille annos præscriberentur: quod innumeris doctorum testimoniis fulcit. Nemo jam non videt, ad usum rei communis intercipiendum nullam quantivis temporis usurpationem prodesse. Cui adjungendum est etiam eorum qui dissentiunt auctoritatem huic quæstioni non posse accommodari. Illi enim de Mediterraneo loquuntur, nos de Oceano: illi de sinu,

per tot. tit. ff. ne quid in flum. pub.

L. Scio. ff. de minor. Vasq. lib. 1. de succ. reso. c. 7.

all. Balbum de præscr. 5. q. pr. in q. 11. illi-us. s. quæst. pr. Gl. in c. inter cætera. 16. q. 3. Alphons. de Castr. de potest. leg. pæn. lib. 2. c. 14. Bal. in sine. & ibi Ang. in omnes. C. de præscr. 30. ann. & c.

D

Chapter VII

did[1] the secondary law of nations cease to produce, when the sea was involved, that separation[2] [of parts privately controlled] which it produced with respect to lands and streams? This question may be answered as follows: 'Because, in the case of lands or streams, it was expedient that the law should operate thus, whereas it was not expedient in regard to the sea'. For it is generally agreed that, if a great many persons hunt or fish upon some wooded tract of land or in some stream, that wood or stream will probably be emptied of wild animals or fish, an objection which is not applicable to the sea. Similarly, the erection of edifices may easily impede or prevent the navigation of streams[a], but not the navigation of the sea[3]. Yet again, it is quite likely that the presence of aqueducts will leave a stream drained of its waters, but no such possibility exists where the sea is concerned. Therefore, the same line of reasoning cannot be followed in the two kinds of cases. Moreover, our preceding statement to the effect that the use of waters (including even springs and streams) constitutes a common right, is not pertinent to the question under consideration, inasmuch as the said statement is understood to refer to drinking and similar acts, by which ownership of the stream or rights possessed over it are impaired very slightly or not at all. For we are not concerned with points of trifling significance[b]. Our opinion is furthermore confirmed by the fact that unjust claims are not validated by prescription, regardless of the lapse of time involved, and that, consequently, an unjust law does not result in prescription, nor is it justified, because of the passage of time[c].

A little farther on[4], Vasquius observes that 'those things which are imprescriptible will not become the objects of prescription in consequence of legal measures, nor on the basis of lapse of time even after the passage of a thousand years'. This observation is supported by the testimony of innumerable Doctores[d].

It will now be clear to every reader that usurpation, no matter how long continued, does not avail to intercept the use of a common thing. We must add[5] that the authority of those who dissent from this general conclusion cannot in any event be applied to the particular question under discussion. For the said dissenters are referring to a Mediterranean sea, whereas we are referring to the Ocean; they

---

[a] per tot. tit. ff. ne quid in flum. pub.: see D. 43, 13, whole title (reference copied from Vasquius).

[b] L. Scio. ff. de minor. Vasq. lib. 1. de suc. reso. c. 7.: D. 4, 1, 4. Vasquius, De successionum resolutione, lib. I, cap. 7, [= § 7], num. 34- 58, ed. p. 32-33 (both allegations copied from Vasquius; in his text the second one is preceded by 'dixi multa').

[c] all. Balbum de praescr. 5. q. pr. in q. II. illius 5. quaest[ionis] pr[incipalis]. Gl. in c. inter caetera. 16. q. 3. Alphons. de Castr. de potest. leg. poen. lib. 2. c. 14.: [Vasquius] refers to Balbus, De praescriptionibus, p. 497, Gloss on Decretum Grat., Causa 16, 3, 9, [and] Alphonsus de Castro, fol. p. 238 v (cf. above p. 44 note b).

[d] Bal. in fine. Et ibi Angelus in [l.] omnes. C. de praescr. 30. ann. etc.: Balbus at the end (ed. p. 496) and – there cited – Angelus de Ubaldis on C. 7, 39, 4, ed. fol. 195v-196r (allegations copied from Vasquius, num. 44, from which Grotius quotes the beginning, cf. above note 4; 'etc.' refers to other allegations following in Vasquius).

sinu, nos de immenso mari, quæ in ratione occupationis plurimum differunt. Et quibus illi indulgent præscriptionem, illi littora mari continua possident, ut Veneti & Ianuenses, quod de Lusitanis dici non posse modo patuit. Imo & si prodesse posset tempus, ut quidam posse putant in publicis quæ sunt populi, tamen non ea adsunt quæ necessario requiruntur. Primum enim docent omnes desiderari, ut is qui præscribit hujusmodi actum, *d. loc. n. 38.* eum exercuerit non longo duntaxat tempore, sed memoriam excedente: deinde ut tanto tempore eundem actum nemo alius exercuerit, nisi concessione illius, vel clandestine: præterea ut alios uti volentes prohibuerit, scientibus quidem & patientibus ijs ad quos ea res pertinebat: nam etsi exercuisset semper, & quosdam exercere volentes prohibuisset semper, non tamen omnes, quia alij fuerunt prohibiti; alij vero libere exercuerunt, id quidem non sufficeret, ex Doctorum sententia.[1] Apparet autem debere hæc omnia concurrere, tum quia præscriptioni publicarum rerum lex inimica est, tum ut videatur præscribens iure suo non autem communi usus, idque non interrupta possessione. Cum autem tempus postulatur, cujus initij non exstet memoria, non semper sufficit, ut optimi interpretes ostendunt, probare sæculi lapsum: sed constare[2]

Chapter VII

are discussing a mere gulf, whereas we are discussing a vast maritime tract, two concepts which differ very widely in so far as occupation is concerned. Moreover, the peoples to whom the right of prescription is conceded by such authorities (for example, to the Venetians and the Genoese) are the possessors of the shores bordering on the sea[1]; but the same cannot be said of the Portuguese, as we have just clearly demonstrated.

Indeed, even if (as some persons believe) the passage of time could avail to establish prescriptive rights over the public possessions of a given nation, certain necessary requisites would still be lacking in the present case. For, first of all, according to the doctrine universally upheld[a], anyone who claims prescription on the basis of such an act must have practised that act, not merely for a long period of time, but for a period stretching back beyond the limits of memory. A second requirement runs as follows: during all of this period, no other person shall have practised the said act, save by permission of the claimant, or else clandestinely. It is furthermore required that the claimant shall have prohibited all other persons who wished to use the possession in question, from so doing; and that he shall have issued this prohibition with the knowledge of and toleration by the parties concerned. For even if he had always practised the act in question and had always prohibited its practice by some, but not all, of the persons desirous of engaging in that activity, the requirements would still not be fulfilled (according to the opinion of the Doctores), since some individuals would have practised the act freely while others would have been forbidden to do so. Then, too, it is apparent that all of the conditions above mentioned must be satisfied concurrently, partly because the law is inclined to oppose the prescription of public things, and partly in order to make it clear that the claimant has exercised a right that is truly his own, not a common right, and that he has exercised it in virtue of uninterrupted possession. Furthermore, since one requirement is the lapse of a period extending back beyond the limits of memory, it does not always suffice (a point brought out by the leading interpreters of the laws[2]) to prove that a century has elapsed; rather,

---

[a] d. loc. n. 38: [This reference seems impossible in combination with 'doctrine universally upheld'. Hamaker simply omits it, Williams interprets it wrongly as 'Angelus de Ubaldis, On Institutes, II, 1, 38'; this was adopted by Armitage. It can, however, be very well understood by noticing that in the ms. 'docent omnes' is a correction for 'docet Vasquius'; it referred to no. 38 of Vasquius Controv. ill. c. 89 (cf. above, p. 44 note a), a paragraph omitted by Grotius in his long quotation from Vasquius (cf. above p. 48 note 1)].

constare oportet famam rei a majoribus ad nos transmissam, ita ut nemo supersit qui contrarium viderit, aut audierit. Occasione rerum Africanarum in ulteriora primum Oceani inquirere cœperunt regnante Iohanne Lusitani, anno salutis millesimo quadringentesimo septuagesimo septimo: viginti post annis sub Rege Emanuele promontorium Bonæ spei præternavigatum est, seriusque multo ventum Malaccam, & insulas remotiores, ad quas Batavi navigare cœperunt anno millesimo quingentesimo nonagesimo quinto, non dubie intra annum centesimum. Iam vero etiam eo quod intercessit tempore aliorum usurpatio adversus alios etiam omnes impedivit præscriptionem. Castellani ab anno millesimo quingentesimo decimo nono possessionem Lusitanis maris circa Moluccas ambiguam fecere. Galli etiam & Angli non clanculum, sed vi aperta eo perruperunt. Præterea accolæ totius tractus Africani aut Asiatici partem maris quisque sibi proximam piscando & navigando perpetuo usuparunt, nunquam a Lusitanis prohibiti. Conclusum igitur sit, jus nullum esse Lusitanis quo aliam quamvis gentem a navigatione Oceani ad Indos prohibeant.

Osorius lib. 1.

Chapter VII

it ought to be manifest that the fame of this thing was handed down to us from our forebears and of such sort that no surviving person has seen or heard any evidence conflicting with it.

It was in connexion with African affairs that the Portuguese first began to investigate the more remote regions of the Ocean during the reign of King John, in the year 1477. Twenty years later, after Emmanuel[a] had ascended the throne, they sailed beyond the Cape of Good Hope. Much later still, they came to Malacca and the more distant islands, whither the Dutch began to sail in 1595, certainly less than a century later. But already during that interval usurpation (of the maritime tract in question) by others against other parties had also created an impediment to prescription by any one of the parties involved. As early as the year 1519, Portuguese possession of the sea in the vicinity of the Moluccas was rendered doubtful by the Castilians. The French and the English also pushed their way into that part of the world, not clandestinely but by employing open force. Then, too, the inhabitants of all these regions, both in Africa and in Asia, continually usurped[1] the part of the sea nearest each of these peoples respectively by fishing and navigation; nor did the Portuguese at any time prohibit that practice.

Therefore, we must conclude that the Portuguese do not possess any right in virtue whereof they may forbid any other nation whatsoever to navigate the oceanic tract extending to the East Indies.

---

[a] **Osorius lib. 1**: Osorius, fol. 15 v.

Capvt VIII.
Iure gentium inter quosvis liberam esse mercaturam.

QVOD si dicant Lusitani cum Indis commercia exercendi jus quoddam proprium ad se pertinere, eisdem fere omnibus argumentis refellentur. Repetemus breviter & aptabimus. Iure Gentium hoc introductum est, ut cunctis hominibus inter se libera esset negotiandi facultas, quæ a nemine posset adimi. Et hoc, sicut post dominiorum distinctionem continuo necessarium fuit, ita originem videri potest antiquiorem habuisse. Subtiliter enim Aristoteles μεταβλητικὴν dixit ἀναπλήρωσιν τῆς κτ Φύσιν αὐταρκείας: hoc est, negotiatione suppleri id quod naturæ deest, quo commode omnibus sufficiat. Oportet igitur communem esse jure gentium, non tantum privative, sed & positive, ut dicunt magistri, sive affirmative. Quæ autem illo modo sunt juris gentium, mutari possunt: quę hoc modo, non possunt. Id ita intelligi potest. Dederat natura omnia omnibus. Sed cum a rerum multarum usu, quas vita desiderat humana, locorum intervallo homines arcerentur, quia, ut supra diximus, non omnia ubique proveniunt, opus fuit trajectione:

Vide c. 1. L. ex hoc iure. ff. de iust. & iure. & ibi Bart.

lib. 1. de republ. c. 9.

Vide Covar. in c. peccatū. §. 8.

Chapter VIII
That by the law of nations trade is free between whomsoever.

If the Portuguese maintain that they have a certain exclusive right to engage in trade with the (East) Indians, their contention will be refuted by practically all of the arguments already advanced. We shall repeat those arguments briefly, adapting them to this particular claim[a].

Under the law of nations, the following principle was established[b]: that all men should have the power to trade freely with one another, nor might they be deprived of that power by any person. Since the need for this principle existed as soon as distinctions of ownership had been drawn, it is clearly quite ancient in origin. For, as Aristotle[c] has acutely observed: μεταβλητικὴ ἀναπλήρωσις τῆς κατὰ φύσιν αὐταρκείας; in other words, barter supplies what nature lacks in order to meet properly the needs of all men. Therefore, according to the law of nations, the privilege of barter must be common to all, not only in a negative [i.e. non-exclusive] sense, but also positively (as the schoolmen say) or, to use another term, affirmatively[d]. Now, the negative dispositions of the law of nations are subject to change, whereas its affirmative dispositions are immutable.

This statement of the case may be clarified as follows. Nature had given all things to all men. Nevertheless, owing to the fact; that the distances separating different regions prevented men from using many of the goods desirable for human life (since not all things are produced in all localities, as we have pointed out in another context), passage to and fro was found to be a necessity.

---

[a] **Vide c. 1.**: See chapter I.
[b] **L. ex hoc iure. ff. de iust. et iure. et ibi Bart.**: D. 1, 1, 5 and the comment on this text by Bartolus in Dig. I, fol. 8 r (num. 8).
[c] **lib. 1. de republ. c. 9.**: [Aristoteles,] Politica I, 9 [3].
[d] **Vide Covar. in c. peccatum. §. 8.**: See Covarruvias in regulam Peccatum, ed. p. 493-499.

LIBERVM. 53

ctione: nec adhuc tamen permutatio erat, sed alijs vicissim rebus apud alios repertis suo arbitrio utebantur: quo fere modo apud Seres diciturrebus in solitudine relictis sola mutantium religione peragi commercium. Sed cum statim res mobiles monstrante necessitate, quæ modo explicata est, in jus proprium transijssent, inventa est permutatio, qua quod alteri deest ex eo quod alteri superest suppleretur. Ita commercia victus gratia inventa ex Homero Plinius probat. Postquam vero res etiam immobiles in dominos distingui cœperunt, sublata undique communio non inter homines locorum spatijs discretos tantum, verum etiam inter vicinos necessarium fecit commercium: quod ut facilius procederet, nummus postea adinventus est, dictus ἀπὸ τοῦ νόμου, quod institutum sit civile. Ipsa igitur ratio omnium contractuum universalis, ἡ μεταβλητικὴ, a natura est. modi autem aliquot singulares ipsumque pretium, ἡ χρηματιστικὴ, ab instituto: quæ vetustiores juris interpretes non satis distinxerunt. Fatentur tamen omnes proprietatem rerum, saltem mobilium a jure gentium primario prodire, itemque contractus omnes quibus pretium non accedit. Philosophi τῆς μεταβλητικῆς, quam translationem vertere licebit, genera statuunt duo: τὴν ἐμποριϰὴν καὶ

Pomponi. Mela. lib. 3. c. 5.

lib. 1. ff. de contrah. emt. lib. 33. c. 1.

d. l. 1.
Aristot. lib. 5. de Morib. c. 8. & lib. 1. de Rep. c. 9. c. Ius naturale. dist. 1. Arist. d. c. 9.
Castr. ex Cyno. & aliis in d. L. ex hoc iure. n. 20. & num. 28. Plato Sophista.

D 3 τὴν

Chapter VIII

Barter in the true sense was not practised as yet in that early epoch, but men followed their own judgement in using what they discovered in one another's territory, very much after the fashion in which commerce is said to be conducted among the Seres (Chinese? some Indians?), who leave their goods[1] in some lonely place and rely entirely upon the scrupulousness of the persons with whom the exchange is made[a]. But as soon as movables had passed into the domain of private property rights (under pressure of necessity, as we have just explained[b]), the process of barter was devised, in order that one person's lack might be remedied by means of another person's surplus[c]. Thus (as Pliny[d] shows, citing Homer) the practice of commerce was developed for the sake of the necessities of life. Moreover, after immovables also began to be divided among different owners, the general abolition of communal ownership made commerce necessary not only among men separated from one another by geographical distance but also among neighbours. Subsequently, with a view to facilitating this commercial activity, money was invented[e] and was given its [Latin] name, [*nummus*,] ἀπὸ τοῦ νόμου, 'from the Greek term νόμος[f] [custom *or* law]', because money was a civil institution.

We find, then, that the general principle underlying all contracts, ἡ μεταβλητική [the principle of exchange], is in itself derived from nature[2]; whereas various specific forms of exchange, and the actual payment of a price, ἡ χρηματιστική [the money-making process], are derived from institution [by law or tradition][g], a distinction which the older interpreters of the law have not made sufficiently clear. Nevertheless, it is universally agreed[h] that private ownership – in the case of movable possessions, at least – has its origin in the primary law of nations, and that the same is true of all contracts not involving the payment of a price.

The philosophers[i] distinguish between two kinds of μεταβλητική, a term which may be translated as 'exchange', namely: ἡ ἐμπορικὴ καὶ

---

[a] **Pompon. Mela. lib. 3.:** Pomponius Mela, III [7].

[b] **c. 5.:** [see] chapter 5. [This reference occurs only in the 1609 and 1618 editions; it is not found in later editions, nor in the ms.].

[c] **lib. 1.** [read 'l. 1' as the ms. has] **ff. de contrah. emt.:** D. 18, 1, 1 [pr.]. The printing error 'lib. 1' occurs in many later editions; it was corrected, however, in 18th century editions.

[d] **lib. 33. c. 1.:** [Plinius, Naturalis historia,] XXXIII, 1.

[e] **d. L. 1.:** D. 18, 1, 1 [pr.], cited above.

[f] **Aristot. lib. 5. de Morib. c. 8. et lib. 1. de Rep. c. 9.:** Aristoteles, Ethica Nicomachea, V, 8 [V, 5, 10], and Politica, I, 9 [I, 3, 15].

[g] **c. Ius naturale. dist. 1. Arist. d. c. 9.:** Decretum Grat., *Dist.* 1 [7]; Aristoteles, c. 9, cited above.

[h] **Castr. ex Cyno et aliis in d. L. ex hoc iure. n. 20. et num. 28.:** [Paulus] Castrensis in Dig. vet. citing Cynus and others on D. 1, 1, 5 (already cited), nos. 20 and 28, ed. fol. 6 v and 7 r.

[i] **Plato Sophista.:** Plato, Sophista [p. 223 D].

MARE

τὴν καπηλικήν: quarum ἐμπορική, quæ est ut vox ipsa indicat inter gentes dissitas, ordine naturæ prior est, & sic a Platone ponitur. Κα-πηλικὴ eadem videtur esse quæ παράστασις Aristoteli, tabernaria sive stataria negotiatio inter cives. Idem Aristoteles τὴν ἐμπορικὴν dividit in ναυκληρίαν & φορτηγίαν, quarum hæc terrestri itinere, illa maritimo merces devehit. Sordidior autem est καπηλική, contra honestior ἐμπορική, & maritima maxime, quia multa multis impertit. Vnde navium exercitionem ad summam rempublicam pertinere dicit Vlpianus: institorum non eundem esse usum: quia illa omnino secundum naturam necessaria est. Aristoteles: ἔστι γὰρ ἡ μεταβλητικὴ πάντων ἀρξαμένη, τὸ μὲν πρῶτον ἐκ τοῦ κατὰ φύσιν, τῷ τὰ μὲν πλείω, τὰ δὲ ἐλάττω τῶν ἱκανῶν ἔχειν τοὺς ἀνθρώπους. Est enim translatio rerum omnium cæpta ab initio, ab eo quod est secundum naturam, cum homines partim haberent plura quam sufficerent, partim etiam pauciora. Seneca: *quæ emeris vendere gentium ius est*. Commercandi igitur libertas ex jure est primario gentium, quod naturalem & perpetuam causam habet, ideoque tolli non potest, & si posset non tamen posset nisi omnium gentium consensu: tantum abest ut ullo modo gens aliqua gentes duas inter se contrahere volentes juste impediat.

CAPVT

Marginalia:
- Plato lib. de Rep. 2. qui locus citatur in L. 2. ff. de nundinis. Arist. lib. 1. de repub. c. 11.
- Cicero offic. 1. Arist. lib. 1. de rep. c. 9.
- d. loco.
- 1. de benef. c. 9.

Chapter VIII

ἡ καπηλική [wholesale commerce and retail trade]. Of these, the former - which is practised between widely separated nations, as the term itself indicates - takes precedence in the natural order, and is so ranked by Plato[a]. The latter form of exchange would seem to be identical with Aristotle's παράστασις, 'shopkeeping', or trade practised on a stationary basis among fellow citizens. That same author[b] makes a division of ἡ ἐμπορική [wholesale commerce] into ναυκληρία [ship-owning] and φορτηγία [hauling], referring in the latter case to merchandise transported by land and in the former case to merchandise transported overseas. Retail trade is of course a comparatively humble pursuit[c]; but wholesale commerce is more creditable, and especially so when maritime transportation is involved, since this phase of commerce enables many people to enjoy a share in many things. Herein lies[1] the reason for Ulpian's assertion[2] that the management of ships (*exercitio*) is a matter of the greatest public importance, whereas with [ordinary] business managers [buying and selling goods for somebody else, *institores*] it is different. In fact[3], the former pursuit is absolutely necessary according to nature's plan. Thus Aristotle[d] has said: ἔστι γὰρ ἡ μεταβλητικὴ πάντων ἀρξαμένη τὸ μὲν πρῶτον ἐκ τοῦ κατὰ φύσιν τῷ τὰ μὲν πλείω, τὰ δὲ ἐλάττω τῶν ἱκανῶν ἔχειν τοὺς ἀνθρώπους; 'For there exists in connexion with all things a process of exchange that originated in the first instance from the natural order, because men had more than enough of some things and less than enough of others'. Seneca[4,e], too, lays down this rule: 'The law of nations decrees that you may sell what you have bought'.

Freedom of trade, then, springs from the primary law of nations, which has a natural and permanent cause, so that it cannot be abrogated. Moreover, even if its abrogation were possible, such a result could be achieved only with the consent of all nations. Accordingly, it is not remotely conceivable that one nation may justly impose any hindrance whatsoever upon two other nations that wish to enter into a contract with each other[5].

---

[a] **Plato lib. de Rep. 2. qui locus citatur. in L. 2. ff. de nundinis.**: Plato, De Republica, II [11-12], which is cited in D. 50, 11, 2.
[b] **Arist. lib. 1. de repub. c. 11.**: Aristoteles, Politica, I, 11 [I, 3, 16].
[c] **Cicero offic. 1. Arist. lib. 1. de rep. c. 9.**: Cicero, De officiis, I [42, 150]; Aristoteles, Politica, I, 9 [I, 3, 12].
[d] **d. loco.**: [Aristoteles] cited above (note c).
[e] **1. de benef. c. 9.**: [Seneca], De beneficiis, I, 9 [4].

Caput IX.

Mercaturam cum Indis propriam non esse Lusitanorum titulo occupationis.

PRIMVM inventio aut occupatio hic locum non habet, quia jus mercandi non est aliquid corporale, quod possit apprehendi: neque prodesset Lusitanis etiamsi primi hominum cum Indis habuissent commercia, quod tamen non potest non esse falsissimum. Nam & cum initio populi in diversa iere, aliquos necesse est primos fuisse mercatores, quos tamen jus nullum acquisivisse certo est certius. Quare si Lusitanis jus aliquod competit, ut soli cum Indis negotientur, id exemplo cæterarum servitutum, ex concessione oriri debuit aut expressa aut tacita, hoc est præscriptione: neque aliter potest.

Vide argumenta. c. 2. & c. 5.

Caput X.

Mercaturam cum Indis propriam non esse Lusitanorum titulo donationis Pontificiæ.

CONCESSIT nemo: nisi forte Pontifex, qui non potuit. Nemo enim quod suum non est concedere potest. At Pontifex, nisi totius Mundi temporalis sit Dominus,

Vide arg. c. 3. & c. 6.

quod

Chapter IX

That trade with the Indians does not belong to the Portuguese by title of occupation.

In the first place, discovery or occupation cannot take place here[a], because the right to trade freely is not a corporeal object, susceptible of seizure. Nor would the Portuguese position be strengthened even if the Portuguese people had been the first to engage in trade with the (East) Indians, although such a claim on their part could be regarded only as an absolute falsehood. For, when in the very beginning different peoples proceeded in different directions, there must be some who were the first traders; yet it is certain beyond all possibility of doubt that those earliest traders did not thereby acquire any right.

Therefore, if the Portuguese do possess any right that gives them an exclusive privilege of trade with the (East) Indians, that right must have arisen, after the fashion of other servitudes, from an express grant, or from a tacit concession (that is to say, from prescription); for under no other circumstances could it exist.

Chapter X

That trade with the Indians does not belong to the Portuguese by title of Papal donation.

But no one made such an express grant, unless perchance Pope did so[b]; and he was not properly empowered to act thus. For there is no person who has the power to bestow by grant that which is not his own; and the Pope – unless he is the temporal master of the whole world,

---

[a] **Vide argumenta. c. 2. et c. 5.**: See the arguments used [above] in chapter 2 and chapter 5 (does not occur in the ms.).

[b] **Vide arg. c. 3. et c. 6.**: See the arguments used [above] in chapter 3 and chapter 6 (does not occur in the ms.).

quod negant sapientes, jus etiam commerciorum universale sui juris dicere non potest. Maxime vero cum res sit ad solum quæstum accommodata, nihilque ad spiritualem procurationem pertinens, extra quam cessat, ut fatentur omnes, Pontificia potestas. Præterea si Pontifex solis illud Lusitanis jus tribuere vellet idemque adimere hominibus cæteris, duplicem faceret injuriam: Primum Indis, quos ut extra Ecclesiam positos Pontifici nulla ex parte subditos esse diximus. His igitur cum nihil quod ipsorum est adimere possit Pontifex, etiam jus illud quod habent cum quibuslibet negotiandi adimere non potuit. Deinde alijs hominibus omnibus Christianis & non Christianis, quibus idem illud jus adimere non potuit sine causa, aut causa indicta. Quid quod ne temporales quidem Domini in suis imperijs prohibere possunt commerciorum libertatem, uti rationibus & auctoritatibus ante demonstratum est? Sicut & illud confitendum est, contra jus perpetuum naturæ gentiumque, unde ista libertas originem sumsit in omne tempus duratura, nullam valere Pontificis auctoritatem.[1]

CAPVT

---

[1] Between the end of chapter 10 and the beginning of chapter 11 the ms. has an addition, which was crossed out, probably when the ms. was prepared for publication: 'multoque minus per Pontificem auferri potuit Venetis ius cum Indis negotiandi, quod illis iam acquisitum erat, praecipue cum satis constet Veneticas ex India merces pro viliori pretio et incorruptiores quam Lusitanicas venisse. Neque vero credendum est unquam Pontifex hoc voluisse, quod ut maxime vellet facere nullo iure potuit'. In the margin there was a reference to 'Ioh. Met[ellus] in Praef. ad Osor'. Probably fol. 5v-6v of this praefatio was meant, where Metellus gives a summary of Pope Alexander's bull 'Inter cetera' of 4 May 1493; cf. E. Staedler, Hugo Grotius über die 'donatio Alexandri', at p. 268-271 (taken from the Osorius edition Coloniae 1586, fol. 5v-6v). See Introduction, notes 191 ff.

Chapter X

an assumption which wise men reject – cannot maintain that even the universal right of trade belongs to him. Especially because this right is a thing relating solely to material gain and has no bearing whatsoever upon spiritual administration outside of which (as is universally admitted) the papal power ceases. Furthermore, if the Pope wished to bestow the said right upon the Portuguese alone, while taking it away from all other men, he would be inflicting a twofold injury. First, he would be injuring the (East) Indians, who (as we have observed) are in no sense subject to the Pope, inasmuch as they were placed outside the Church. Thus the Pope has no power to deprive the latter people of anything that belongs to them; and therefore he cannot have had the power to take from them that right (which they do possess) to carry on trade with whomsoever they please. Secondly, the Pope would be injuring all other men, both Christians and non-Christians; for he has not been empowered to deprive those others of the right in question, without cause or notifying a cause. Indeed, how can such a papal claim be sustained, in view of the fact (which we have already demonstrated both on a logical basis and by citation of authorities) that not even temporal lords have the power to prohibit freedom of trade within their own domains? By the same token, it must also be acknowledged that no papal authority is effective against the eternal law of nature and of nations, the source of that very freedom which is destined to endure for all time[1].

Caput XI.

Mercaturam cum Indis non esse Lusitanorum propriam iure præscriptionis aut consuetudinis.

RESTAT præscriptio, seu consuetudinem mavis dicere. Sed nec hujus nec illius vim esse aliquam inter liberas nationes, aut diversarum gentium Principes, nec adversus ea quæ primigenio jure introducta sunt, cum Vasquio ostendimus. Quare & hic ut jus mercandi proprium fiat, quod proprietatis naturam non recipit, nullo tempore efficitur. Itaque nec titulus hic adfuisse potest, nec bona fides, quæ cum manifesto desinit, præscriptio secundum Canones non jus dicetur sed injuria. Quin & ipsa mercandi quasi possessio non ex iure proprio contigisse videtur, sed ex iure communi quod ad omnes æqualiter pertinet: sicut contra, quod aliæ nationes cum Indis contrahere forte neglexerunt, id non Lusitanorum gratia fecisse existimandi sunt, sed quia sibi ita expedire crediderunt: quod nihil obstat quo minus ubi suaserit utilitas, id facere possint, quod antea non fecerint. Certissima enim illa regula a doctoribus traditur, in his quæ sunt liberi ar-

Vide argumenta, c. 7.

glos. & Bart. in l. viam.

Chapter XI

That trade with the Indians does not belong to the Portuguese by right of prescription for custom.

There remains for consideration the question of prescription, or custom, if the reader prefers the latter term. But we have shown[a], in agreement with Vasquius, that neither custom nor prescription has any force in the relations between free nations or between the rulers of different peoples; and again, that these two factors are likewise without force when opposed to the principles introduced by the earliest form of law. Accordingly, in this connexion, too, we find that no lapse of time avails to make a private property of the right to trade, a right which is in itself incapable of assuming the character of private property. Consequently, in the case under discussion, neither a title nor good faith can have been present; and when these elements are clearly lacking[1], prescription will, according to the canonists, be regarded not as a right but as a wrong.

Furthermore, the very concept of quasi-possession of trade would seem to be based, not upon a private right, but upon a common right which pertains to all men alike; so that, conversely, it should not be supposed, merely because non-Portuguese peoples may have neglected to engage in commerce with the (East) Indians, that they refrained from so doing out of deference to the Portuguese, since one ought rather to assume that they considered the omission expedient for themselves. This attitude on their part will by no means prevent them from undertaking, at any time when such a course shall seem advantageous, the activity from which they previously abstained. In fact, the Doctores[b] have laid down an infallible rule regarding these matters which involve free judgement

---

[a] **Vide argumenta. c. 7.**: See the arguments in chapter 7 (does not occur in the ms.).

[b] **glos. et Bart. in l. viam.**: this is the beginning of a long marginal note which continues on p. 58 and is dealt with in note a of that page. The full stop after 'viam' is of course a printer's error; it has been maintained, however, in the 1618 and 1633 editions. I found it corrected for the first time in ed. 1667, followed by ed. 1689. The ed. 1712 changed 'L. viam publ.' into 'L. 2', which was taken over by the 1720, 1735 and 1773 editions.

58 MARE

publ. ff. de via publ.
Balb. in 4. par. 5. par. princ. qu. 1.
Panorm. in c. ex parte Astens. de concess. præben. Doct. in l. qui iure familiaritatis. ff. de acq. poss. & alleg. per Covar. in c. possessor. parte. 2. § 4. in 6. contr. usu freq. c. 4. n. 10. & 12. d. n. 12.

bitrii seu meræ facultatis, ita ut per se actum tantum facultatis ejus, non autem jus novum operentur, nec præscriptionis nec consuetudinis titulo annos etiam mille valituros: quod & affirmative & negative procedit, ut docet Vasquius. Nec enim quod libere feci facere cogor, nec quod non feci omittere. Alioquin quid esset absurdius quam ex eo quod singuli non possumus cum singulis semper contrahere, salvum nobis in posterum non esse jus cum illis, si usus tulerit, contrahendi? Idem Vasquius & illud rectissime, ne infinito quidem tempore effici, ut quid necessitate potius, quam sponte factum videatur. Probanda itaque Lusitanis foret coactio, quæ tamen ipsa cum hac in re juri naturæ sit contraria, & omni hominum generi no-

Vasq. de loco. n. 11.

xia, jus facere non potest. Deinde illa coactio durasse debuit per tempus, cujus initij non extet memoria: id vero tantum hinc abest, ut ne centum quidem anni exierint, ex quo tota fere negotiatio Indica penes Venetos fuit, per Alexandrinas tra-

Guicc. lib. 19. histor. Vide 5. c. 7. sub finem.

jectiones. Debuit etiam talis esse coactio, cui restitum non sit. At restiterunt Galli & Angli, aliique. Neque sufficit aliquos esse coactos, sed ut omnes coacti sint requiritur, cum per unum non coactum servetur

Chapter XI

or a simple optional faculty[a], to the effect that acts falling within this sphere represent merely the exercise of that power or faculty and do not constitute any new right, nor will the passage of so much as a thousand years avail in such cases to create a title based upon prescription or upon custom. This principle operates (as Vasquius[b] maintains) both affirmatively and negatively. For I am not compelled to continue doing what I have done voluntarily, nor am I compelled to refrain from doing that which hitherto I have voluntarily left undone. What could be more absurd than the conclusion which would necessarily follow upon any other line of reasoning, namely, that in consequence of our inability as individuals to enter at all times into contracts with other individuals, the right to conclude such contracts at some future time, if occasion should arise, will not be preserved to us? Moreover, that same Vasquius[c] quite rightly declares that not even the passage of immeasurable time will cause a given course of conduct to be regarded as compulsory rather than voluntary.

Therefore, in order to establish any claim of this kind, the Portuguese will have to prove that an element of coercion was involved. But coercion – since it would in the present case be contrary to the law of nature and injurious to mankind as a whole – could not of itself create the right claimed. It would also be necessary[d] for that coercion to have persisted throughout a period extending back beyond the limits of memory; and this is so far from being a fact, that not even a hundred years have passed since the time when almost the entire trade with the (East) Indies was in the hands of the Venetians, who conducted it by way of Alexandria[e]. Another requisite would be the absence of resistance to such coercion; but the French, the English, and others did resist it[f]. Neither will the requirements be met by the fact that some persons were coerced. On the contrary, all persons must have been subjected to the coercion, since by failure to coerce one man,

printer's error see Err.; it was, however, maintained in all 17th century editions and was only corrected in the 1712 and other 18th century editions. Magoffin simply omits this reference.

[e] **Guicc. lib. 19. histor.:** Guicciardinus, Historiae, lib. 19, ed. p. 689-724 (passage not found).

[f] **Vide 5. [read: 'Vide s[upra].'], c. 7. sub finem.:** See above chapter 7 at the end. For the printer's error cf. Err.; it was maintained in all 17th century editions and was only corrected in the 1712 and other 18th century editions. Magoffin simply omits the reference.

servetur in causa communi libertatis possessio. Arabes autem & Sinenses a sæculis
aliquot ad hunc usque diem perpetuo cum
Indis negotiantur. Nihil igitur prodest ista
usurpatio.

CAPVT XII.

Nulla æquitate niti Lusitanos in prohibendo commercio.

EX his quæ dicta sunt satis perspicitur eorum cęca aviditas, qui, ne quenquam
in partem lucri admittant, illis rationibus
conscientiam suam placare student, quas
ipsi magistri Hispanorum qui in eadem
sunt causa manifestę vanitatis convincunt.
Omnes enim qui in rebus Indicis usurpan-
tur colores injuste captari quantum ipsis licet, satis innuunt, adduntque nunquam
eam rem serio Theologorum examine pro-
batam. Illa vero querela quid est iniquius,
quod dicunt Lusitani quæstus suos exhauriri copia contra licentium? Inter certissima enim Iuris enuntiata est necin dolo eum
versari, nec fraudem facere, ne damnum
quidem alteri dare videri qui iure suo utitur: quod maxime verum est, si non ut alteri noceatur, sed rem suam augendi animo quippiam fiat. Inspici enim debet id
quod

Vasq. contr. illustr. c. 10. n. 10. Vict. p. 1. de Indis. rel. 1. n. 3.
l. sin autem. §. pen. de rei vind. l. nullus videtur. de Reg. iuris. l. illud constat. Quæ in fr. credit. l. fluminum. §. ult. de damno infecto. l. nemo damnum: de reg. iur. Bart. in. l. 1. n. 5. ff. de flum. Castr. in l. si tibi. C. de servit.

possession of freedom is maintained in a common cause. But the Arabs and the Chinese have traded continuously with the (East) Indians throughout several centuries, and are still trading with them at the present day. Consequently, the claim based upon usurpation is not valid.

Chapter XII

That the Portuguese cannot appeal to any equity in their prohibition of trade.

The foregoing comments reveal clearly enough the blind covetousness of those [the Portuguese] who, in an attempt to prevent admittance of any other person to a share of the gains, are striving to placate their consciences with arguments which exactly the learned authorities of the Spaniards – who are doing the same thing [as the Portuguese] – have convincingly demonstrated to be evidently vain[a]. For the said authorities intimate, that all of the pretexts advanced [by those people] in connexion with the Indian questions are – ad libitum – seized upon unjustly; and they add that the matter has never been seriously examined and approved by the theologians.

Indeed, what could be more unjust than the complaint of the Portuguese that their own profits are drained away by the multitude of persons bidding against them? For among the most incontrovertible principles of law[b] we find the following presumption: he who is availing himself of his own right is not engaged in deceitful wrongdoing, nor in contriving a fraud, nor even in the infliction of loss upon another. This presumption holds good particularly for cases wherein an act is committed, not for the purpose of causing harm to another person, but rather with the intention of advancing the interests of the agent himself[c]. For attention should be fixed

[116]

---

[a] Vasq. contr. illustr. c. 10. n. 10. Vict. p. 1. de Indis. rel. 1. n. 3.: Vasquius, Controv. I, p. 118; Victoria, De Indis, I, num. 3, ed. p. 221-222.

[b] l. sin autem. §. pen. de rei vind. l. nullus videtur. de Reg. iuris. l. illud constat. Quae in fr. credit. l. fluminum. §. ult. de damno infecto. l. nemo damnum. de reg. iur. Bart. in l. 1. [read 'l. 2'] n. 5. ff. de flum. Castr. in l. si tibi. C. de servit.: D. 6, 1, 27, 4; D. 50, 17, 55; D. 42, 8, 13; D. 39, 2, 24, 12; D. 50, 17, 151; Bartolus on D. 43, 12, 1, num. 5, ed. V, fol. 135 v; Paulus Castrensis on C. 3, 34, 10, ed. I, fol. 167 r. In the 1633 edition, followed by all later editions, these references are wrongly added to those mentioned in note a; the ms. clearly shows that they should be linked to 'certissima … iuris enunciata' (see above, note 1).

[c] See below, p. 60 note a.

MARE

l.1.§. denique de aq. & aq. plu.
Vide Vafq. contr. ufu fr.c.4.n.3. & feq.
l. Proculus de damno infecto.

quod principaliter agitur, non quod extrinsecus in consequentiam venit. Imo si proprie loquimur cum Vlpiano, non ille damnum dat, sed lucro quo adhuc alter utebatur eum prohibet. Naturale autem est & summo juri atque etiam æquitati conveniens, ut lucrum in medio positum suum quisque malit quam alterius, etiam qui ante perceperat.

Vafq.d.loco.

Quis ferat querentem opificem quod alter ejusdem artis exercitio ipsius commoda evertat? Batavorum autem causa eo est justior, quia ipsorum hac in parte utilitas cum totius humani generis utilitate conjuncta est, quam Lusitani eversum eunt.

ibidem. n.5.

Neque hoc recte dicetur ad æmulationem fieri, ut in re simili ostendit Vasquius: aut enim plane hoc negandum est, aut asseverandum non ad bonam modo, verum etiam ad optimam æmulationem fieri, iuxta Hesiodum, ἀγαθὴ δ᾽ ἔρις ἥδε βροτοῖσι, *Bona lis mortalibus hæc est*.[1] Nam etiam si quis pietate motus, inquit ille, frumentum in summa penuria vilius venderet, impediretur improba durities eorum hominum qui sæviente penuria suum carius fuerant venditurt. Verum est talibus modis minui aliorum reditus: nec id negamus, ait,[2] *sed minuuntur cum universorum hominum commodo: Et* VTINAM *omnium* PRINCIPVM *&* TYRAN-

---

[1] 'Hesiodum': Hamaker and Williams add the source of the quotation: Hesiodus, Opera et dies, vs. 24.
[2] 'ait': the following quotation from Vasquius is found in num. 5, cited below note e, ed. p. 54.

Chapter XII

upon the basic purpose of the act[a], not upon its extrinsic consequences[b]. As a matter of fact, according to the strict interpretation placed upon such cases by Ulpian[c], the agent does not inflict a loss, but merely prevents another person from continuing to enjoy a benefit which the latter was enjoying hitherto. Furthermore, it is natural, and compatible with the highest form of law as well as with the principle of equity, that every individual should prefer to have for himself a commonly accessible source of profit, rather than to see it in the hands of another, even when previously the profit may have been enjoyed by that other[d]. Who would have patience with any artisan given over to complaining that his profits are being cut off by another artisan's practice of the same craft? Yet the cause of the Dutch is more just than that of such a competitor, inasmuch as their own profit in this case is bound up with profit to the entire human race, a universal benefit which the Portuguese are attempting to destroy.

Nor can it fairly be said that the activities of the Dutch are motivated by the spirit of rivalry, a point also brought out by Vasquius[e] in connexion with a similar case. For such an assertion must be roundly denied, unless it is taken as referring to a kind of rivalry that is not merely good but even excellent in the highest degree: the kind described by Hesiod[1] when he declares that, ἀγαθὴ δ' ἔρις ἥδε βροτοῖσι, 'Such strife is wholesome for mankind'. For, Vasquius says, if any man, moved by compassion, should sell grain at a comparatively low price during a time of extreme scarcity, the shameless hard-heartedness of individuals who had intended to sell their own grain at a higher price than usual because of the cruel lack would be opposed. It is true that such charitable measures lessen the proceeds accruing to other persons. 'Nor do we deny this', Vasquius[2] adds, 'but the diminution of those proceeds is advantageous for the human race as a whole. *Would that* the profits accruing to all *the princes*

---

[a] l. 1. §. denique de aq. et aq. plu.: D. 39, 3, 1, 12 [not: 39, 3, 1, 23, as Hamaker and Williams have it]. In the 1633 edition, followed by all later editions, this reference, is wrongly added to those mentioned in notes a and b on p. 59; the ms. clearly shows that it should be linked to 'sed rem suam agendi animo quippiam fiat' (on p. 59, where apparently, there was no place left to put it, see p. 59 note 2).

[b] Vide Vasq. contr. usu fr. c. 4. n. 3. et seq.: Vasquius, Controv. II, p. 52 ff.

[c] l. Proculus de damno infecto.: D. 39, 2, 26.

[d] Vasq. d. loco.: Vasquius, cited above (note b).

[e] ibidem. n. 5.: [Vasquius] at the same place (above note b) num. 5, ed. p. 53-56.

LIBERVM. 61

*& * TYRANNORVM ORBIS *reditus ita minuerentur.* Quid ergo tam iniquum videri potest, quam Hispanos vectigalem habere Terrarum Orbem, ut nisi ad illorum nutum nec emere liceat nec vendere? In cunctis civitatibus dardanarios odio atque etiam pœnis prosequimur: nec ullum tam nefarium vitæ genus videtur quam ista annonæ flagellatio. Merito quidem. Naturæ enim faciunt injuriam, quæ in commune fæcunda est: neque vero censeri debet in usus paucorum reperta negotiatio, sed ut quod alteri deest alterius copia pensaretur, justo tamen compendio omnibus proposito qui laborem ac periculum transferendi in se suscipiunt. Hoc ipsum igitur quod in republica, id est minore hominum conventu, grave & perniciosum judicatur, in magna illa humani generis societate ferendum ne est? ut scilicet totius Mundi Monopolium faciant populi Hispani? [1] Invehitur Ambrosius in eos qui maria claudunt: Augustinus in eos qui itinera obstruunt: Nazianzenus in coemtores suppressoresque mercium, qui ex inopia aliorum soli quæstum faciunt, & ut ipse facundissime loquitur καταπραγματευόντων τῆς ἐνδείας. [2] Quin & divini sapientis sententia publicis diris devovetur, sacerque habetur, qui alimenta

l.1.C. de monop.

Caiet. ad sum.Thom.2. 2.q.77. ar.1. quod ad tertium. Arist. 1. de rep.c. 9.

5. Hex. c. 10. lib.4.q. 44. sup. Num. In sun, Basil.

---

[1] The passage beginning with 'Invehitur Ambrosius' and ending (on p. 62) with 'δημοκατάρατος' is a marginal addition in the ms., at fol. 116 v, copied from fol. 119 v., where it occurs in a part of the text of Djp that was crossed out when the ms. was being prepared for the publication of Ml; cf. Williams, p. 261 n. 1 (who does not specify, however, that it occurs on p. 265 of her translation) and van Ittersum, Preparing Mare liberum, p. 280 n. 95.

[2] 'divini sapientis sententia': a reference should have been added (as was done in the Dutch translation 1614, p. 79) to Proverbia, XI, 26, a Bible text implicitly cited by Gregorius of Nazianzum. It is clear that 'divini sapientis' does not refer to Gregory (as is suggested by the translations of Magoffin, Williams and some others) but to the author of Proverbia (Solomon); cf. the Italian translation 1933 ('La divina sapienza') and the Spanish translation ('por sentencia divina'). The ms. has 'divini Sapientis sententia' on fol. 116 v and 'divina sententia' on fol. 119 v (cf. above, note 1).

Chapter XII

and tyrants of this world might be lessened in like manner!'

What, then, can be so manifestly unjust as a situation in which the Spaniards would hold the entire world tributary, in such fashion that neither buying nor selling would be permissible save in accordance with their pleasure? In every state, hatred and even punishment are loosed upon speculators in grain[a]; nor is any other way of life held to be so abominable as this practice of whipping up the market-price of produce[b]. Assuredly, that hatred is justified. For such speculators are committing an offence against Nature, who is fruitful for all in common. Moreover, it is not to be supposed that the institution of trade was devised for the benefit of a few persons. On the contrary, it was established in order that one person's lack might be compensated by recourse to the abundance enjoyed by another[c], though not without a just profit for all individuals taking upon themselves the labour and peril involved in the process of transfer. Shall we say, then, that the above-mentioned practice, which is regarded as gravely pernicious when carried on within a single state (that is to say, within a comparatively small unit of humanity), should be tolerated within that great community made up of the human race, thus enabling the Spanish nations to establish a monopoly over the whole earth?

Ambrose[d] inveighs[1] against those who block entry to the seas; Augustine[e] against those who obstruct the highways; [Gregory of] Nazianzum[f] against those who buy up and keep back merchandise, who make profits for themselves alone out of the need of all others, and, as he himself puts it most eloquently, *καταπραγματεύονται τῆς ἐνδείας*, 'employing want as a means to an end'. Indeed, also in the opinion of the divine Wise Man [Solomon][2], that person is marked out for public execration and is held to be

---

[a] l. 1. C. de monop.: C. 4, 59, 1.
[b] **Caiet. ad sum. Thom. 2. 2. q. 77. ar. 1. quod ad tertium:** Caietanus in S. Thomam, III, p. 258.
[c] **Arist. 1. de rep. c. 9.:** Aristoteles, Politica, I, 9 [I, 3].
[d] **5. Hex. c. 10.:** [Ambrosius,] Hexaemeron, V, 10 (cf. also above, p. 25 note f).
[e] **lib. 4. q. 44. sup. Num.:** [Augustinus,] Quaestiones in Heptateuchum, IV, qu. 44 on Numeri [see above p. 3 note g.].
[f] **In fun. Basilii:** [Nazianzenus,] In Funus Basilii [Orationes XLIII, § 34].

62 MARE

menta supprimendo vexat annonam : ὁ συνέχων σῖτον δημοκαταάρατος. Clament igitur Lusitani quantum & quam diu libebit : lucra nostra dediscitis. Respondebunt Batavi : Imo nostris invigilamus. Hocne indignamini in partem nos venire ventorum & maris ? Et quis illa vobis lucra mansura promiserat ? Salvum est vobis, quo nos contenti sumus.

Capvt XIII.

Batavis ius commercij Jndicani qua pace, qua induciis, qua bello retinendum.

Qvare cum & jus & æquum postulet, libera nobis ita ut cuiquam esse Indiæ commercia, superest ut sive cum Hispanis pax, sive induciæ fiunt, sive bellum manet, omnino eam quam a natura habemus libertatem tueamur. Nam ad pacem quod attinet, notum est eam esse duûm generum: aut enim pari federe, aut impari coitur. Græci istam vocant συνθήκην ἐξ ἴσου: hanc σπονδὰς ἐξ ἐπιταγμάτων. illa virorum est, hæc ingeniorum servilium. Demosthenes in oratione de libertate Rhodiorum : καί τοι χρὴ τοὺς βουλομένους ἐλευθέρους εἶναι τὰς ἐκ τῶν ἐπιταγμάτων συνθήκας φεύγειν, ὡς ἐγγὺς δουλείας οὔσας ; *eos qui volunt esse liberi oportet omnes*

Thucydes Isocrat. Andocides.

[1]

---

[1] 'Demosthenes in oratione de libertate Rhodiorum': the quotation in Greek which the edition gives before the Latin translation is not from this work of Demosthenes but from Isocrates, Archidamos 51 (see note a). Magoffin saw the error and corrected it by adding in the Latin text the reference to Isocrates (which does not occur in the 1633 edition) and by commenting in his translation 'Grotius probably quoted here from memory'; this last remark was not taken over by his followers (Armitage, p. 57, as well as the Polish, Spanish and Italian (2007) translations) with the exception of the Korean translation, p. 128.

accursed, who forces up the market-price by holding back food supplies (ὁ συνέχων σῖτον δημοκατάρατος; who withholds grain is held to be accursed by the people). In short, let the Portuguese cry out, as loud and as long as they will: 'You are cutting off our profits!' The Dutch will answer: 'Not at all! We are looking out for our own profit! Are you indignant because we are acquiring a share in the winds and the sea? Besides, who promised that you would retain those profits of yours? You still possess unimpaired the same benefits with which we are content'.

CHAPTER XIII

That the Dutch are to maintain the right to carry on Indian trade by peace, by truce or by war.

Wherefore since both law and equity require that (East) Indian trade be as free to us as to anyone else, it follows that we are to maintain at all hazards that freedom which is ours by nature, either by coming to a peace agreement with the Spaniards, or by concluding a truce, or by continuing the war. So far as peace is concerned, it is well known that there are two kinds of peace, one made on terms of equality, the other on unequal terms. The Greeks[a] call the former kind συνθήκην ἐξ ἴσου, a compact between equals, the latter σπονδὰς ἐξ ἐπιταγμάτων, an enjoined truce; the former is meant for high souled men, the latter for servile spirits. Demosthenes in his speech on the liberty of the Rhodians says[1] that it was necessary for those who wished to be free to avoid all conditions whereon laws are imposed as those are almost the same as slavery.

---

[a] **Thucydes [read: Thucydides], Isocrat. Andocides.**: The printer's error was corrected in ed. 1633 (the ms. has 'Thucyd.'). – No specifications are given for the texts of the three authors mentioned. They can be reconstructed by means of passages in Djbap, II, 15, 6 (and II, 15, 5, 3), citing Thucydides, De bello Peloponnesiaco III, 75; Isocrates, Archidamos 51; Andocides, Orationes III, 4. These three references could also fit for the passage in Ml. As to Thucydides, there is another text, I, 44, which perhaps seems more relevant. For the error in mentioning Demosthenes instead of Isocrates in the text, see note 2; this error has been repeated in Djbap, II, 15, 6, as was discovered already by Jean Barbeyrac in the beginning of the 18th century, see footnotes in his 1720 and 1735 editions of Djbap (in which, however, he did not correct the error in the text of Mare liberum) cf. Djbap 1993, p. 393 n. 5: 'Error huc translatus ex Mari libero cap. 13' Cf. also Introduction, note 15.

LIBERVM. 63

tet omnes conditiones quibus leges imponuntur ita fugere tanquam quæ proximæ sunt servituti. Tales autem sunt omnes quibus pars altera in jure suo imminuitur, juxta Isocratis definitionem, προςάγματα vocantis ἃ τοῖς ἑτέροις ἐλαττοῦντα παρὰ τὸ δίκαιον. Si enim, ut inquit Cicero, suscipienda bella sunt ob *off. 1.* eam causam, ut sine injuria in pace vivatur, sequitur eodem auctore, pacem esse vocandam, non pactionem servitutis, sed tranquillam libertatem: quippe cum & Philosophorum & Theologorum complurium judicio pax & justitia nominibus magis quam re differant, sitque pax non qualiscunque, sed ordinata concordia. Induciæ autem si fiunt satis apparet ex ipsa induciarum natura non debere medio earum tempore conditionem cujusquam deteriorem fieri, cum ferme Interdicti uti possidetis instar obtineāt Quod si in bellum trudimur hostium iniquitate, debet nobis causæ æquitas spem ac fiduciam boni eventus addere. Nam ὑπὲρ μὲν ὧν ἂν *Demosthenes.* ἐλαττῶνται μέχρι δυνατοῦ πάντες πολεμοῦσι, περὶ δὲ τοῦ πλεονεκτεῖν οὐχ οὕτως: *pro his in quibus iniuria afficiuntur omnes quantum omnino possunt depugnant: at propter alieni cupiditatem non item.* quod & Alexander Imperator ita expressit: τὸ μὲν ἄρχειν ἀδίκων ἔργων οὐκ ἀγνώμονα ἔχει την πρόκλησιν, τὸ δὲ τοὺς ὀχλοῦντας

Polus Lucanus apud Stob. de iust. Clem. Alex. Strom. 4. August. 15. de civit.

---

[1] 'juxta Isocratis definitionem': [Isocrates, Panegyricus, 176; reference added to the Latin text by Magoffin].

[2] 'τοῖς ἑτέροις' is a printer's error for 'τοὺς ἑτέρους', see Err.

[3] 'Alexander Imperator': the emperor Alexander Severus (222-235) is meant; the quotation is from Herodianus, Historiae ab excessu Divi Marci libri octo, VI, 3, 4. This text is quoted by Grotius in Djp, ch. XIV, fol. 146 v (identified by Williams, p. 324), but without reference and in a different version.

Chapter XIII

Such conditions are all those by which one party is lessened in its own right, according to the definition of Isocrates who called προστάγματα τὰ τους ἑτέρους¹ ἐλαττῶντα παρὰ τὸ δικαιον². For if, as Cicero says[a], wars must be undertaken in order that people may live in peace unharmed, it follows that peace ought not to be called an agreement which entails slavery but an undisturbed liberty, especially as peace and justice according to the opinion of many philosophers and theologians[b] differ more in name than in fact, and as peace is not any agreement whatsoever but a well ordered regulation.

If however a truce is arranged for, it is quite clear from the very nature of a truce, that during its continuance no one's condition ought to change for the worse, because it takes effect more or less as an equivalent of the interdict *uti possidetis*.

But if we are driven into war by the injustice of our enemies, the justice of our cause ought to bring hope and confidence in a happy outcome. 'For', [as Demosthenes[c] has said,] 'every one fights his hardest for things wherein he is injured but for the greedy desire of that which is another's this is not so'. The Emperor Alexander has expressed his idea in this way³: 'To be the initiator of an unjust action is most spiteful,

---

[a] **off. 1.**: [Cicero,] De officiis, I [35].
[b] **Polus Lucanus apud Stob. de iust. Clem. Alex. Strom. 4. August. 15. de civit.**: Stobaeus, [Florilegium, IX, 54]; Clemens Alexandrinus, Stromata, IV [6]; Augustinus, De civitate Dei, XV [4].
[c] **Demostenes.**: Demosthenes, [De libertate Rhodiorum, XV, 10].

τας ἀπὸ σείεσθαι, ἔκτε τῆς ἀγαθῆς συνειδήσεως ἔχει τὸ θαρραλέον, κὶ ἐκ τοῦ μὴ ἀδικεῖν ἀλλ' ἀμύνασθαι, ὑπάρχει τὸ εὔελπι. Eius a quo cœpit iniuria provocatio maxime invidiosa est: at cum depelluntur aggressores, sicut bona conscientia fiduciam secum fert, ita quia de vindicanda non de inferenda iniuria laboratur, spes etiam adsunt optimæ. Si ita necesse est, perge gens mari invictissima, nec tuam tantum, sed humani generis libertatem audacter propugna;

Propertius lib. 4. eleg. 6.

> Nec te quod classis centenis remigat alis
> Terreat (INVITO labitur illa MARI.)
> Quodve vehunt proræ Centaurcia saxa minantes,
> Tigna cava & pictos experiare metus.
> Frangit & attollit vires in milite causa,
> Quæ nisi iusta subest excutit arma pudor.

Vide 5. c. 1. Si justa multi, & ipse Augustinus, arma crediderunt eo nomine suscipi, quod per terras alienas iter innoxium negaretur, quanto illa erunt justiora, quibus maris, quod naturæ lege commune est, usus communis & innoxius postulatur? Si juste oppugnatæ sunt gentes quæ in suo solo commercia alijs interdicebant, quid illæ quæ populos ad se nihil pertinentes per vim distinent, ac mutuos earum commeatus intercludunt? Si res ista in judicio agitaretur, dubitari non potest quæ a viro

Chapter XIII

but when agressors are repelled, not only good conscience creates confidence, but also, because we go about to revenge and[1] not to act in an unjust way, there is reason for highest hope'.

Therefore, if it be necessary, arise, O nation unconquered on the sea, and fight boldly, not only for your own liberty, but for that of the human race.

> Nor let it fright thee that their fleet is winged, each ship, with an hundred oars. The sea whereon it sails will have none of it. And though the prows bear figures threatening to cast rocks such as Centaurs[2] throw, thou shalt find them but hollow planks and painted terrors. 'Tis his cause that makes or mars a soldier's strength. If the cause be not just, shame strikes the weapon from his hands[a].

If many writers, Augustine himself[b] among them, believed it was right to take up arms because innocent passage was refused across foreign territory, how much more justly will arms be taken up against those from whom the demand is made of the common and innocent use of the sea, which by the law of nature is common to all? If those nations which interdicted others from trade on their own soil are justly attacked, what of those nations which separate by force and interrupt the mutual intercourse of peoples over whom they have no rights at all? If this case should be taken into court, there can be no doubt what opinion ought to be anticipated from a good man.

---

[a] **Propertius lib. 4. eleg. 6.**: Propertius, Elegia, IV, 6 [47-52].

[b] **Vide 5. c. 1. [read: 'Vide s[upra]., c. 1.']**: See above chapter 1 [p. 3 note g, where a reference to the text of Augustinus is given]. For the printer's error cf. Err.; it was maintained in all 17th and 18th century editions. Magoffin simply omits the reference.

viro bono expectari deberet sententia. ait Prætor : *Quo minus illi in flumine publico navem agere, ratem agere, quove minus per ripam exonerare liceat, vim fieri veto.* De mari & littore in eandem formam dandum interdictum docent interpretes, exemplo Labeonis, qui cum interdiceret Prætor : *Ne quid in flumine publico ripave eius facias, quo statio iterve navigio deterius sit, fiat :* simile dixit interdictum competere in mari: *Ne quid in mari inve littore facias, quo portus, statio, iterve navigio deterius sit, fiat.* Imo & post prohibitionem, si quis scilicet in mari navigare prohibitus sit, aut non permissus rem suam vendere, aut re sua uti, iniuriarum eo nomine competere actionem Ulpianus respondit. Theologi insuper & qui tractant casus, quos vocant, conscientiarum, concordes tradunt, eum qui alterum vendere aut emere impediat, utilitatemve propriam publicæ ac communi præponat, aut ullo modo alterum in eo quod est juris communis impediat, ad restitutionem teneri omnis damni viri boni arbitrio. Secundum hæc igitur Vir bonus judicans Batavis libertatem commerciorum adjudicaret, Lusitanos & cæteros qui eam libertatem impediunt vetaret vim facere, damna restituere juberet. Quod autem in judicio obtineretur, id ubi judicium haberi non potest, iu-

Chapter XIII

The Praetor says[1]: 'I forbid the use of force to prevent a boat or raft from sailing over a public stream, or to prevent the loading or unloading of such a vessel along the bank of that stream'[a]. The interpreters[b] of this prohibition, following the example set by Labeo, maintain that an interdict should be granted in a similar form with respect to the sea. For Labeo, in commenting upon the Praetor's edict 'Nothing shall be done in a public stream nor on the bank thereof, that may be detrimental either to the anchorage or to the transit of boats'[c], makes the observation that a similar interdict will lie when applied to the sea in these terms: 'Nothing shall be done in the sea nor on the seashore, that may be detrimental to the use of ports by boats or to anchorage or to the transit of boats'[d].

Furthermore, after the prohibition has been imposed, in cases where a given person has been forbidden to sail upon the sea, to sell his own property, or to make use thereof, Ulpian says that he can have recourse to an action for injuries[e]. Also the theologians and those who are dealing with cases of conscience (as they call them) agree[f] that he who prevents another from buying or selling, or who puts his private interests before the public and common interests, or who in any way hinders another in the use of something which is his by common right, is bound to make restitution of all the loss by the arbitration of a good man.

Following these principles an arbitrating good man would adjudge to the Dutch the freedom of trade, and would forbid the Portuguese and others from using force to hinder that freedom, and would order the payment of just damages. But that which in a judgement could be obtained, should, where a judgement cannot be given,

---

'L. iniuriarum', see ms.] actio. et l. si quis propr. ff. de iniur.: D. 43, 8, 2, 9; D. 47, 10, 13 [7] and D. 47, 10, 24.

f Silv. in verbo restitutio parte 3. sub finem, alleg. Gerar. Oldradum. et Archid. argum. l. 2. ff. ad l. Iuliam de annona et l. annonam. de extraord. crimin. et ibi glos.: Sylvester Prierias, verbo Restitutio, III, p. 368 [§ 11 in fine], referring to Gerardus [Othonis, a French theologian], Oldradus and Archidiaconus, and arguing from D. 48, 12, 2 and D. 47, 11, 6 and the [Accursian] gloss 'proventus' on that text.

De civ. lib. 4.
Off. 1.
Cassiod. 3.
Var. 1.17.

l. quamvis quod in littore. ff. de acq. rer. dom. Henric. Gorich. de bello iusto. prop. 9.

sto bello vindicatur. Augustinus: *Iniquitas partis adversæ iusta ingerit bella.* Et Cicero: *cum sint duo genera decertandi, unum per disceptationem, alterum per vim, confugiendum ad posterius si uti non licet priore.* Et Rex Theodoricus: *veniendum tunc ad arma, cum locum apud adversarium iustitia nõ potest reperire.* Et quod propius est nostro argumento, Pomponius cum qui rem omnibus communem cum incommodo cæterorum usurpet MANV PROHIBENDVM respondit. Theologi quoque tradunt sicuti pro rerum cujusque defensione bellũ recte suscipitur, ita non minus recte suscipi pro usu earum rerum quæ naturali jure debent esse communes, Quare ei qui itinera præcludat evectionemq; mercium impediat, etiam non expectata ulla publica auctoritate, via facti, ut loquũtur, posse occurri. Quæ cum ita sint, minime verendum est, ne aut Deus eorum conatus secundet, qui ab ipso institutum jus naturæ certissimum violant, aut homines ipsi eos multos patiantur, qui solo quæstus sui respectu communem humani generis utilitatem oppugnant.

FINIS.

Chapter XIII

be claimed by a just war. Augustine[a] acknowledges this when he says: 'The injustice of an adversary brings a just war'. Cicero also says[b]: 'There are two ways of settling a dispute; first, by discussion; second, by physical force; we must resort to force in case we may not avail ourselves of discussion'. And King Theodoric says[c]: 'Recourse must then be had to arms when justice can find no lodgment in an adversary's heart'. And – a statement which has more bearing on our argument – Pomponius has declared[d] that the man who seized a thing common to all to the prejudice of everyone else must be resisted by a strong hand. The theologians[e] also say that just as war is righteously undertaken in defense of individual property, so no less righteously is it undertaken in behalf of the use of those things which by natural law ought to be common property. Therefore he who closes up roads and hinders the export[1] of merchandise ought to be prevented from so doing by way of fact, as they say, even without waiting for any public authority.

Since these things are so, there need not be the slightest fear that God will prosper the efforts of those who violate that most undoubted law of nature which he himself has instituted, or that even men will allow those to go unpunished[2] who for the sake alone of private gain oppose themselves against the common benefit of mankind.

END

---

[a] **De civ. lib. 4.**: [Augustinus,] De civitate Dei, IV.

[b] **Off. 1.**: [Cicero,] De officiis, I [34].

[c] **Cassiod. 3. Var. 1. 17.**: Cassiodorus, Variarum libri XII, lib. III, cap. 1 [and] cap. 17, ed. p. 54 and 62. Cap. 1 has the passage quoted by Grotius; in cap. 17 a similar idea can be found. In chapter VIII of Djp Grotius quotes the same passage of Cassiodorus, also referring to '3. Var. 1. 17' (see ms. fol. 44 v, Hamaker, p. 97 (omitting '3') and Williams, p. 97. In the 1633 and later 17th century editions it was wrongly linked and mutilated (omission of 'Cassiod. 3' before 'Var. 1. 17'). This error was only corrected in the 1712 and later 18th century editions. Magoffin omits the whole reference.

[d] **l. quamvis quod in littore. ff. de acq. rer. dom.**: D. 41, 1, 50.

[e] **Henric. Gorich. de bello iusto. prop. 9.**: Henricus Gorcumensis, Tractatus de iusto bello, propositio 9, ed. fol. 56 r.

Cum sub hoc tempus plurima Regis Hispaniarum literæ in manus nostras venissent, quibus ipsius & Lusitanorum institutum manifeste detegitur, operæpretium visum est ex iis, quæ pleræque eodem erant argumento, binas in Latinum sermonem translatas exhibere.

DOMINE Martine Alphonse de Castro Prorex amice, ego Rex multam tibi salutem mitto. Cum hisce literis perveniet ad te exemplum typis impressum Edicti quod faciendum curavi, quo ob rationes quas expressas videbis, aliasque meis rebus conducentes prohibeo commercium omne externorum in ipsis partibus Indiæ aliisq; regionibus tramarinis. Quandoquidé res hæc est mométi atq; usus maximi, & quę effici summa cum industria debeat, impero tibi, ut simulatque literas has & edictum acceperis, publicationem eius omni diligentia procures in omnibus locis ac partibus istius imperii, idq; ipsum quod edicto continetur exequaris sine ullius personæ exceptione, cuiuscunque qualitatis ætatis conditionisve sit, citra omnem moram atq; excusationem, procedasq; ad impletioné mandati via meræ executionis, nullo admisso impedimento, appellatione, aut grauamine in contrarium: cuiuscunque materiæ generis aut qualitatis. Iubeo itaq; hoc ipsū impleri per eos ministros ad quos executio pertinet, iisque significari non modo eos qui contra fecerint malam operam mihi navaturos, sed eosdem me puniturum privatione officiorum in quibus mihi seruiunt. Quia autem relatum est mihi commorari in istis partibus externos multos variarum nationum

E 2   Italos,

[APPENDIX]

As several letters of the King of Spain have come of late into our hands, in which his design and that of the Portuguese is clearly disclosed, it seemed worthwhile to translate into Latin two of them (there were many of the same argument) and to append them here.

[LETTER I]

Don Martin Alphonse de Castro, our beloved viceroy, I, the King, send you many greetings.

Together with this letter will come to you a copy printed in type of an edict which I have taken much pains to draw up, by which, for reasons which you will see expressed, and for other reasons which are expedient for my affairs, I prohibit all commerce of foreigners in India itself, and in all other regions across the seas. As this matter is of the greatest importance and use, and ought to be carried out with the highest zeal, I command you, as soon as you shall have received this letter and edict, to further with all diligence its publication in all places and districts under your jurisdiction, and to carry out the provisions of the edict without exception of any person whatsoever, no matter what his quality, age, or condition, and without delay and excuse, and to proceed to the fulfilment of this command with the full power of your authority, no delay, appeal, or obstacle to the contrary, being admitted, of any kind, sort, or quality.

Therefore I order that this duty be discharged by those officers to whom its execution belongs, and that they be informed that not only will those who disobey serve me ill, but that I will punish them by depriving them of the offices in which they now serve me.

Further, inasmuch as it has been reported to me that within your jurisdiction there are sojourning many foreigners of different nations,

Italos, Gallos, Germanos, Belgas, quorũ pars maior, quãtum intelligimus, eo venit per Persida & Turcarũ imperium, non per hoc regnũ, adversus quos si ex huius Edicti præscripto ac rigore procedatur, posse inde nonnullas difficultates sequi, si illi ad Mauros inimicos perfugiant, vicinisq; munitionum mearũ dispositionem indicent, rationesque monstrent quæ rebus meis nocere possent, exsequi te hoc edictum volo prout res & tempus ferent, atq; ea uti prudentia qua illæ difficultates evitentur, curãdo ut omnes externos in potestate tua habeas eosque custodias pro cuiusque qualitate, ita ut adversus imperium nostrũ nihil valeant attentare, utq; ego omnino eum finem consequar quem hoc Edicto mihi proposui. Scriptæ Vlyssipone xxvIII. Novẽbris. anno cIɔIɔcvI. subsignatum erat, Rex. Inscriptio. Pro Rege. Ad Dominum Martinum Alfonsum de Castro consiliarium suum, & suum Proregem Indiæ.

Prorex amice Rex multam salutem tibi mitto. Etsi pro certo habeo tua præsentia iisq; viribus cum quibus in partes austrinas concessisti, perduelles Hollãdos, qui illic hærent, nec minus indigenas qui eis receptũ prębent, ita castigatos fore, ut nec hi nec illi tale quicquam in posterum audeant, expediet tamẽ, ad res tuendas, ut iustam classem eiq; operi idoneã, cum tu Goam redibis, in istis Maris partibus relinquas, eiusque imperium & summã præfecturã mandes Andreę Furtado Mendosæ, aut si quẽ ei muneri aptiorem iudicabis, quemadmodum pro tuo in me affectu confido, ea in re non aliud te respecturũ quã quod rebus meis erit utilissimum. Scriptæ Madritii xxvII. Ianu. cIɔIɔcvII. Signatũ Rex. Inscriptio. Pro Rege. Ad Dominum Martinum Alfonsum de Castro suum consiliarium & suum proregẽ Indiæ.

[Appendix]

Italians, French, Germans, and men of the Low Countries, the larger part of whom as we know came there by way of Persia and the Empire of the Turks, and not through our realm; and inasmuch as, if this edict be rigidly enforced against those persons to the letter, some inconveniences might follow, if they should escape to the Moors, our enemies, and make known to our neighbors the disposition of my forces, and thus show the means by which they might be able to harm my affairs; therefore I wish you to carry out the provisions of this edict as the matter and the time will permit, and to use all prudence necessary in order to avoid those difficulties, taking especial pains to keep all foreigners in your power, and to guard them in accordance with their quality, so that they may have no opportunity to attempt anything prejudicial to our Empire, that thus I may attain fully that end which I have set forth in this edict.

Given at Lisbon, on the 28th of November in the year 1606. Signed by the king, and addressed: For the king, to Don Martin Alphonso de Castro, his Councillor, and Viceroy of India.

[LETTER II]

Beloved viceroy, I, the King send you many greetings:
Although I consider it absolutely certain that by your presence and the forces which you took with you into the southern regions, our enemies, the Dutch, who remain there as well as the natives who give them a welcome reception, will be so thoroughly chastised that neither the one nor the other will ever dare such a thing in the future: still it will be expedient for the protection of our interests, that, when you shall return to Goa, you leave in those parts of the sea a convenient fleet, capable enough to do the business, and also that you delegate the supreme command and chief managing thereof to Andrea Furtado de Mendoza, or to any one else whom you shall consider better fitted for this post, as I trust for your affection towards me that in this matter you will do nothing but what will be most useful to my interests.

Given at Madrid the 27th day of January in the year 1607. Signed by the king, and addressed: For the king, to Don Martin Alfonso de Castro, his Councillor, and Viceroy for India.

ABBREVIATIONS USED FOR REFERENCES IN THE EDITOR'S INTRODUCTION, IN HIS NOTES AND HIS LIST OF SOURCES

Armitage: The Free Sea, Hugo Grotius, Translated by Richard Hakluyt with William Welwod's Critique and Grotius's Reply, edited and with an introduction by David Armitage, [Natural Law and Enlightenment Classics – Major Legal and Political Works of Hugo Grotius], Liberty Fund, Indianapolis [2004] (cf. also below at 'Hakluyt')

Beaufort: D. Beaufort, Alphonsus a Castro als bron voor Hugo de Groot's Mare liberum, in: Collectanea Franciscana Neerlandica uitgegeven bij het zevende eeuwfeest van Sint Franciscus, 1226-1926, 's Hertogenbosch 1927, p. 205-218

Bensly: Edward Bensly, review of the Magoffin edition/translation of Mare liberum in The English Historical Review, vol. 33, no. 129 (January 1918), p. 115-118

Blok: F. F. Blok, Contributions to the History of Isaac Vossius's Library [= Verhandelingen der Koninklijke Nederlandse Akademie van Wetenschappen, Afd. Letterkunde, Nieuwe reeks, 83], Amsterdam-London 1974

Borschberg (1994): Peter Borschberg, Hugo Grotius "Commentarius in Theses XI", an Early Treatise on Sovereignty, the Just War, and the Legitimacy of the Dutch Revolt, Berne etc. [1994], p. 47-101

Borschberg (2005): Peter Borschberg, Hugo Grotius' Theory of Trans-Oceanic Trade Regulation, Revisiting Mare Liberum (1609), in: Itinerario, vol. 29 (2005), number 3, p. 31-53

Boschan: Hugo Grotius, Von der Freiheit des Meeres, übersetzt und mit einer Einleitung, erklärenden Anmerkungen und Register versehen von Richard Boschan, [Der Philosophischen Bibliothek Band 97], Leipzig 1919

Briefwisseling: Briefwisseling van Hugo Grotius, ed. by P. C. Molhuysen et al., vol. I, [Rijks Geschiedkundige Publicatiën, Grote Serie, vol. 64], 's Gravenhage 1928, Nrs. 148, 149, 151-156, 159, 161, 164, 165

De Sat.: Hugo Grotius, Defensio fidei catholicae de satisfactione Christi adversus Faustum Socinum Senensem, edited with an introduction and notes by Edwin Rabbie [= Hugo Grotius, Opera theologica, edited by the Grotius Institute of the Royal Netherlands Academy of Arts and Sciences, vol. I], Assen-Maastricht 1990

Defensio: Hugonis Grotii Defensio Capitis quinti Maris liberi oppugnati a Guillielmo Welwodo [edited as an Annex in] S. Muller Fz., Mare clausum, Bijdrage tot de geschiedenis der rivaliteit van Engeland en Nederland in de zeventiende eeuw, Amsterdam 1872, p. 331-361

Djbap [or Djbap 1993]: Hugo Grotius, De iure belli ac pacis libri tres, curavit B.J.A. de Kanter - van Hettinga Tromp, Editionis anni 1939 … exemplar photomechanice iteratum, Annotationes novas addiderunt R. Feenstra et C. Persenaire adiuvante E. Arps - de Wilde, Aalen 1993 (now available at Kloof Booksellers & Scienta Verlag, Amsterdam; www.kloof.nl); cf. also **Feenstra, Djbap**

Djp: Hugonis Grotii de jure praedae commentarius, ex Auctoris Codice descripsit et vulgavit H. G. Hamaker, Hagae Comitum 1868 (also cited as 'Hamaker'). Sometimes the abbreviation Djp is also used to refer to the collotype reproduction of Grotius' manuscript (Leiden University Library, BPL 917; the original is cited as 'ms.'), published in 1950, see Introduction, note 63. For an English translation see **Williams**; a Dutch translation (without the marginal references) is mentioned in Introduction, note 61.

Djp o.p.: used in the List of Sources to indicate the 'other parts' (i.e. not the Mare liberum part) of Grotius' manuscript in giving the number of citations of a work mentioned in this List

Dovring (I and II): F. Dovring, Une partie de l'héritage littéraire de Grotius retrouvée en Suède, Mededelingen der Koninklijke Nederlandsche Akademie van Wetenschappen, Afd. Letterkunde, Nieuwe reeks, 12 (1949), p. 237-250, and id., Nouvelles recherches sur la bibliothèque de Grotius en Suède et en Italie, ibidem 14 (1951), p. 331-340

Dutch translation 1614: Vrije zeevaert ofte Bewys Van 't recht dat de In-gesetenen deser genieerde Landen toecomt over de Indische coophandel ten tweede mael oversien ende verbetert door den Auteur selffs tot vorderinge des Vaderlants. Tot Leyden, Bij Ian Hubertsz, Boeckvercooper, Anno 1614 [second issue, TMD 553; see for other issues Introduction, at note 66 ff., for another edition at note 71 and for other Dutch translations note 72]

Ed. 1609: Mare liberum sive de iure quod Batavis competit ad Indicana commercia dissertatio, Lugduni Batavorum, ex officina Ludovici Elzevirij, 1609. [TMD 541; for a counterfeit (TMD 542) see Introduction, at note 38 f.]

Ed. 1618: Hugonis Grotii Mare liberum sive de iure quod Batavis competit ad Indicana commercia dissertatio, Ultima editio, Lugduni Batavorum, ex officina Elzeviriana, 1618. [TMD 543; reprint: Hugo Grotius, Mare liberum … Neudruck der Ausgabe Leiden 1618; John Selden, Mare clausum … Neudruck der Ausgabe London 1635; Mit einer Einführung zu beiden Schriften von F. Krügel - Sprengel [Bibliotheca rerum militarium, Quellen und Darstellungen zur Militärwissenschaft und Militärgeschichte, 42], Biblio Verlag, Osnabrück 1978, see Introduction, at note 40 f.]

Ed. 1632: Hugonis Grotii Mare liberum … [title as in ed. 1618] … dissertatio, Ultima editio, Amsterdami, apud Iohannem Ianssonium, 1632 [TMD 544; see Introduction, at note 42]

Abbreviations Used for References in the Editor's Introduction, in his Notes and his List of Sources

Ed. 1633 I (308 p.): Hugo Grotius de Mari libero et P. Merula de Maribus, Lugd. Batavorum, ex officina Elzeviriana, 1633 [TMD 545; see Introduction, at note 46 f.]

Ed. 1633 II ([XV], 267 p.): Hugo Grotius de Mari libero et P. Merula de Maribus, Lugd. Batavorum, ex officina Elzeviriana, 1633 [TMD 546; see Introduction, at note 48]

Ed. 1633 III (Amsterdam): Hugonis Grotii Mare liberum sive de jure quod Batavis competit ad Indicana commercia dissertatio, Editio nova, prioribus longe emendatior, Amsterdami, apud Gulielmum Blaeuw 1633 [TMD 547; see Introduction, at note 43]

Ed. 1667: Hugo Grotius De mari libero [annex to: Hugonis Grotii De iure belli ac pacis libri tres ... Accesserunt Annotata in Epistolam Pauli ad Philemonem et Dissertatio de Mari libero, Amstelaedami, apud Ioannem Blaeu, 1667; TMD 579] (VI, 28, I, p.)

Ed. 1689: see description in TMD 585-586; cf. Introduction, note 54

Ed. 1712: see description in TMD 596-597; cf. Introduction, note 54

Ed. 1720: see description in TMD 601-603; cf. Introduction, note 54

Ed. 1735: see description in TMD 605-606; cf. Introduction, note 54

Ed. 1773: Hugonis Grotii Mare liberum ... [title as in ed. 1618] ... dissertatio [first part of annex to: Hugonis Grotii De iure belli ac pacis libri tres, cum adnotationibus selectis Ioann. Frid. Gronovii et auctioribus Ioannis Barbeyracii, Accedit H. Grotii Dissertatio de mari libero et Libellus singularis De aequitate, indulgentia et facilitate, Edidit atque praefatus est Meinardus Tydeman, [2 tom.], Trajecti ad Rhenum, ex officina Ioannis a Schoonhoven et Soc., 1773; TMD 611] (p. 1-30 [p. 31-43 = Libellus ... De aequitate])

English translation ca. 1615, see **Hakluyt**

English translation 1916, see **Magoffin**

English translation (of Djp, ch. XII), see **Williams**

English translation (of Ml, ch. V), see **Wright**

Err.: Errata, see above fol. 6 verso of the edition of the text

Eysinga, see **Van Eysinga**

Feenstra, Djbap: Feenstra, Introduction to Annotationes novae in **Djbap 1993**

Feenstra 1978: R. Feenstra, Hugo de Groot's eerste beschouwingen over dominium en over de oorsprong van de private eigendom: Mare liberum en zijn bronnen, in: Acta Juridica 1976 [published in 1978 = Essays in honour of Ben Beinart, I], p. 269-282

Feenstra 1992-1996: R. Feenstra, Ius commune et droit comparé chez Grotius, Nouvelles remarques sur les sources citées dans ses ouvrages juridiques, à propos d'une réimpression du De iure belli ac pacis, in: Rivista internazionale di diritto comune, 3 (1992), p. 7-36); reprinted in R. Feenstra, Legal Scholarship and Doctrines of Private Law, 13th-18th Centuries, [Variorum Collected Studies Series, CS 556], Aldershot 1996, as nr. VI

Feenstra 1996-2005: R. Feenstra, Les origines du 'dominium' d'après Grotius et notamment dans son 'Mare liberum', in: Homenaje al profesor Alfonso García Gallo, I, Madrid 1996, p. 179-190; reprinted in R. Feenstra, Histoire du droit savant (13e-18e siècle), Doctrines et vulgarisation par incunables, [Variorum Collected Studies Series, CS 842], Aldershot 2005, as nr. III

French translation, see **Guichon de Grandpont**

German translation, see **Boschan**

Guichon de Grandpont: Dissertation de Grotius sur la liberté des mers, traduite du latin, avec une préface et des notes, par A. Guichon de Grandpont, avocat, in Annales maritimes et coloniales, 30e Année, 3e Série, tome I, 1845, p. 653-717; for a reprint, published in 1990 under a wrong title see Introduction, notes 75 and 76

Hakluyt: 'Mare liberum / The Free Sea, Translated into English by Mr Rich. Hakluyt etc.' [London, Inner Temple Library, ms. Petyt 529, text published as 'The Free Sea, Hugo Grotius' by David Armitage. For the full title see above at 'Armitage'. The abbreviation 'Hakluyt' serves for references to the text; for the annotation and commentary the abbreviation 'Armitage' is used]

Hamaker, see **Djp**

Inv.: Inventory of Grotius' library compiled on 25 March 1620, see **Molhuysen**

Italian translation 1933: Dissertazione sulla libertà del mare o del diritto che hanno gli Olandesi al commercio con le Indie (prima traduzione italiana), Introduzione del Prof. Manfredi Siotto Pintor, Traduzione e note del Dott. Francesco Carfì, Firenze [1933] [cf. Introduction, note 91]

Italian translation 2007: Ugo Grozio, Mare liberum, a cura di Francesca Izzo, [Quaderni del Dipartimento di Filosofia e Politica, Università di Napoli "L'Orientale"], [Napoli 2007] [this publication also includes an edition of the Latin text, taken over from the Magoffin edition, see Introduction, at notes 27 f.]

Ittersum, see **Van Ittersum**

Magoffin: The Freedom of the Seas or the Right which Belongs to the Dutch to Take Part in the East Indian Trade, a Dissertation by Hugo Grotius, translated with a revision of the Latin text of 1633 by Ralph Van Deman Magoffin, edited with an introductory note by James Brown Scott, [Carnegie Endowment for International Peace, Division of International Law], New York [etc.] 1916. NB. The page

Abbreviations Used for References in the Editor's Introduction, in his Notes and his List of Sources

numbers XIV-XV and 1-79 are used twice: for the left pages (Latin text) and the right pages (English translation). For the two different issues of the book see Introduction, notes 84 ff.; references are to the second issue.

Meijers: E. M. Meijers, Boeken uit de bibliotheek van De Groot in de Universiteitsbibliotheek te Leiden, in: Mededelingen der Nederlandsche Akademie van Wetenschappen, Afd. Letterkunde, Nieuwe reeks, 12 (1949), p. 251-279

Mem. 1607: [Memorandum in Latin, written by Grotius for the government of the United Provinces in 1607, edited by] W. J. M. van Eysinga, Eene onuitgegeven nota van De Groot, in: Mededelingen der Nederlandsche Akademie van Wetenschappen, Afd. Letterkunde, Nieuwe reeks, 18 (1955), p. 235-252, reprinted in his Sparsa collecta, Leiden 1958, p. 488-504

Ml.: Mare liberum

Ms.: Manuscript Leiden University Library, BPL 917, cf. **Djp**. References to the ms. can be checked by using the indications of the pages in the margin of my edition of the English translation

Molhuysen: P. C. Molhuysen, De bibliotheek van Hugo de Groot in 1618, in: Mededeelingen der Nederlandsche Akademie van Wetenschappen, Afd. Letterkunde, Nieuwe reeks, 6 (1943), p. 45-63

Nellen: H. Nellen, Hugo de Groot, Een strijd om de vrede, 1583-1645, Amsterdam 2007

Rabbie: E. Rabbie, The History and Reconstruction of Hugo Grotius' Library, a Survey of the Results of Former Studies with an Indication of New Lines of Approach, in: Bibliothecae selectae da Cusano a Leopardi, ed. E. Canone, Firenze 1993, p. 119-137

Spanish translation: Hugo Grocio, De la libertad de los mares, Prólogo de Luis García Arias, Traducción de V. Blanco García y L. García Arias, Madrid 1979 (first edition 1956 with a slightly different title, see Introduction, note 94)

Staedler: E. Staedler, Hugo Grotius über die donatio Alexandri von 1493 und der Metellus-Bericht, in: Zeitschrift für Völkerrecht, 25 (1941), p. 257-274

STCN: Short-title Catalogue, Netherlands (on-line); see Introduction, note 36

Straumann: Benjamin Straumann, Is Modern Liberty Ancient? Roman Remedies and Natural Rights in Hugo Grotius' Early Works on Natural Law, in: Law and History Review, 27 (2009), p. 55-85 (previous version under the title 'Natural rights and Roman Law in Hugo Grotius' Theses LVI, De iure praedae and Defensio capitis quinti maris liberi, in: Grotiana, 26-28 (2005-2007), p. 341-365)

TMD: J. ter Meulen and P. J. J. Diermanse, Bibliographie des écrits imprimés de Grotius, La Haye 1950 (reprint Zutphen 1995)

Van Eysinga, see **Mem. 1607**

Van Ittersum, Dating the Manuscript: M. J. van Ittersum, Dating the Manuscript of De Jure Praedae (1604-1608): What Watermarks, Foliation and Quire Divisions Can Tell Us about Hugo Grotius' Development as a Natural Rights and Natural Law Theorist, in: History of European Ideas, 35 (2009), p. 125-193

Van Ittersum, Mare Liberum in the West Indies?: M. J. van Ittersum, Mare Liberum in the West Indies? Hugo Grotius and the Case of the Swimming Lion, a Dutch Pirate in the Caribbean at the Turn of the Seventeenth Century, in: Itinerario, 31 (2007), no. 3, p. 59-94

Van Ittersum, Preparing Mare Liberum: M. J. van Ittersum, Preparing Mare Liberum for the Press: Hugo Grotius' Rewriting of Chapter 12 of De Jure Praedae in November-December 1608, in: Grotiana 26-28 (2005-2007) [published in one volume in 2008], p. 246-280

Van Ittersum, The Wise Man: M. J. van Ittersum, The Wise Man is Never Merely a Private Citizen: the Roman Stoa in Hugo Grotius' De Jure Praedae (contribution to a conference 'Cosmopolitan Politics: on the History of a Controversial Ideal' (Frankfurt am Main, December 2006) [still forthcoming? See Introduction, note 105])

Williams: De iure praedae commentarius by Hugo Grotius, [The Classics of International Law, 22], vol. I: A Translation of the Original Manuscript of 1604, by Gwladys L. Williams with the collaboration of Walter H. Zeydel, Oxford-London 1950 (reprints New York 1964 and 1995). For a new edition in 2006 by Martine Julia van Ittersum see Introduction, note 64

Wright: Herbert F. Wright, Some Less Known Works of Hugo Grotius, [first part: 'The Works of Hugo Grotius on Fisheries in his Controversy with William Welwood', nr. 1: 'Chapter V of the Mare Miberum'], in: Bibliotheca Visseriana Dissertationum ius internationale illustrantium, tom. VII (Lugduni Batavorum 1928), p. 131-238, at p. 137-153). Cf. Introduction, note 78

Title page of the 1633 Amsterdam edition, published by Blaeuw.

LIST OF SOURCES

For the purpose and character of this List of Sources, I refer in general to sections 6–10 of my Introduction (above, p. LI-LXIV) and particularly to sections 8, 9 and 10 (above p. LV - LXIV). The system I have followed in indicating references to pages of the *editio princeps* (and of the English translation) is basically that of the 'List of Sources' in the 1993 edition of *De iure belli ac pacis*. This applies particularly to the markers *bis*, *ter* etc., which are used not only when there is more than one note containing a reference to the source, but also when a note contains two consecutive references to passages that are not connected. If the name of the author or source occurs in the text (that is, not simply in a note) I put the page number in italics.

For abbreviations used see above, p. 161-163 (Abbreviations Used for References in the Editor's Introduction, his Notes and his List of Sources). The sigla in capitals after each title of a source refer to the libraries where I have found a copy. It concerns:

KB	Koninklijke Bibliotheek, Den Haag
MPI	Max-Planck-Institut für europäische Rechtsgeschichte, Frankfurt am Main
UBL	Universiteitsbibliotheek, Leiden
UBLM	Universiteitsbibliotheek Leiden, Meijers Collection
UBM	Universiteitsbibliotheek, Maastricht
UBN	Universiteitsbibliotheek, Nijmegen
VP	Bibliotheek van het Vredespaleis, Den Haag

Accursius: see Gl. [= Glosa] in CJCiv.
Alciatus, Consilia: Andreas Alciatus, Responsa, libris novem digesta, Basileae 1582. UBL.
    4 ('Alci.' printer's error for 'Alex.', see editor's note on p. 4)
Alexander Imolensis, see **Alexander Tartagnus**
Alexander Tartagnus, Consilia: Alexander [Tartagnus] Imolensis, Consiliorum prima secunda, tertia, quarta, quinta, sexta, septima] pars, cum annotationibus Caroli Molinaei, 7 tom., Lugduni 1549. UBL. – Cf. Inv. 13 (?), Djbap (2)
    4
Alphonsus de Castro: Alfonsus a Castro. De potestate legis poenalis libri duo, Salmanticae 1550 (Repr. Madrid 1961. MPI). – See Introduction, section 9, at note 161. Cf. Inv. 321 and Djbap (bis); De sat. (1) [cf. p. 61, 134 and 358]
    44, 49
Alvarotus, see **Jacobus Alvarotus**
Andreas de Isernia, Super feudis: Andreas de Isernia, Super feudis, [Lugduni] 1532. UBL. – See Introduction, section 10, note 185
    28
Angelus Aretinus in Inst.: Angelus a Gambilionibus Aretinus, In quatuor Institutionum libros commentaria, Venetiis 1570. UBLM. – See Introduction, section 10, at note 180. Cf. Inv. 95 and Djbap (1)
    42, 50 (in editor's note)
Angelus de Ubaldis, Consilia: Angelus de Ubaldis Perusinus, Consilia, Francofurti 1575.
UBLM. – Cf. Inv. 8 and Djbap (1). – On the author see Introduction, section 10, at note 180
    39, *40*, *41* (bis), *44*, *47*
Angelus de Ubaldis in Cod.: Angelus Ubaldus, In Codicem commentaria, Venetiis 1579. UBLM. – Cf. Inv. 8, Djbap (1) and Djp o.p. (1)
    49
Angelus de Ubaldis in Dig.: Angelus Ubaldus, In I atque II Digesti novi partem et in tit. de Interdictis commentaria, Venetiis 1579. UBLM. – Cf. Inv. 8
    27
Archidiaconus [= Guido de Baysio]: second hand reference without specification. – Canonist, died 1313.
    65
Aretinus, see **Angelus Aretinus**
Auth. [= Authenticum], see Introduction, section 8
Ayala: Balthazar Ayala, De iure et officiis bellicis et disciplina militari libri III, Antverpiae 1597. KB. – See Introduction, section 9, note 147. Cf. Djbap (6), Djp o.p. (14) and Mem. 1607 (3)
    9, *10*
Balbus, De praescr.: Ioannes Franciscus Balbus Taurinensis, Tractatus de praescriptionibus, Eiusdem repetitio l. Celsus, D. de usucapionibus, Coloniae Agrippinae 1590. UBL. – See Introduction, section 10, at note 198
    28, *40*, 41, 42, *47*, 49 (bis, cf. editor's note), 58
Baldus: mentioned in text without specification
    47
Baldus, Consilia: Baldus Ubaldus, Consiliorum sive responsorum volumen primum [secundum, tertium, quartum,

quintum], 5 tom., Venetiis 1575 [Reprint Torino 1970]. UBL. – Cf. Djbap (5) and Djp o.p. (4)

3

Baldus in Dig.: Baldus Ubaldus, In primam [secundam] Digesti veteris partem, in primam et secundam Infortiati partem [et] in Digestum novum commentaria, 3 tom., Venetiis 1568. UBLM. – Cf. Djbap (10) and Djp o.p. (2)

26, 36

Baldus in Feud.: Baldus de Perusio, Super feudis, [Lugduni], 1545. UBLM. – Cf. Djbap (1), Djp o.p. (5) and Mem. 1607 (1)

27

Bartolus in Cod.: Bartolus de Saxoferrato, Commentaria in primam [in secundam atque tertiam] Codicis partem, [Commentariorum] tomus septimus [octavus], Venetiis 1596. UBLM. – Cf. Inv. 100, Djbap (2) and Djp o.p. (1)

4, 10

Bartolus in Dig.: Bartolus a Saxoferrato, Commentaria in primam [secundam] Digesti veteris, in primam [secundam] Infortiati, in primam [secundam] Digesti novi partem, [Commentariorum] tomus primus [secundus, tertius, quartus, quintus, sextus], Venetiis 1596. UBLM. – Cf. Inv. 100, Djbap (23) and Djp o.p. (31)

40, 46, 52, [57-]58, 59

Baysio, see **Guido de Baysio**

Bernardus Clarevallensis, De consideratione ad Eugenium: Bernardus Clarevallensis, De consideratione ad Eugenium, in his Opera omnia, Parisiis 1602. KB. – Probably Grotius has taken over the reference from Victoria and not seen an edition

9

C. [= Codex Justinianus], see Introduction, section 8

Caietanus in S. Thomam: Thomas de Vio Caietanus, Commentaria [in Summam S. Thomae Aquinatis universam sacram theologiam complectentem], in **Thomas Aquinas, Summa** – Cf. Djbap (23) and Djp o.p. (14)

9, 11-12 (full quotation), 61

Canonistae [= Interpreters of the Canon Law, after the **Gl. in CJCan.**]

9, 10, 35

Cassiodorus, Variarum libri XII: Aurelii Cassiodori Variarum libri XII, in his [Opera], Parisiis 1589, p. 1-283. UBL. – Cf. below at 'Theodoricus'

66

Castrensis, see **Paulus Castrensis**

Castro, see **Alphonsus de Castro**

Celsus (Roman jurist), see Introduction, section 8, note 139

22, 23, 26

Cinus, see **Cynus**

Clem. [= Clementinae], see Introduction, section 8

14

Codex Justinianus, see Introduction, section 8

Connanus, Commentaria iuris civilis: Franciscus Connanus, Commentaria iuris civilis, 2 tom., Lutetiae 1553. KB. – Cf. Inv. 70, Djbap (10) and Djp o.p. (1)

5, 20

Corpus iuris canonici, see Introduction, section 8

Corpus iuris civilis, see Introduction, section 8

Covarruvias in reg. Peccatum: Didacus Covarruvias, Regulae Peccatum, de regulis iuris, libro Sexto, relectio, in his Opera, tom. I, Antverpiae 1610, p. 462-518. KB. – Cf. Djbap (30) and Djp o.p. (15)

3, 4, 6, 9 (ter), 10, 52

Covarruvias in reg. Possessor malae fidei: Didacus Covarruvias, Relectio regulae Possessor malae fidei, de regulis iuris, libro VI, in his Opera, tom. I, Antverpiae 1610, p. 400-461. KB. – Cf. Djbap (4)

42 (bis), 50, 58

Cujacius, Commentaria in Pandectarum titulos: Iacobus Cuiacius, Commentaria in Pandectarum titulos, in his Opera, Francofurti 1623, tom. II, col. 103-376. KB. – Cf. Inv. 60

40

Cujacius, Observationes: Iacobus Cuiacius, Observationum et emendationum libri XXVIII, in his Opera, Francofurti 1623, tom. IV. KB. – Cf. Inv. 60, Djbap (6) and Djp o.p. (4)

25

Cynus [cited by Paulus Castrensis on D. 1, 1, 5], see Introduction, section 9, note 157

53

D. [= Digesta (Justiniani)], cited by Grotius with the medieval abbreviation 'ff.', see Introduction, section 8

Dd. [= Doctores, see below]

Decretal. [= Decretales (Gregorii IX), also called Extra or Liber Extra]: see Introduction, section 8

35, 43, 48, 57

Decretum Grat. [= Decretum Gratiani], see Introduction, section 8
   3, 10, 14, 48, 49, 53
Doctores [mainly on Corpus iuris civilis], see Introduction, section 8, note 141, and section 10, at the end
   26, *31*, *35*, *50*, 57, 58
Doctores Hispani, see Introduction, section 10, at the end
   5, 13
Donellus, Commentaria de iure civili: Hugo Donellus, Commentaria de iure civili viginti octo, 5 tom., Francofurti 1596 [1595-1597]. KB. – Cf. Djbap (1) and Djp o.p. (2)
   5, 21, 22, 25, 38, 40
Duarenus in Dig.: Franciscus Duarenus, In Digesta seu Pandectas et Codicem commentarii,
in his Omnia quae quidem hactenus edita fuerunt opera, Francofurti 1607, p. 1-1222. UBL. – Cf. Djbap (1) and Djp o.p. (3). I was unable to check the references in the ed. Lugduni 1578, mentioned Djbap, p. 1042
   18, 40
Extra, see **Decretal.**
Extravag. Joan. XXII [= Extravagantes Johannis XXII], see Introduction, section 8
   16
Faber, see **Johannes Faber**
Fachinaeus, Controv.: Andreas Fachineus, Controversiarum iuris libri decem, [two parts], Coloniae Agrippinae 1604. MPI. – See Introduction, section 10, at note 202
   42 (bis)
Felinus Sandeus: Felinus Sandeus, Commentariorum in Decretalium libros V pars prima [secunda, tertia], 3 tom., Basileae 1567. KB. – Cf. Djbap (5) and Djp o.p. (1)
   40
Feud. [= Libri Feudorum], see Introduction, section 8
   27
Ff., see **D.** [= Digesta (Justiniani)]
Gentilis, De iure belli: Albericus Gentilis, De iure belli libri III, Hanoviae 1612. [Reprint in The Classics of International Law, no. 16, 1933]. UBL. – I have also consulted – in VP – the first edition of this work, Hanoviae 1598 (the only one Grotius could have seen); the difference between the two editions is minimal as far as lib. I, cap. 19 is concerned. See Introduction, section 10, at notes 206 ff. Cf. Djbap (15), Djp o.p. (7) and Mem. 1607 (2)

2, 35, 43; cf. also 3 (in editor's note)
Gentilis, De iure belli (Italian translation): Alberico Gentili, Il diritto di guerra (De iure belli libri III, 1598), Introduzione di Diego Quaglioni, Traduzione di Pietro Nencini, Apparato critico a cura di Giuliano Machetto e Christian Zendri, Milano 2008. VP
   3, 39 (both in editor's note)
Gerardus [Othonis]: second hand reference without specification. – French theologian, died 1336
   65
Gl. [= Glosa] **in CJCan.:** Gloss on Corpus juris canonici (Decretal., Decretum Grat. and Sextus), see Introduction, section 8, at the end, and section 10, at note 208
   35 (bis), 49
Gl. [= Glosa] **in CJCiv.:** Gloss of Accursius on Corpus juris civilis (Digesta), see Introduction, section 8, at note 141 and section 10, at note 208
   14, 26, 36, 40, *42* (Accursius), 43, 58, 65 (bis); cf. also 40 (in editor's note)
Gorcumensis, see **Henricus Gorcumensis**
Gratianus, see **Decretum Grat.**
Guicciardinus: Franciscus Guicciardinus, Historiarum sui temporis libri viginti, ex italico in latinum sermonem conversi, Basileae 1566. KB. – Cf. Inv. 199 [!] and Djbap (14)
   58 (passage not found)
Guido de Baysio, see **Archidiaconus**
Henricus Gorcumensis: Henricus de Gorychum, Tractatus de iusto bello, in his Tractatus consultatorii, [Coloniae 1503], fol. 50 r – [57] v. KB. – Cf. Djbap (1) and Djp o.p. (3)
   66
Hermogenianus (Roman jurist), see Introduction, section 8, note 139
   17
Hugo [Pisanus], see **Huguccio**
Huguccio [Hugo Pisanus], **Summa decretorum:** reference taken over from Victoria, original text only available in ms. – Canonist, died 1210
   9
Innocentius IV ad Decretal.: Innocentius IV papa, Apparatus super primo, secundo, tertio, quarto et quinto Decretalium libris, [Lugduni 1520]. UBLM (copy now lost). – Cf. Inv. 94, Djbap (9) and Djp o.p. (23)
   9, 10

Inst. [= Institutiones (Justiniani)], see Introduction, section 8

Isernia, see **Andreas de Isernia**

Jacobus Alvarotus, Super feudis: Jacobus Alvarotus, Super feudis, [Lugduni] 1530. UBL. – See Introduction, section 10, at note 184
28

Jason de Maino in Dig.: Jason Maynus, In primam [secundam] Digesti veteris partem commentaria, In primam [secundam] Infortiati partem commentaria, In primam [secundam] Digesti novi partem commentaria, 6 tom., Venetiis 1598. UBLM. – See Introduction, section 9, note 147. Cf. Inv. 97, Djbap (6) and Djp o.p. (20)
46

Johannes [Bassianus]: mentioned in text without specification. – See Introduction, section 10, at note 167
40

Johannes Faber, In Institutiones: Ioannes Faber, In Institutiones Iustinianeas commentarii autographo collati, Lugduni 1565. UBL. – See Introduction, section 10, at note 177. Cf. Djp o.p. (3)
26, 31, 47

Johannes de Turrecremata: Ioan. de Turrecremata, Summa de Ecclesia, Venetiis 1561. UBN. – Probably Grotius has taken over the reference from Victoria and not seen an edition. Spanish canonist and theologian, died 1468. Cf. Djp o.p. (2)
9

Justinianus, see Introduction, section 8

Labeo (Roman jurist), see Introduction, section 8, note 139
65

Leges Hispanicae, see **Siete Partidas**

Liber Extra, see **Decretal.**

Libri Feudorum, see **Feud.**

Liber Sextus, see **Sextus**

Marcianus (Roman jurist), see Introduction, section 8, note 139
24 (bis), 39, 40

Maynus, see **Jason de Maino**

Menchaca, see **Vasquius**

Metellus, Praefatio ad Osorium: Johannes Metellus, praefatio ad Osorium, see below at **Osorius**
10, 12, 56 (all three in editor's notes)

Neratius (Roman jurist), see Introduction, section 8, note 139
20

Nov. [= Novellae Justiniani], see Introduction, section 8

Nov. Leonis [= Novellae Leonis], see Introduction, section 8
25 (quater)

Oldradus: second hand reference without specification. – Italian civilist, died 1335 (or later?). Cf. Djbap, where his Consilia are cited
65

Osorius: Hieronymus Osorius Lusitanus, De rebus Emmanuelis Lusitaniae Regis virtute et auspicio annis sex ac viginti domi forisque gestis libri duodecim, item Io. Matalii Metelli in eosdem libros praefatio et commentarius, Coloniae 1586. KB. – See Introduction, section 10, at notes 192 ff. Cf. Djbap (2) (from ed. in Opera omnia, Romae 1592); cf. also Djp o.p. (3)
8, 51; cf. also above at **Metellus**

Panormitanus in Decretal. III: Nicolai Tudeschii vulgo Abbatis Panormitani Commentaria in tertium Decretalium librum, Venetiis 1588. UBM. – Cf. Inv. 102 and Djbap (where another ed. is cited for 15 passages from the five books of the Decretales, not including the passage cited in Ml), Djp o.p. (23) and Mem. 1607 (1)
58

Papinianus (Roman jurist), see Introduction, section 8, note 139
39, 40, 41

Paulus (Roman jurist), see Introduction, section 8, note 139
24 (bis), 42, 43

Paulus Castrensis in Cod.: Paulus Castrensis, In primam [secundam] Codicis partem commentaria, Venetiis 1582. UBLM. – Cf. Inv. 92 [!] and Djbap (1)
59

Paulus Castrensis in Dig. nov.: Paulus Castrensis, In primam [secundam] Digesti novi partem commentaria, Venetiis 1582. UBLM. – Cf. Inv. 92
40 (bis)

Paulus Castrensis in Dig. vet.: Paulus Castrensis, In primam [secundam] Digesti veteris partem commentaria, Venetiis 1582. UBLM. – Cf. Inv. 92, Djbap (5) and Djp o.p. (7)
14, 53

Placentinus: mentioned in text without specification. See Introduction, section 10, at notes 165 ff.
26

Pomponius (Roman jurist), see Introduction, section 8, note 139
22, 26

Prierias, see **Sylvester Prierias**

Sandeus, see **Felinus Sandeus**

Scaevola (Roman jurist), see Introduction, section 8, note 139
22

Scholastici, see Introduction, section 10, at note 210
  14, 21

Sextus [= Liber Sextus Decretalium], see Introduction, section 8
  14, 35 (bis), 39

Siete Partidas: Las Siete Partidas del rey Alonso el nono, glosadas por Gregorio Lopez, 7 tom., Salamanca 1555. MPI. – See Introduction, section 10, at notes 169 ff. Cf. Djbap (5)
  36 (bis), *41*

Sigonius: Carolus Sigonius, De regno Italiae quinque reliqui libri, Venetiis 1591. [not seen]. – Identification borrowed from Gentilis, De iure belli (Italian translation)
  3

Silvester Prierias, see **Sylvester Prierias**

Suarez, see **Zuarius**

Sylvester Prierias: Sylvestrinae Summae pars prima [secunda], 2 tom., Antverpiae 1569. KB. – Cf. also Djbap and Djp on other entries
  verbo **Infidelitas.** Not in Djbap
    9
  verbo **Papa.** Cf. Djbap (1)
    37
  verbo **Restitutio.** Cf. Djbap (3) and Djp o.p. (6)
    65

Tartagnus, see **Alexander Tartagnus**

Theodoricus [Rex –], Constitutions transmitted by **Cassiodorus** (see above)
  66

Thomas Aquinas, Summa: S. Thomas Aquinas, Summa universam sacram theologiam complectens, in tres partes divisa, cum commentariis Thomae de Vio Caietani, 4 tom., [I: Prima pars; II: Prima Secundae partis; III: Secunda Secundae partis; IV: Tertia pars], Lugduni 1581. KB. – See Introduction, section 9, note 157. Cf. Inv. 258. Cf. also Djbap (30) and Djp o.p. (50)
  6, 9 (bis), *10*, 11, 16; see also 11 (in editor's note)

Turrecremata, see **Johannes de Turrecremata**

Ubaldis, see **Angelus de Ubaldis** and **Baldus** [de Ubaldis]

Ulpianus (Roman jurist), see Introduction, section 8, note 139
  19, 23, 25, 27, 36, 43, 54, 60, 65

Vasquez, see **Vasquius**

Vasquius, Controv. I: Fernandus Vasquius Menchacensis, Illustrium controversiarum aliarumque usu frequentium pars prima, tres priores libros continens, [Genevae] 1599. UBL. – See Introduction, section 9, at notes 157 and 161. Cf. Djbap o.p. (circa 50) and Mem. 1607 (2)
  7, 9, 10, 38, 42, *43,* 44-49 (full quotations in text, cf. also editor's notes), *57,* 59; cf. also 50 (in editor's note)

Vasquius, Controv. II: Fernandus Vasquius, Controversiarum usu frequentium secunda pars, tres posteriores libros continens, [Genevae] 1599. UBL. – Cf. Djbap (3) and Djp o.p. (3)
  14, *58* (ter), *60* (ter)

Vasquius, De successionum resolutione: Fernandus Vasquius Menchacensis, De successionum resolutione [= Tractatus de successionibus, Augustae Senorum 1624, tom. III]. UBL. – Cf. Djbap (3: other part of Tractatus)
  49

Victoria, De Indis: Franciscus de Victoria, De Indis et de iure belli relectiones, edited by E. Nys [The Classics of International Law], Washington 1917, p. 217-268 [= the critical edition by H.F. Wright of De Indis relectio]. This edition, which I have sometimes cited as 'the Wright-edition', is based on the first edition of *De Indis*, Lugduni 1557, and some other editions. It should be noted that the Wright-edition (as the ed. Ingolstadt 1580 and subsequent edd.) is divided into three sections whereas the ed. Lugduni 1557 and the ed. Salamanca 1565 are divided into two sections. Section I in the two early edd. has subsequently been divided into two sections in the later edd. Thereby I, 25-40 was reconstituted as II, 1-16, while the former section II became section III. In *Mare liberum* Grotius usually cites the earlier numbering, probably from the 1557 edition, cf. Introduction, section 9, at note 149. – Cf. Djbap (14) and Djp o.p. (4)
  3, *7,* 8, *9* (sexies), 10, 12, 13, 37, 59; cf. also editor's notes at p. 6 and 7

Victoria, De potestate civili: Franciscus a Victoria, Relectio de potestate civili, in his Relectiones tredecim in duos tomos distributae, Ingolstadii 1580, p. 119-147. MPI. – Cf. Djbap (2) (from ed. Lugduni 1557) and Djp o.p. (3)
  6

Zuarius, Consilia: Rodericus Zuarius, Consilia duo de usu maris et navibus transvehendis, in Tractatus de mercatura seu mercatore Benvenuti Stracchae, Coloniae Agrippinae 1595, p. 850-868. MPI – See Introduction, section 10, at notes 172 ff. Cf. Djbap (other ed., 1)
  36, 41; cf. also 26, 27, 35 (in editor's notes)

H. GROTI
VRYE ZEEVAERT,
Ofte
BEWYS
Van het Recht dat de Inghesetenen deser vereenighde Nederlanden toekomt / over den Oost ende West-Indische Koop-handel.

Nu uyt den Latijne op een nieuw vertaeld door A. Iekerman.

Ghedruckt te HAERLEM,

By Adriaen Roman, Boeck-drucker woonende inde Groote Hout-straet inde verguide Parsse. 1641.

Title page of *Vrije Zeevaert*, the second Dutch translation of *Mare liberum* by A. Iekerman, second edition published in 1641 by Roman in Haarlem. The first edition appeared in Haarlem in 1639.

INDEX OF SOURCES NOT MENTIONED IN THE LIST

Numbers in red refer to the upper pagination of the English translation and the Latin text, in particular to the editor's notes on these pages.

1 ROMAN AND CANON LAW SOURCES
See Introduction, section 8

a. Corpus iuris civilis

Codex

C. 3, 28, 35, 1   47
C. 3, 34, 10   59 (Castrensis on –)
C. 3, 44, 7   47
C. 4, 59, 1   61
C. 4, 63, 4 [3]   3
C. 6, 43, 2   47
C. 7, 39, 4   49 (Angelus on –)
C. 8, 11 (12), 6   39
C. 8, 40 (41), 13   5
C. 11, 13 (12), 1   27
C. 11, 43 (42), 4   40
C. 11, 43 (42), 9   39, 40

Digesta

D. 1, 1, 5   14 (Gloss and Castrensis on –), 17, 45, 52 (also Bartolus on –)
D. 1, 3, 1 and 2   48
D. 1, 3, 32 ff   48
D. 1, 5, 4   47
D. 1, 8, 1   20
D. 1, 8, 2   20, 26 (Gloss and Baldus on –)
D. 1, 8, 4   3, 22, 24, 35
D. 1, 8, 5, 1   22
D. 1, 8, 10   20 (bis), 22
D. 4, 1, 4   49
D. 4, 6, 28, 2   47
D. 5, 1, 9   26
D. 6, 1, 27, 4   59
D. 7, 5   16
D. 8, 4, 4   27
D. 8, 4, 13   19, 27
D. 9, 2, 32   47
D. 14, 1, 1, 20   54 (note 2)
D. 14, 2, 9   26 (Doctores on –)

D. 18, 1, 1   53 (bis)
D. 18, 1, 6   38
D. 23, 5, 16   39
D. 30, 11   46 (also Bartolus and Jason on –)
D. 39, 2, 24 [pr.]   22
D. 39, 2, 24, 12   59
D. 39, 2, 26   60
D. 39, 3, 1, 12   60
D. 39, 4, 15   26
D. 41, 1, 3   6
D. 41, 1, 14   20 (bis), 22, 40, 44
D. 41, 1, 50   20, 22 (bis), 66
D. 41, 2, 3, 3   6
D. 41, 2, 41   58 (Doctores on –)
D. 41, 3, 4, 27   46
D. 41, 3, 9   38
D. 41, 3, 25   39
D. 41, 3, 45   20, 25, 39, 40 (Cujacius on –), 41, 44
D. 42, 8, 13   59
D. 43, 8, 2 pr   22
D. 43, 8, 2, 8   22
D. 43, 8, 2, 9   36, 65
D. 43, 8, 2, 10   22
D. 43, 8, 2, 16   22
D. 43, 8, 3   20, 22 (bis), 26 (also Gloss on –)
D. 43, 8, 4   20, 22
D. 43, 9, [1]   28
D. 43, 11, 2   39, 58 (Gloss and Bartolus on –)
D. 43, 12, 1 [pr.]   65
D. 43, 12, 1, 17   23, 65
D. 43, 12, 2   59 (Bartolus on –)
D. 43, 13   49
D. 43, 14, 1   36 (Gloss on –), 65
D. 43, 20, 3, 4   40
D. 43, 29, 1 and 2   47
D. 44, 3, 7   24, 40, 44-45
D. 44, 5, 1, 5   47

171

Index of Sources Not Mentioned in the List

D. 47, 10, 13, 7   20, 25 (bis), 28, 43 (also Gloss on –), 65
D. 47, 10, 14   24, 27 (Angelus on –), 42 (Gloss on –), 44
D. 47, 10, 24   65
D. 47, 11, 6   65 (also Gloss on –)
D. 48, 12, 2   65
D. 50, 11, 2   54
D. 50, 16, 28   39
D. 50, 17, 55   59
D. 50, 17, 151   59

Institutiones

Inst. 1, 2, 1 and 2   45
Inst. 1, 3, 1   47
Inst. 2, 1, 1   2, 20, 26 (Gloss on –)
Inst. 2, 1, 2   44
Inst. 2, 1, 5   20, 22, 26 (Johannes Faber on –), 50 (see editor's note 1)
Inst. 2, 1, 13   5
Inst. 2, 1, 40   8
Inst. 4, 6, 14   46

Novellae (Authenticum)

Nov. 134, 1 [= Authenticum 9, 17, 1]   43

Novellae Leonis

Nov. Leonis 56   25
Nov. Leonis 57   25 (see editor's note)
Nov. Leonis 102, 103, 104   25

Libri Feudorum

Feud. I, 16, 1   27 (Baldus on –)
Feud. II, 56   27

b. Corpus iuris canonici

Decretum Gratiani

Dist. 1, 7   14, 53
Dist. 4, 2   48
Dist. 45, 3   10
Dist. 45, 5   10
Causa 16, 3, 9   49 (Gloss on –)
Causa 23, 2, 3   3

Decretales (Liber Extra)

Decretal. 1, 4, 11   43
Decretal. 2, 9, 3   35 (Gloss on –)
Decretal. 2, 26, 20   48
Decretal. 3, 8, 10   57

Sextus

Sextus 1, 6, 3, 2   35 (Gloss on –)
Sextus 5, 12, 3   14
Sextus 5, ult. 3   39

Clementinae

Clem. 5, 11, 1   14

Extravagantes Johannis XXII

Extravag. 14, 3   16
Extravag. 14, 5   16

Index of Sources Not Mentioned in the List

2 ANCIENT NON-LEGAL SOURCES

I would like to remind the reader that for the sources mentioned in this section I have simply adopted the verifications given by Williams and Magoffin (see Editor's Introduction, section 6).

Ambrosius
   De officiis I, 28 [132]   43
   Hexaemeron V, 10 [27]   25, 61
   Nabuthe III [12]   24
Andocides
   Orationes III, 4   62
Antipater, Caelius (cited by Plinius)   32
Apollodoros
   Bibliotheca, II, 7, 7   3
Aristoteles
   Ethica V, 8 [V, 5, 10]   53
   Politica I, 9 [I, 3]   52, 61
      I, 9 [I, 3, 12]   54 (bis)
      I, 9 [I, 3, 15]   53 (bis)
      I, 11 [I, 3, 16]   54
Athenaeus
   Deipnosophistae VIII, 35 (in fine)   20
Augustinus
   Quaestiones in Heptateuchum
      IV, qu. 44   3, 61
   De civitate Dei, XV [4]   63
      IV   66
   Numeri XX [14-22]   3 (bis)
Avienus
   Arataea 301 f.   16
   [302 f.]   15

Bible
   Ad Corinthos I, 5 in fine   9
   Johannes VI, 15   9
      XVIII, 36   8
   Liber iudicum 6   12
   Lucas X, 3   11
      XII, 14   8

   Matthaeus X, 16   11
      X, 23   10
      XVII, 27   9
      XX, 26   9
      XXIII, 15   12
      XXVIII, 18   11
   Numeri   3, 61
   Proverbia XI, 26   61
Boethius
   De consolatione philosophiae, IV, 4 [7 ff.]   10

Cassiodorus   (see List of Sources)
Cicero
   De officiis, I [7, 20]   21
      I, 7, 21   14, 17, 18
      I [16, 51]   19, 20
      I [16, 52]   30 (bis)
      I [34]   66
      I [35]   63
      I [42, 150]   54
   Pro Sexto Roscio Amerino XXVI, 72   20
Clemens Alexandrinus
   Stromata IV [6]   63
Columella
   De re rustica, VIII, 16   23
      VIII, 17   23

Demosthenes   62, 63
   De libertate Rhodiorum, XV, 10   63
Diodorus Siculus, XI [XII, 39]   3

Ennius [in Cicero, *De officiis*, I [16, 52]   30

Gregorius Nazianzenus
   In Funus Basilii [*Orationes* XLIII § 34]   61

Index of Sources Not Mentioned in the List

Herodianus
  Historiae ab excessu Divi Marci libri octo,
  VI, 3, 4   63
Hesiodus
  Opera et dies, vs. 24   60
Horatius
  [*Epistulae*] I, 1 [45 f.]   6
  Odae, III, 1, 33 f   23
  Sermones, II, 2, 129 f.   14

Isocrates
  Archidamos 51   62
  Panegyricus 176   63

Martialis
  Epigrammata X, 30 [19-20]   24
Mela, Pomponius
  III [7]   53
  III [9]   32

Nepos, Cornelius (cited by Plinius)   32
Nonius Marcellus
  De compendiosa doctrina IV   5

Ovidius   46
  Metamorphoses I [121, 135 f.]   17
    I, 134   18
    VI [349 ff.]   19

Plato
  De Republica, II [11-12]   54
  Sophista [p. 223 D]   53
Plautus
  Rudens [IV, 3, vs. 975 ff., 985]   21
Plinius (the Elder)
  Naturalis historia, II, 69 [67]   32
    VI, 22 [24]   6
    VI, 23 [24]   32, 33
    VI, 31   32
    X, 54 [X, 80, 170]   23
    XII, 19 [18]   33
    XXXIII, 1   53

Plinius (the Younger)
  Panegyricus [XXIX, 7]   2
Plutarchus
  Pericles [XXIX, p. 168 B]   3
  Pompeius, LXX, 3   7
Propertius
  Elegia, IV, 6 [47-52]   64

Quintilianus
  Declamationes, XIII [8]   17

Seneca
  De beneficiis, I, 9 [4]   54
    III, 28   30
    VII, 4   18
    VII, 12   17
  Naturales quaestiones, III, 4 [V, 18]   2
  Octavia [402 f.]   15, 18
  Thyestes [203-204]   17
Sophocles
  Trachineae (cited by Apollodorus)   3
Stobaeus
  Florilegium, IX, 54   63
Strabo
  Geographica, II [5, 12]   33
    XVII   33

Tacitus
  Historiae, IV [64]   4
Thucydides
  De bello Peloponnesiaco, I, 44   62
    I [139]   18
    III, 75   62

Varro
  De re rustica, III, 17, 9   23
Vergilius
  Aeneis, I [539 f.]   3, 20
    [VI, 847 f.]   2
    VII [229 f.]   3, 20
  Georgica, I [139-140]   17
    [II, 109]   2

GENERAL INDEX

Please note that in addition to this General Index this book is provided with two other specific indexes: the 'List of Sources' and the 'Index of Sources Not Mentioned in the List'. The General Index contains additional entries on subjects and names which occur in both introductions, including the footnotes. For the subject entries we have selected only some (mainly) legal terms and notions, but in adding names of persons, places and sources, some overlap with the other indexes could not be avoided. In these cases the entries refer to these indexes with the abbreviations 'LS' for 'List of Sources' and 'IS' for 'Index of Sources Not Mentioned in the List'.

Roman numerals refer to both Introductions and their notes. Numbers in red refer to the upper pagination of the English translation and the Latin text (in some exceptional cases also to the editor's notes, both numbered and lettered). References to the List of Abbreviations are indicated by the page numbers of that section. A semi-colon is used to distinguish between the above mentioned sections.

Accessory (*accessio*), LII; fol. 4 verso
Accursian Gloss, LIX, LXIII, *see also* LS (and IS)
Actio iniuriarum, 36
Alciatus, LXII, *see* LS
Alexander the Great, 32
Alexander Severus, Emperor, 63
Alexander VI, *see* Pope
Alexander Tartagnus, *see* LS
Alvarez (Alvarus), XLVIII, LXI, LXII
Alvarotus, *see* Jacobus Alvarotus
Alvotus, LXI
Ambrosius, *see* IS
Andreas de Isernia, LXI, *see also* LS
Angelus (de Gambilionibus) Aretinus, LIX, LXI, *see also* LS
Angelus de Ubaldis, LIX, LX-LXI, *see also* LS
Antipater, Caelius, *see* IS
Apprehension (*apprehensio*), 17
Arabia(n) Gulf, 32, 33
Arabs, 6, 32, 33, 59
Archidiaconus, *see* LS
Aretinus, *see* Angelus Aretinus
Armitage, David, XXII, XXIV, XLV, XLIX, L, LIII, LXI, LXIII; 161
Athenaeus, *see* IS
Authenticum, LV, *see also* IS
Ayala, Balthazar, LVII, *see also* LS
Azo, LIX

Balbus, Johannes Franciscus, LXI, LXII, *see also* LS
Baldus de Ubaldis, LX, *see also* LS
Bartolus, *see* LS
Batavians (*Batavi*), 1

Baudius, Dominicus, LI
Beaufort, D, 44; 161
Bellum iustum, *see* Just War
Bensly, Edward, XXXII, XXXIV, XLIV, XLVIII, LIX, LX, LXII; 161
Bernardus Claravellensis, *see* LS
Bertius, Petrus, XLIII
Bible, *see* IS
Biblical texts, LII
Bijnkershoek, Cornelis van, XXXI
Blaeu(w), (publisher), XXXII, XXXVI, XLVIII; 164
Blok, F. F., LVII; 161
Boethius, *see* IS
Boreel, Johan, X
Borschberg, Peter, IX, XI, XVIII, XX, XXI, XXV, XXXI, LVI; 161
Boschan, Richard, XLV, LXI; 161

Cadiz, 32
Caesar, Gaius, 32
Caietanus, *see* LS
Canonists, 9, 10, 57
Carfì, F., XLVIII; 162
Carnegie Endowment for International Peace, VII, XXXI, XXXII, XXXIV, XXXV, XL
Cassiodorus, LII, *see also* LS
Castilians, 8, 51
Castro, Alfonso de, LVIII, *see also* LS
Castro, Martin Alphonse de, [67]
Celsus, *see* LS
Charles V, Emperor (and king of Spain), 12
China, XI; 33
Christian IV (king of Denmark), XXVII

Christina (queen of Sweden), LVI
Cicero, *see* IS
Civilians, 10
Civil law, XVIII, XXII, LVI, LXII, LXIII; 36 ff.
Clementinae, LV, *see also* LS (and IS)
Codex, LV, *see also* LS (and IS)
Colonial Conferences, XX
Columella, *see* IS
Comines, Philippe de, 20
Common good, XV, XXII, XXV, XXVIII
Corpus iuris canonici, LIII, LV, LXIII, *see also* IS
Corpus iuris civilis, LII, LIII, LV, LVI, LXIII, *see also* IS
Counterfeit of first edition, see Grotius, *Mare liberum*, editions
Courtin, Antoine de, XLIV
Covarruvias, Didacus, *see* LS
Cujacius, Jacobus, LIX, *see also* LS
Custom, XVIII, XXVI, fol. 2 recto ff.
Cynus, *see* LS

Damsté, Onno, XXXIX
Decretales, LV, *see also* LS (and IS)
Decretum Gratiani, LV, *see also* LS (and IS)
Defensio capitis quinti Maris liberi, *see* Grotius, other works
De jure belli ac pacis, *see* Grotius, other works
De jure praedae, *see* Grotius, other works
Demosthenes, *see* IS
Diermanse, P. J. J., *see* TMD
Digesta, LV, *see also* LS (and IS)
Discovery, X, XV, XXV; 4, 5, 6, 34, 36, 55

175

General Index

Divine Justice, 2
Divine Providence, 44
Doctores, LVI, LVIII, LXIII, *see also* LS
Doctores Hispani, LXIV, *see also* LS
Dominicans, 12
Dominion, XIV, XXVII; 4 ff.
Dominium, *see* Ownership
Donatio (*Pontificis*) *Alexandri*, *see* Papal donation
Donellus, Hugo, *see* LS
Dovring, F., LVI, LVII; 161
Duarenus, Franciscus, *see* LS
Dutch East India Company (VOC), IX, X, XI, XIII, XIV, XVIII, L
Dutch Provinces, 1
Dutch Revolt, IX

East Indies, X, XIV, XVIII, XX; 6 ff.
Editio princeps, *see* Grotius, *Mare liberum*, editions
Elzevirius, Ludovicus (publisher of edd. 1609, 1618, 1633), IX, XXXII, XXXV
Emmanuel (king of Portugal), 51
Equity, 35
Errata (list of), XXXV, XLIX, LI; fol. 6 verso
Estius (Willem van Est), XLVIII, LIX; 3
Exchange, principle of, 2, 53, 54
Exercitio, XLIX; 54
Extravagantes, LV, *see also* LS (and IS)
Eyffinger, A., LXIV
Eysinga, W. J. M. van, X, XIII, XIV, XIX, XX, XXI, LVIII; 163

Faber, *see* Johannes Faber
Fachinaeus, Andreas, LXIII, *see* LS
Fachinham, Nicholas, LXIII
Feenstra, Robert, *see* Grotius, *Mare liberum*, editions
Feenstra, Robert, other works, XV, XXXI, LVI, LXI, LXIII, LXIV; 162
Felinus Sandeus, 40, *see* LS
Feud., *see* *Libri feudorum*
Finch, George A., XXXII, XXXIV, XL
First edition, *see* Grotius, *Mare liberum*, editions
Fishery Edict of 1609, XXI
Freitas, Seraphin de, XIX, XXIV, XXV
Fruin, Robert, XIV

Genoese, 39 ff.
Gentilis, Albericus, XIX, XXVI, LVI, LVIII, LXIII, *see also* LS
Gerardus [Othonis], *see* LS
Glosa, LXIII, *see also* LS
Glossators, LIX, LXIII
Gordianus, Emperor, LIX; 5
Gothofredus edition (of *Corpus iuris civilis*), LVI
Graswinckel, Dirck, XXVIII
Gregory of Nazianzum, 10, 61, *see also* IS
Grewe, W. G., XVIII, XXI, XXV, XXVII
Grootenhuis, Jan ten, LVII
Grotius, *Mare liberum*
  Manuscript, *see* Manuscript Leiden BPL 917
  Editions
    1609, first edition (*editio princeps*), VII, IX, XXXV, LI; 161
    1609, counterfeit of first edition, XXXV; 161
    1618, Leiden edition, IX, XXXV, LIV; 161
    1632, Amsterdam edition, XXXVI; 161
    1633, Leiden editions, XXXVI, XLIV, LIV; 162
    1633, Amsterdam edition, XXXVI, XLVIII; 162, 164
    1667 (as appendix to *De jure belli ac pacis*), XXXVI; 162
    1689 (idem), XXXIX; 162
    1712 (idem), XXXIX; 162
    1720 (idem), XXXIX; 162
    1735 (idem), XXXIX; 162
    1773, Utrecht edition (idem), XXXVI, LXI; 162
    1916, *see* Magoffin
    2007, *see* [Longobardi]
    2009, *see* Eyffinger
    2009, by Feenstra, III
  Online editions, XXXIV, XLV
  Translations, XLIII-XLVIII;
    into Dutch, *see* Bertius;
    see Eyffinger; by Iekerman, A, XLIII; 170; by Gorius, Joan, XLIII
    into English, *see* Hakluyt; *see* Magoffin
    into French, *see* Courtin; *see* Guichon de Grandpont
    into German, *see* Boschan
    into Italian, of 1931-1933, *see* Carfi; of 2007, *see* [Longobardi];
    into Korean, by Kim, Seok Hyun, XLVI, XLVIII
    into Norwegian, by Aure, Andreas, XLVIII
    into Polish, by Bierzanek, R., XLVI, XLVIII
    into Spanish, by García Arias, L. and Blanco García, V., XLVI, XLVIII, LXII; 163
Grotius, other works
  Defensio capitis quinti Maris liberi, IX, XXII-XXIV, XXVI, XXXIX; 161
  De jure belli ac pacis, XXV-XXVI; editions of, XXXI, XXXIX; 161
  De jure praedae, X, XI, XIII, XIV, XXXIX-XLIII; edition of, *see* Hamaker; translation into Dutch, *see* Damsté; into English, *see* Williams
  Florum sparsio ad jus Justinianeum, LVIII
  Inleidinge tot de Hollandsche Rechtsgeleerdheid, LVIII
  Letters (Correspondence), L-LI; 161
  Memorandum (Mem. 1607), LVIII; 163
Guicciardinus, Franciscus, *see* LS
Guichon de Grandpont, Alfred, XXXII, XLIV; 162
Guido de Baysio, *see* LS

Hakluyt, Richard, XLV, XLIX, L, LII, LIII; 162
Hamaker, H. G., XIV, XXXVI, XXXIX, XL, LIV, LVII, LXII; 161, 162
Hauling, 54
Heemskerck, Jacob van, XI, XV
Heinsius, Daniel, L, LI
Henricus Gorcumensis, *see* LS
Henry IV (king of France), XIII
Hermogenianus, *see* LS
Hesiodus, *see* IS
Hesperion Ceras, *see* Western Horn
Holland, states of, X
Horatius, *see* IS
Huguccio, *see* LS
Huybertsz., Jan (printer), XLIII

Ianssonius, Iohannes (publisher), XXXV, XXXVI
Imperium, XXII, XXIV, XXVI
Indians, IX, XXII; 1 ff.
Iniuria, LII

Innocentius IV, *see* LS
Institores, 54
Institutiones, LV, *see also* LS (and IS)
Interdict(um), *de loco publico fruendo*, 28; *utile*, 36; *uti possidetis*, XLIX; 24, 63
Inventio, *see* Discovery
Isernia, *see* Andreas de Isernia
Ittersum, M. J. van, IX, XI, XIII, XIV, XVIII, XX, XXI, XXII, XXVI, L, LI, LX; 163
Ius commerciandi, *see* Trade
Ius communicandi, *see* Trade
Ius navigandi, *see* Right of navigation

Jacobus Alvarotus, LIX, LXI, *see also* LS
James I (king of England), XX, XXI, XXVI, XXVII
Japan, XI; 33
Jason de Maino, LVII, *see also* LS
Java, 4
Jean Faure, *see* Johannes Faber
Johannes Andreae, LIX
Johannes Bassianus, LIX, *see also* LS
Johannes Faber, XLVIII, XLIX, LIX, LX, *see also* LS
Johannes de Turrecremata, *see* LS
John (king of Portugal), 51
Jus gentium, *see* Law of nations
Justinian, XXIV, LII, *see also* LS
Just War, XIII, XV; 66

Labeo, *see* LS
Lathyrus (king of Alexandria), 32
Law of nations, primary, XVIII; 1, 38, 44, 45, 48, 53, 54; secondary, XVIII; 49
Leges Hispanicae, LIX, LX, *see also* LS
Leo VI (Byzantine emperor), LVI; 25
Library, Grotius' –, LVI; inventory of, LVI-LVII, LVIII; 162
Libri feudorum, LVI, LXI, *see also* LS (and IS)
Literary texts of classical antiquity, LII
Longobardi, F., XXXIV

Magoffin, Ralph Van Deman, VII, XXXI, XXXII, XXXIV, XXXV, XXXVI, XXXIX, XL, XLIV, XLV, XLVI, XLVIII, LII, LIX, LX, LXI, LXII, LXIII; 162
Malacca, XI; 5, 51

Manuscript Leiden BPL 917, L-LI, LII, LVII; 163
Marcianus, *see* LS
Mare clausum, *see* Selden, John
Mare liberum, *see* Grotius, *Mare liberum*
Martialis, *see* IS
Meijers, E. M., LVII; 163
Mem. 1607, *see* Grotius, other works, *Memorandum*
Merula, P., XXXII, XXXVI, XLIV
Metellus, Johannes, LXII, *see also* LS
Meulen, J. ter, *see* TMD
Molhuysen, P. C., L, LVI; 163
Moluccas, 4, 51
Moors, 33, [68]

Nellen, H., VII, XIII, XX, XXVIII, XLIII, L, LI; 163
Neratius, *see* LS
Novellae, *see also* LS (and IS)
Nys, Ernest, XIX

Objectives of present edition, LI-LIII
Occupation (*occupatio*), X, XV, XXI, XXII, XXV, XXVII, XXVIII, LII; 10 ff.
Oldenbarnevelt, Johan van, X
Oldradus, *see* LS
Online versions, *see* Grotius, *Mare liberum*, online editions
Osorius, Hieronymus, LXII, *see* LS
Oudendijk, J. K., XX, XXI, XXII, XXIV, XXV, XXVI
Ovidius, *see* IS
Ownership, XV, XVIII, XXI, XXII, XXIV, XXV, XXVI, XXVII, XXXI; 5 ff.

Panormitanus, *see* LS
Papal donation, XI, XV, XVIII, LXII; 7, 36, 55
Papinianus, *see* LS
Paragraphs, LII
Paulus (Roman jurist), *see* LS
Paulus Castrensis, *see* LS
Placentinus, LIX, *see also* LS
Plinius (the Elder), *see* IS
Plinius (the Younger), *see* IS
Plutarchus, *see* IS
Pomponius, *see* LS
Pope Alexander VI, LXII; 7
Pope Paul III, 12

Positive law, 11, 38, 43, 44
Possession, XV, XXI, XXII, XXVIII; 5 ff.
Praetor, 65
Prescription, XI, XV, XVIII; 38 ff.
Printer's errors, LI, LIV; fol. 6 verso
Property, XV; 14; common, 3, 13, 14, 15, 18, 21, 30, 40, 45, 47, 66; private, XVIII; 14 ff.
Proprium, *see* Property

Quintilianus, *see* IS

Rabbie, E., LVI; 163
References, linking of, XXXII; marginal, VII, XXXII, XXXVI, XXXIX, XL, XLIII, XLIV, XLV, LI; verification of, XXXII, LII, LIII-LIV
Res communis, *see* Common good
Res extra commercium, XV
Res nullius, XV, 13
Right of navigation, XVIII; fol. 4 verso, 13, 36, 37, 38, 42
Rhodians, 62
Roelofsen, C. G., XLV
Roman and Canon Law, *see Corpus iuris canonici* and *Corpus iuris civilis*

Santa Catarina, XI, XIII, XVIII
Scholastici, LXIV, *see also* LS
Scott, James Brown, XIV, XXXI, XXXII, XXXIV, XXXIX, XL
Selden, John, XIX, XXVI-XXVIII, XXXV
Seneca, *see* IS
Seres, 53
Sextus, LV, *see also* LS (and IS)
Siete Partidas, LX, *see also* LS
Sigonius, *see* LS
Sources, *see* IS and LS
Staedler, E., LXII; 163
Strabo, *see* IS
Straccha, Benvenuto, LX
Straumann, Benjamin, XVIII; 13; 163
Suarez, *see* Zuarius, *see* LS
Sumatra, *see* Taprobane
Sweden, XXVII
Sylvester Prierias, *see* LS

Tacitus, *see* IS
Taprobane, 4, 6, 33
Telders, B. M., XXV

Theodoric (king of the Ostrogoths), LII; 66; *see also* LS
Theologians, 7, 9, 10, 12, 59, 63, 65, 66
Thomas Aquinas, LVII, *see also* LS
Thucydides, *see* IS
TMD: J. ter Meulen and P. J. J. Diermanse, *Bibliographie des écrits imprimés de Grotius, La Haye 1950 (reprint Zutphen 1995)*, XXXV, XXXVI, XXXIX, XLIII, XLIV, XLV, XLVIII; 163
Trade, freedom of, XI, XIV, XV, XVIII, XX; fol. 4 verso, 54, 56, 65; prohibition of, 59 ff.
Tuning, Gerard, LI
Twelve Years' Truce, IX, XXIV
Tydeman, Meinard, XXXIX

Ulpianus, *see* LS
United Nations Convention on the Law of the Sea, XXVIII
Usus, 14
Usurpation, 43, 46, 49, 51, 59
Uti possidetis, *see* Interdictum *uti possidetis*

Varro, *see* IS
Vasquius, Fernandus, LVIII, LXI, *see also* LS
Venetians, 3 ff.
Vergilius, *see* IS
Veteres, 28
Victoria, Franciscus de, LVII, LVIII, *see* LS
Vissering, Simon, XIV
VOC, see Dutch East India Company
Vollenhoven, C. van, LI

Welwood, William, IX, XIX, XXI-XXII
Western Horn, the, 32
Wholesale commerce, 54
Williams, Gwladys L., VII, XXXIX, XL, XLIII, XLIV, XLV, XLIX, LII, LIII, LIV, LVII, LX, LXI, LXII, LXIII; 163
Wright, Herbert F., XIV, XXII, XLIV, XLV, LII; 163; *see also* LS, at Victoria, *De Indis*

Zeydel, H, LIX, *see also* Williams
Zuarius, Rodericus, (Rodrigo Suárez) *Consilium*, XLV, XLVIII, LVIII, LIX, LX, LXI, *see also* LS